THE INSTITUTIONAL ECONOMICS OF THE INTERNATIONAL ECONOMY

THE INSTITUTIONAL ECONOMICS OF THE INTERNATIONAL ECONOMY

Edited by

JOHN ADAMS
Northeastern University

and

ANTHONY SCAPERLANDA
Northern Illinois University

KLUWER ACADEMIC PUBLISHERS
Boston / Dordrecht / London

Distributors for North America:
Kluwer Academic Publishers
101 Philip Drive
Assinippi Park
Norwell, Massachusetts 02061 USA

Distributors for all other countries:
Kluwer Academic Publishers Group
Distribution Centre
Post Office Box 322
3300 AH Dordrecht, THE NETHERLANDS

Library of Congress Cataloging-in-Publication Data

A C.I.P. Catalogue record for this book is available from
the Library of Congress.

ISBN-13: 978-94-010-7311-0 e-ISNB-13: 978-94-009-1820-7
DOI: 10.1007/978-94-009-1820-7

Printed on acid-free paper.

To Wendell C. Gordon, a mentor and colleague who planted many of the intellectual seeds that grew into the insights and understandings that are found in the chapters of this book

CONTENTS

FIGURES

TABLES

CONTRIBUTORS

JOHN ADAMS earned his Ph.D. in economics at the University of Texas in 1966. He taught at the University of Maryland (1965-1990) before accepting a position as Professor of Economics and Chair of the Department at Northeastern University. He has authored *International Economics* and has edited *The Contemporary International Economy*. He has written, with Sabiha Iqbal, *Exports, Politics, and Economic Development: Pakistan, 1970-1982* and *India: The Search for Unity, Democracy, and Progress* with Walter C. Neale. He is a past president of the Association for Evolutionary Economics and is the current president of the Eastern Economic Association.

WILLIAM E. COLE, Professor of Economics at the University of Tennessee, Knoxville, joined that faculty after completing his Ph.D. in economics at the University of Texas in 1965. His research, emphasizing economic development, rural-urban migration, and integrated rural development has been published in the *Journal of Economic Issues*, the *Journal of Development Economics*, *International Economic Journal, World Development, Land Economics,* and the *American Economic Review*. In 1995 he published *The Economics of Total Quality Management: Clashing Paradigms in a Global Market*.

THOMAS R. DEGREGORI, Professor of Economics at the University of Houston, received his Ph.D. in economics from the University of Texas in 1965. His books and articles on development include *A Theory of Technology* (1985). He has done development work in more than 40 countries in Africa, Asia, and the Caribbean, specializing in issues of technological and scientific policy, programs, and projects. His advisory work has frequently been at the cabinet or senior administrative level.

WILLIAM P. GLADE, following the completion of his Ph.D. at the University of Texas in 1955, taught at the Universities of Maryland and Wisconsin before returning to his alma mater as Professor of Economics and Director of the Institute of Latin American Studies. His main research interests have been Latin American economic history and development, entrepreneurship in developing economies, and the role of public enterprises in development. Some of his recent research has focussed on the process of privatization during economic restructuring. Representative publications include *The Latin American Economies: A Study of their Institutional Evolution* and *State-shrinking: A Comparative Inquiry into Privatization*.

WENDELL GORDON is a retired Professor of Economics at the University of Texas, where he was a member of the faculty from 1940 to 1984. He obtained his Ph.D. in 1940 at New York University in Political Science under the supervision of Clyde Eagleton. His work has been in international economics, with emphasis on Latin America, and in the field of institutional economics. He is a past president of the Association for Evolutionary Economics and a recipient of its Veblen-Commons Award.

DILMUS D. JAMES is a Professor of Economics at the University of Texas at El Paso. After completing a B.A. and an M.A. (1958) at the University of Texas, he earned the Ph.D. in 1970 at Michigan State University. He is past president of the North American Economics and Finance Association and of the Association for Evolutionary Economics. His research and writing have centered on technology capacity-building and science and technology policy in developing countries.

HANS E. JENSEN, Professor Emeritus at The University of Tennessee, Knoxville, received the Ph.D. from The University of Texas in 1961. His teaching and research interests lie in the history of economics. In his publications, he has inquired into the nature and causes of new departures in economics. He is president of the Association for Social Economics.

PETER KARL KRESL is Professor of Economics at Bucknell University where he has taught since receiving his Ph.D. from the University of Texas in 1969. His interests have focused on Canada-U.S. economic relations, on the European Union, and recently on urban economies and their internationalization efforts.

MILTON D. LOWER, retired senior economist, U.S. House of Representatives, now lives and writes in Austin, where he completed a Texas Ph.D. under C. E. Ayres in 1970. In Washington, Lower spent two years at the Economic Policy Institute after leaving government service. Earlier, he taught economics at The University of Texas at Austin, and at the Universities of Maryland and Houston, as well as labor education for the United Steelworkers. Lower is a past president of the Association for Evolutionary Economics.

ANNE MAYHEW, Professor of Economics and History at the University of Tennessee, Knoxville, received the Ph.D. from the University of Texas in 1966. Her specialties are economic history and the history of economic thought (with emphasis on institutionalist thought). She has served as editor of the *Journal of Economic Issues* since 1992 and is a past president of the Association for Evolutionary Economics.

ANTHONY SCAPERLANDA, who holds the Ph.D. in economics from the University of Texas, 1964, is Professor of Economics and Chair of the Department of Economics at Northern Illinois University. His primary work on the determinants of foreign direct investment and multinational enterprise expansion appears in journals such as the *Journal of Economic Issues*, *Review of Social Economy*, *Eastern Economic Journal*, *European Economic Review*, *Economic Journal*, and *The American Economic Review*.

PREFACE

This book is the outgrowth of the editors' conviction that there is a need for a current and comprehensive examination of international economic issues within the framework of institutional economics. The volume covers the most important international topics that institutional economists historically have addressed. We hope that our initiative and necessarily limited choice of subjects will encourage additional applications of institutional economic theory to the international economy. For other economists, the analyses contained in the volume's dozen chapters afford an opportunity to become more aware of the theoretical work and policy recommendations of institutional economists.

It may be surprising that, to an extent, evolutionary and neoclassical thinking converge and even sometimes overlap on the matter of trends and problems of the international economy. A case in point is the increased attention both schools devote to the role of technology in shaping patterns of world trade and specialization. In the past few decades, global shifts in comparative advantages, the widespread adoption of more flexible exchange-rate systems, and the remarkable shifts in institutional arrangements and policy regimes in the former Soviet Union and East Asia have compelled a reassessment of conventional static trade theories based on neoclassical assumptions. Links among trade, international investment, and the diffusion of economic growth are being more closely scrutinized and better understood. This volume is an effort to expand and stimulate this discourse on the economics of international relations, including global economic development. We are deeply grateful to our contributors for providing lucid, provocative essays that push the frontiers of our knowledge.

The editors began planning the book and organizing its contents in 1991. Early conversations led to a panel on institutional international economics, organized for the spring 1994 meeting of the Association for

Institutional Thought, held in Albuquerque. This session confirmed the potential value of the project as a useful contribution and we moved ahead to solicit additional chapters. A double-session mini-conference was held during the March 1995 meeting of the Eastern Economic Association in New York City. At both conferences the draft papers were strengthened as a result of critiques by other contributors and audience participants. The editors appreciate the willingness of the contributors to be involved in this intensive way in the book's creation. The editors admire the scholarly enthusiasm with which the contributors vetted their ideas and policy recommendations. The editors also appreciate the substantial comments and criticisms provided by the other participants in the three lively conference sessions. The unity of the volume was significantly enhanced by our collective interaction.

This book could not exist without the positive encouragement received from Zachary Rolnick, economics editor of Kluwer Publishing. Nor would it have emerged without the extraordinary dedication and precision of Susan Harshman, who prepared the final copy for publication. Susan is a manuscript editor in the Manuscript Services Office of the College of Liberal Arts and Sciences at Northern Illinois University, directed by Karen M. Blazer. Susan was not only expeditious and precise but unusually effective in editing the editors' editing to insure consistency and clarity. Susan was assisted by Karen and by Elizabeth Mehren. We thank, as well, Mary Suzanne Schriber, Distinguished Professor of English at Northern Illinois University, for selective editing of portions of the manuscript.

1 February 1996

John Adams,
Northeastern University

Anthony Scaperlanda,
Northern Illinois University

INTRODUCTION

THE INSTITUTIONAL ECONOMICS OF THE INTERNATIONAL ECONOMY

John Adams and Anthony Scaperlanda

As the twenty-first century approaches, all national economies are operating within shared global parameters. It is no longer possible to design and implement an autarkic, or nearly autarkic, program of development, drawing exclusively on indigenous resources, skills, and technologies. Interdependence and codetermination are universal features of economic life among all countries, large and small, industrial and industrializing, rich and poor. A closed economy, if such ever truly existed, is a phenomenon of the past. Economic destinies and many aspects of the globe's manifold cultures and political systems continue to converge. Revolutionary changes in communications, travel, and transportation have greatly lowered the time and distance barriers to economic and social interaction. Economists, other social scientists, historians, and political leaders must confront the challenges to theory and policy generated by rapid and powerful changes that demand new theoretical understandings. Shifts in comparative advantage, the accelerating dispersion of transnational enterprises, experimentation with varying exchange-rate mechanisms, and the globalization of labor markets cannot be encompassed within static models that do not put technological and institutional processes on center stage. Theoretical foundations must be broadened if international economic policy-making is to address present and future conditions and needs.

This volume grew out of our perception that it would be opportune to assemble, in a single, convenient source, a current depiction of how institutional economists think about the evolving international economy. A period of unprecedented structural and technological change certainly offers an ideal laboratory for the extension and application of institutionalist ideas. Institutional economists have made significant contributions to our understanding of trade flows, investment mechanisms, the role of multinational corporations, technology diffusion, and economic growth and development. Some have made useful recommendations for the progressive reform of international institutions. Each of these strands of evolutionary thought appears in this book, a set of twelve original essays that reestablish and update the institutional theoretical base, and provide examples of applications of evolutionary theory to international issues. Section I contains three essays on the Theoretical Foundations of International Economic Relations. The three chapters in section II examine International Trade and Foreign Investment in depth. Labor, Resources, and Technology in the International Economy are the rubric for the three chapters in section III. The final triplet of chapters in section IV is devoted to Institutional Change in the International Economy. In greater or lesser degree, each of the dozen contributions integrates theory and policy.

INSTITUTIONAL ECONOMICS

Two early chapters of this collection offer an entre to institutional, or evolutionary, economics. In chapter 1, Hans Jensen provides an excellent overview of the foundations of modern evolutionary theory. In chapter 3, Milton Lower connects early institutional theorizing about the international arena to present-day topics and lays a foundation for the contributions that follow. The references in these two chapters constitute an introductory road map to relevant, standard institutionalist sources. Before a reader, unfamiliar with contemporary institutional economics takes up the road map, a brief outline of the cardinal perspectives of institutional economic thought may be helpful.

Methodological pluralism informs the work of institutionalists, and individual writers weight differently the perspectives of institutionalist thought (as they do the use of mathematics, graphics, or empirics to reinforce their line of argument). Institutionalist thought typically manifests five perspectives or orientations: evolutionary, institutional, technological, political economy, and democratic.

The *evolutionary perspective* is the trademark of social and economic analysis. This perspective takes process rather than equilibrium as the normal mode of human activity. It assumes that because historical time is irreversible, a set of interactions does not lead back to an original or stable equilibrium state. John Adams's chapter, elucidating the institutional theory of inter-social exchange, including international trade, relies heavily on the notion of instituted processes.

The *institutional perspective* entails recognizing the simultaneous and continuous interplay of individual and collective (families, interest groups) action and pre-existing institutional formations. From this perspective, individual action cannot be taken as prior to the creation of institutions, for instance by positing a preceding social contract, nor can individual choice or decision-making be understood apart from a particular social and economic context. This set of views is more or less consistent with neo-institutional ruminations on bounded rationality, limited information, repeated games, and path dependence. William Cole's contribution on Third-World migration, contrasting Mexican and Indian family and tenurial institutions, exemplifies this perspective.

The third orientation, the *technological perspective*, assumes that social and technological change are mutually determining. Improvements in the human condition stem from the progressive and cumulative advance of technology, which is understood to include human skills and ideas as well at the material dimensions of culture such as tools, structures, and machines. Changes in technology result from the human predisposition to explain, explore, and experiment, and are especially rapid when the prevailing institutions permit or encourage inquisitiveness and the diffusion of new techniques, as has been the case in modern industrial societies. Differences in levels of technology are the primary reason for the wide global differences in national standards of living, and technological change is the preeminent source of economic growth. Thomas DeGregori's essay on national resources and Dilmus James's chapter on technology and economic development show the technological perspective at work; and Anne Mayhew's essay, stressing the distinction between technology transfers and financial capital movements, unmasks the largely mythical role of foreign investment transfers in histories of national economic growth.

The fourth orientation, usually called the *political economy perspective*, is holistic. This means that rather than creating an abstract context of an idealized set of economic relations, such as a competitive self-regulating market system, economic relations are analyzed within their national political and social matrixes in order to gain understanding or to assess policy options. The political economy perspective assumes that any economic system must be studied in its distinctive historical context where the economic, social, and political realms are complexly interdependent. As is seen so vividly today in the territories of the former Soviet Union, a market economy cannot exist and function in a socially useful fashion without a supporting web of institutionalized property rights, commercial conventions, and judicial enforcement. William Glade's chapter, with apt comparisons of the former Soviet Union to Latin America, particularly Mexico, compellingly demonstrates this point. Making a case for the global licensing of multinational corporations, Anthony Scaperlanda's essay demonstrates the gains to internationalizing firms and timorous host nations of establishing clear rules of the game.

Fifth and last, many institutionalists have embraced a *democratic perspective*, endorsing to greater or less degree the importance of the role of publicly guided governmental oversight of the market process and of market agents, such as currency traders or corporations, to correct market failures or aberrations, or to engage in socially desirable redistributions of wealth or incomes. This democratic perspective is embedded in the chapters contributed by Peter Karl Kresl on urban planning in a changing global economy, by Scaperlanda on making the IMF a true central bank for the world, and by Wendell Gordon on a reformed United Nations.

INSTITUTIONS AND TECHNOLOGY IN THE INTERNATIONAL ECONOMY

Although institutional and orthodox economists have followed different paths in their study of international economic relationships for more than a century now, this was not always the case. Rather, what are now identified as institutionalist and orthodox approaches were mingled in early economic analysis such as Adam Smith's *Wealth of Nations* (1776), as Lower points out in chapter 3 of this book. Even as late as John Stuart Mill's *Principles of Political Economy* (1848), institutional and cultural elements remained in the forefront, explaining patterns of global exchange and comparative levels of development. This line of thought, however, was ignored thereafter in the British-American mainstream. Orthodox and institutionalist thought parted company. The orthodox departure had begun with David Ricardo's statement of the principle of comparative advantage in 1817. In the language used by today's orthodoxy, Ricardo formalized the classical theory and in so doing imposed a number of restrictive assumptions in the interests of rigor. Among these were international factor immobility, pure competition, institutional homogeneity, and technological identity. After Ricardo, orthodox trade theorists have usually treated technology as given, institutions as passive, natural resources as fixed, labor skills as homogenous, and businesses as competitive, short-term profit maximizers. Consumers are conceptualized as simply atomistic utility maximizers with unchanging tastes, able to purchase products from any source of supply without transport or other transactions costs. Unions, business combines, and consumer interest groups do not operate to affect trade policies.

Institutional economists find these assumptions unrealistic, even if the rejection of them means dealing with the world as a more complex and indeterminate place, less amenable to mathematical and geometrical modeling. Institutionalists believe that technological gaps underlie national income differences and that levels of technology and skills are crucial in determining global trade and investment flows. National and international institutional arrangements matter mightily, as does the evolving nature of corporate enterprises and their transborder activities. Natural and human resources constantly change in abundance and availability as a result of the progress of technology and knowledge. Trade policy formation cannot be understood without considering the influence of business, labor, and consumer interest groups. Generally, institutional policy recommendations do not flow from an ideal-type model, grounded in a vision of how the world *ought* to operate, but from an on-going process of assessment of how the world *does* operate, and application of what is feasible, therefore at the moment. Policy prescriptions incorporate knowledge of what is, and are responsive to the conditions actually encountered. They are in this sense pragmatic and instrumental, and subject to constant revision. No policy, including free trade, is taken as always the best, under any circumstances, for any nation.

The foundations for modern neoclassical economists' work in international trade theory were laid by Eli Heckscher and Bertil Ohlin. Neither Heckscher nor Ohlin was himself overly narrow or mindlessly technical in approach, but their joint development of what is known as the factor proportions-factor intensity explanation of trade advantages foreshadowed 50 years of orthodox extensions.

As we enter the 1990s, there are signs of revisions in orthodox thinking about international trade, foreign investment, and other international factor movements that are broadening the range of inquiry and bringing this tradition back into conjunction with institutional thought, and with that of such fields as international relations and international political economy. There is agreement that technology, skills, enterprise strategies, work place practices, and cooperative government-business links are crucial determinants of a nation's trade level and pattern. Orthodox trade theorists have realized, over the past several decades, that institutional factors cannot be ignored if the pattern of trade is to be understood. The foremost source of this return to Smith's more comprehensive perspective was perhaps the inability to find convincing empirical support for the Heckscher-Ohlin theory. A second factor prompting a return to Smith's vision has been the rapid rise to prominence in world trade of a roster of newly industrializing nations such as Korea, Taiwan, India, and China, where human-capital variables are having a crucial impact. Often encouraged by forms of governmental protection and support that foster economies of scale and economies of agglomeration, this route to trading effectiveness draws attention to the institutional arrangements that facilitate the growth of trade. A third element in the picture is the increasingly dominant position of multinational corporations in international flows of goods, capital, and technologies, another development requiring institutional analysis.

Creating strong international agencies, such as the new International Trade Organization, and working within regional trade blocs such as the European Union or the North American Free Trade Agreement put institution-building at the heart of international political economy. Structuring appropriate exchange-rate regimes remains a central challenge to national governments and regional trade and payments unions. In any case, the orthodox excursion after Ricardo mostly had affected international trade theory. All along, international monetary economics has been concerned with the appropriate design and operation of global financial institutions. As far as international factor flows are concerned, it is evident that the motivations for the transfer of capital and location of production range far beyond simple rate-of-return comparisons, and embrace such things a long-run market-share strategies. The movement of people is much more responsive to political and cultural factors than to wage differentials.

CONTRIBUTIONS OF THE BOOK

Each chapter in this book employs the hallmark features of institutional analysis in extending the fundamental theory and in demonstrating the effectiveness of institutional policy investigation. Theory and its applications are interlaced throughout the four sections. The nine chapters in the first three sections are more heavily weighted towards the theoretical, and the final three chapters, in the fourth section, illustrate the institutionalist handling of specific policy issues. The three chapters in section I present the ideas of Thorstein Veblen and Clarence Ayres that are fundamental to institutional thought about international economic relations; examine how the collation of financial capital with transfers of real machines and technologies confuses the historical interpretation of long-term capital movements; and integrates these sets of concepts in a comprehensive dissection of the modern international economy. Section II provides an in-depth treatment of institutional trade theory; introduces a spatial dimension by highlighting the role of cities; and considers the dispersion of multinational enterprises and its impact on global welfare. Section III demonstrates the close integration in institutional thought of international linkages and national development. Natural resource abundance is scrutinized from the institutional viewpoint;

the importance of technology in national growth programs is described; and the relationship between migration patterns, inheritance practices, and other institutions is examined. Section IV applies institutional analysis to three topics: the need for institutional reform and institution-building in the emerging economies of the former Soviet Bloc and Latin America; the reform of the International Monetary Fund; and the redefinition and expansion of the functions of the United Nations.

The book opens with Hans Jensen's introduction to the Veblen-Ayres tradition of American institutionalism. Thorstein Veblen and one of his leading followers, Clarence E. Ayres, identified the dichotomy between technology and ceremonialism as the key and necessary understanding upon which to predicate study of long-run social change and progress. Ceremonialism encompasses all past-binding aspects of institutions, while technology is the dynamic force in human history. Jensen's detailed treatment of Veblen's and Ayres's concepts establishes a firm foundation for the ensuing chapters. In chapter 2, Anne Mayhew argues convincingly that foreign investment is neither a sufficient nor necessary requirement for economic growth. She demonstrates that historical evidence concerning capital movements to the young United States and to other nations in the early stages of development does not support the conventional idea that such transfers were an important source of growth. Orthodox economists, according to Mayhew, have failed to be clear, even in their own minds, in drawing a distinction between different types of international financial claims and flows and the actual movements of physical capital. Further, their theorizing, Mayhew contends, greatly overstates the influence of capital and savings on national growth. In the third chapter of the book, Milton Lower argues that conventional theory erred in turning its face from the "forces of technology and organization that have reshaped cultures and nations toward a global industrial system." Yet these forces, in conjunction with radical alterations in communications, are transforming today's global economy. According to Lower, any meaningful calculus of understanding contemporary international economic relationships must consider the emerging nature of the multinational corporation as an engine of non-market exchange.

The chapters in section II look closely at three phenomena: the institutionalized processes through which international exchange occurs; the function of cities as nodes of world trade; and the operations and oversight of multinational corporations. In chapter 5, John Adams develops a theory of inter-social exchange in which institutional convergence and divergence are key to explaining the long-term waxing and waning of international commerce among nations in the world economy. He argues that the transactions costs associated with institutional patterns determine the level, composition, and direction of trade flows. Adams finds that reductions in these costs have historically created an environment in which trade has expanded most rapidly, as in the late nineteenth century and after World War II. In the next essay, Peter Karl Kresl connects international trade with city location and function. He draws heavily on the institutional conviction that democratic planning functions must be sited at the most appropriate level of government, and he concludes that for many purposes urban loci and networks are the right venues in which to shape international commercial outcomes. Capital and firm mobility and challenges to the nation-state make it imperative in Kresl's view that the place of cities be fully considered. Completing this section, Anthony Scaperlanda delves into the reasons for multinational corporate growth and global spread in chapter 6. He maintains that the choice between trading in foreign markets or expanding into them by direct investment is critically dependent on technological variables. Scaperlanda proposes global chartering of transnational firms by the United Nations as one means of resolving conflicts between corporate and country interests, and of creating a consistent operating environment for business enterprises throughout the world.

The three chapters of section III together provide a comprehensive analysis of the implications of natural resources, technology, and labor-market dynamics for economic development in the context of a changing world economy. In chapter 7, Thomas DeGregori succinctly presents the institutional conceptualization of resources. He demonstrates that the volume of resources constantly evolves as science, technology, and human needs advance. DeGregori examines the effects of modern and traditional energy and resource use on local environments. In the end, he does not argue for reduced resource use; rather, he emphasizes that resource creation through the application of science and technology lies at the center of any economic development policy. Dilmus James begins chapter 8 by remarking that "for institutional economists, technology has always been viewed as a core element in economic development." While his perspective closely parallels DeGregori's, James devotes attention predominantly to the process of technology transfer, particularly to poor countries. James traces the evolution of the heterodox position toward technology transfer; describes recent experiences; and synthesizes the present heterodox viewpoint. He concludes that inadequate government, business, and research institutions severely impede inward technology transfer, while the character of the labor force complements resources and technology in the development process. In chapter 9, William Cole observes how differences in the institutional context of the labor market affect families' migration decisions. He demonstrates how the tenurial and inheritance systems of Mexico and India lead to different labor market and migration outcomes, even when both societies have strong rates of population growth.

Section IV provides three applications of institutional analysis to international issues. In chapter 10, William Glade reflects on the multidimensional process through which a country must pass as it restructures institutions that have become unworkable in the modern world context. He devotes particular attention to the cases of Mexico and the former Soviet Union, beginning their stories with their common political revolutions of 1917. Glade concludes that Mexico's current restructuring has proved successful, whereas Russia's (the Soviet Union's) is still in flux, because Mexico has made a more effective institutional transformation that entails "an impressive accumulation of human and organizational capital." According to Glade, this has laid a base for further development, propelled in part by domestic and in part by foreign investors. In chapter 11, Anthony Scaperlanda applies institutional analysis to the evolving international monetary regime. He finds that the International Monetary Fund has moved substantially in the direction of an international central bank, and contends that completion of this transformation would usefully accommodate future needs that are emerging around advances in communication and transportation technologies. In chapter 12, Wendell Gordon reflects on institutional refinements to recompose the United Nations as a more effective instrument for the maintenance of world peace and to foster global economic development. He carefully considers how governmental functions may be divided among the international, national, and local levels. Gordon maintains that a reduction in the importance of national sovereignty would facilitate the more efficient use of the world's resources and contribute to a more just distribution of its product. Like Scaperlanda he favors an international currency.

AN APPRECIATION

When we conceived this book, we aimed to provide comprehensive coverage of the institutional economics of the international economy. We were fortunate in enlisting the participation of a distinguished set of institutionalists whose overlapping interests made this collection of essays an unusually coherent one. On average, each contributor to this collection has spent over three decades as an active professional, engaged not only in academic pursuits but in front-line applied policy work in Washington and around the globe. The contributors to *The Institutional Economics of the International Economy*, however, share more than a multi-gauge evolutionary and institutional approach to international economic issues and years of pragmatic application in the field. With one exception, each of the authors studied for an advanced degree in the Department of Economics at the University of

Texas, Austin, between 1950 and 1970. The exception is Wendell C. Gordon, who influenced each of us during his tenure as professor at The University of Texas when it possessed the leading institutional economics department in the United States after World War II. His inclusion as an author makes this book a shared expression of the application of the institutional method rather than a festschrift, an encomium he would have rejected in any case as excessively ceremonial, no matter how high its technological competence (to use the Veblen-Ayres vernacular). It is relevant and timely to again articulate and extend the work of this singularly prescient institutional economist, and particularly at this moment, when the global economic system is being transformed by technological, political, and commercial forces of uncommon thrust. As we conclude work on this project, we are more aware than ever of the depth and substance of what he taught us. Accordingly, John Adams recalls, in the epilogue to this book, memorable and influential elements of Wendell's teaching that continue to reverberate in the minds of his students and to inform the work he motivated them to pursue.

I. THEORETICAL FOUNDATIONS OF INTERNATIONAL ECONOMIC RELATIONS

CHAPTER 1

INTERNATIONAL ECONOMIC AFFAIRS AS VIEWED FROM A VEBLEN-AYRES PERSPECTIVE

Hans E. Jensen
University of Tennessee

Aside from studies of the developmental process in the less developed countries,[1] institutionalists have not, at least until very recently, "devoted much attention to international economic issues" [Adams 1984, 289]. Wendell Gordon stands out as an early exception to this rule. When it was published nearly 40 years ago, his *International Trade: Goods, People, and Ideas* [1958] was "the fullest expression [in international economics] of several aspects of the institutionalist theory, and his ideas have strongly influenced the arguments" of a number of latter-day institutionalists when they turned their attention to international economic affairs [Adams 1988, 423].[2]

The institutionalist point of view from which Gordon and his followers study international economic processes is one that they inherited from "Thorstein Veblen [1857-1929] and C. E. Ayres [1891-1972]" [Gordon 1958, viii]. These two scholars anchored their analyses in a particular "bedrock . . . position" [Klein 1993, 19], namely in the proposition that human beings display two principal behavioral patterns that "oppose each other" [Ayres 1952, 59]. One pattern manifests itself in the form of a "problem-solving (hence forward-looking) activity (instrumental or technological)" and the other one is shaped by "belief systems or attitudes that are essentially backward looking (ceremonial)" [Klein 1993, 31]. In the words of Ayres, this "distinction of the technological and the ceremonial aspects of organized behavior is a dichotomy but not a dualism. That is, it undertakes to distinguish two aspects of what is still a single, continuous activity both aspects of which are present all the time" [Ayres 1944, 101].

Ayres admitted readily that it was "Veblen [who] made the dichotomy of technology and ceremonialism . . . [a] master principle" of institutionalism and that in his "later efforts to clarify the 'Institutionalist conception' of economic processes and economic policy," he had "followed . . . [Veblen's] lead" [1973, v]. Some of Ayres's followers have found it necessary to clarify his clarification of Veblen's concepts. Inasmuch as it all started with Veblen, I shall now turn to a consideration of the Veblenian origins of some of those Ayresian propositions on which it might be logical to base "an agenda of work" for those economists of today and tomorrow who strive to develop an institutionalist theory of the external sector [Adams 1988, 423].

VEBLENIAN ORIGINS

The dichotomy, which has been characterized as "the central analytical tool of institutional economists in the Veblen-Ayres tradition" [Waller 1982, 757], was given several forms by Veblen.[3] Although he may never have employed the term himself, Veblen began to construct the dichotomy as an instrument of inquiry when he observed that the modern community is characterized by a "bifurcate scheme of culture." This bifurcation has come about in consequence of an historically evolved process in the course of which two major types of occupation have become dominant, namely "industrial and pecuniary employments." The experiences that people have gained in these two realms of activity have resulted in a "concomitant two-cleft systematisation of knowledge" [Veblen 1942, 45-46, 404].

One part of man's bisected knowledge has been systematized by, and in, a set of "habits of thought" that Veblen characterized as "technological use and wont," or "industrial use and wont," because these particular habits are "imposed [on man] by the modern technology" of his society [Veblen 1942, 17; 1966, 110; 1918, vii]. Hence those individuals whose behavior is shaped by industrial use and wont are technologically adequate for being employed in "industry" where they are "mechanically engaged in the production of goods" that are "serviceable to the community" at large [Veblen 1942, 292-293].

The other part of knowledge has been systematized by, and in, a set of "received habits of thought-use and wont" that are of a "ceremonial nature" [Veblen 1966, 6; 1942 109]. That is so, because this type of habits has been formed in the crucible of "law and [legendary] custom, politics, and religion," "status," "coercive control" and, especially in the modern age, "pecuniary reputability" [Veblen 1942 44-45; 1924, 100]. Hence "ceremonial adequacy" [Veblen 1942, 65] is the standard by which performance is measured in the realm of status and, especially, pecuniary employments. As Veblen saw it, these "employments have to do with wealth in point of ownership" [1942, 307]; and, said he, the "owners own . . . things because they own them." Ownership rests on "the ancient feudalistic ground of privilege and prescriptive tenure, vested interest, which run back to the right of seizure by force and collusion" [Veblen 1954, 51]. Hence ownership has become "the conventional basis of esteem. Its possession in some amount becomes necessary in order to [have] any reputable standing in the community." Wealth "is now itself intrinsically honourable and confers honour on its possessor" [Veblen 1924, 29], and not only honor, but also rules of conduct. In short, "conventions out of the past" [Veblen 1966, 30] "delimit and prescribe the behavior that is proper" to property owners as well as "to persons of every [other] social rank" [Ayres 1962, xiv].

A convention is "always in the nature of a precipitate of past habituation" [Veblen 1966, 30]. According to Veblen, habituation is closely associated with what he called "institutions." Thus he referred to institutions as "human relations governed by use and wont" [1942, 45, 236]. An institution is therefore "of the nature of a usage which has become axiomatic and indispensable by habituation and general acceptance" [1954, 101n].[4] "[I]nstitutions are an an outgrowth of habits." "That is what is meant by calling them institutions," said Veblen, "they are settled habits of thought" [1942, 241, 239]. He emphasized that any institution "is a body of habits of thought [that has] bearing on a given line of conduct" [1945, 91]. Thus "human conduct takes place under institutional norms and only under stimuli that have an institutional bearing." It means, said Veblen, that the "wants and desires, the end and aim, the ways and means, the amplitude and drift of the individual's conduct are functions of an institutional variable that is of a highly complex . . . character" [1942, 242-243]. In short, it is the function of institutions to govern human behavior.

There is a reciprocal relationship between individuals and the control mechanism of institutions. Veblen put it in this way:

> The growth and mutations of the institutional fabric are an outcome of the conduct of the individual members of the group, since it is out of the experience of the individuals, through the habituation of individuals, that institutions arise; and it is in this same experience that these institutions act to direct and define the aims and end of conduct. It is, of course, on individuals that the system of institutions imposes those conventional

standards, ideals, and canons of conduct that make up the community's scheme of life [1942, 243].

As mentioned above, Veblen maintained that habituation is molded by experience in two different realms: pecuniary and industrial employments, "business and industry" for short [1942, 292]. The former breeds ceremonial use and wont and the latter inculcates technological use and wont. Veblen argued, therefore, that "institutions that are primarily and immediately of an economic character" may be "distinguished into two classes or categories, according as they serve one or the other of two divergent purposes of economic life" [1924, 208], namely improvement of the "life process," on the one hand [1942, 70] and its "retardation," on the other [1966, 32]. The institutions in question, said Veblen,

are institutions of acquisition or of production; or [to put it differently] . . . they are pecuniary or industrial institutions; or in still other terms, they are institutions serving either the invidious[5] or the non-invidious economic interests. The former category have to do with "business," the latter with industry, taking the latter word in the mechanical sense [1924, 208].

The industrial or "technological institutions . . . enforce their discipline upon the population" in such a manner that "their thinking on other matters [is bent] . . . in consonance with the frame of mind inbred in the industrial system" [1966, 99]. In conformity with this view, Veblen made it clear that he did not identify technology solely with tools and gadgets. This is what he said:

Wherever a human community is met with, as, *e.g.* among any of the peoples of the lower cultures, it is found in possession of . . . fire, of a cutting edge, of a pointed stick, of some tool for piercing, of some form of cord, thong, or fiber. . . . [But] together with [these artifacts is found] some skill in the making of knots and lashings. Coordinate with this knowledge of ways and means, there is also uniformly present some matter-of-fact knowledge of the physical behavior of the materials with which men have to deal in the quest of a livelihood, beyond what any individual has learned or can learn by his own experience alone [1942, 325].

In any society, this kind of "information and proficiency in the ways and means of life" constitutes "a common stock of immaterial equipment" that Veblen called "technological knowledge." It is "embodied in the material contrivances," such as "tools, vessels, vehicles, raw materials, [and] buildings," by means of which "the members of the community make their living. Only by such means does technological efficiency go into effect."

Veblen reiterated, that tools "are useful--in other words, that they are economic goods--means that they have been brought within the sweep of the community's knowledge of ways and means" [1942, 325-326, 328-329].

Thus it is apparent that Veblen conceived of technology as the sum of the tools in existence plus the volume of knowledge available for the production and use of tools. Moreover, as he saw it, the interaction of material and immaterial equipments results in "inventions and discoveries of more and better ways and means" of doing things. Such technological advancement occurs in a process in which "[s]cience and technology play into one another's hands" [1942, 328, 17].

In the first place, the "machine process [is] . . . the archetype in whose image causation is conceived by the scientific investigator." Although he "thinks in the same terms, and applies the same tests of validity" as the practitioners of technology [Veblen 1942, 16-17], unlike the acts of technologists, the scientist's inquiry is propelled by "an Idle Curiosity"--idle "in the sense that no utilitarian aim enters in its habitual exercise" [Veblen 1957, 3; 1918, 88]. Secondly, and fortunately for the fate of humankind, the scientist pays off his debt to technology, as it were, because "much of the knowledge gained under machine-made canons of research can be turned to practical account" in the very same machine process in which the said canons originated. "This employment of scientific knowledge for useful ends *is* technology," said Veblen. Inasmuch as economic "development" is in the nature of "a change in the community's methods of turning material things to account," he concluded that the developmental process must be rooted in the "easy copartnership between . . . [s]cience and technology" [1942, 16-17, 75].

In Veblen's opinion, the impact of technological institutions "is very far-reaching." As he put it in 1904, the "ubiquitous presence" of technology, "with its spiritual concomitant--workday ideals and scepticism of what is only conventionally [i.e., ceremonially] valid--is the unequivocal mark of the Western culture of to-day as contrasted with the culture of other times and places." There has occurred, therefore, a "loosening of the bonds, a weakening of conviction as to the full truth and beauty of the received . . . [ceremonial] institutions" [1904, 323, 358]. Veblen admitted, however, that continued technology-spawned "progress," i.e. "divergence from the archaic position" of ceremonial institutions, could not be taken for granted [1924, 196].

Thus although it is an object pursued by "inventors, engineers, [and other] experts" on technology, "[s]erviceability, industrial advisability, is not the decisive point" that animates pecuniary institutions [1904, 36, 39]. On the contrary, these "disserviceable institutions" control the "production of goods and services . . . [solely] with a view to gain." The "end is pecuniary gain, and the means is disturbance of the industrial system" [1918, 49; 1904, 50, 28].

According to Veblen, the perceived need for disturbance is rooted in two aspects of the industrial economy. One is ceremonial and the other one is technological. The former is actually a conglomerate of interlocking features. In the first place, it is "in terms of [monetary] price that . . . [a businessman] keeps . . . accounts, and in the same terms he computes his output of products." Secondly, the "vital point of production with him is the vendibility of the output, its convertibility into money values not its serviceability for the needs of mankind." Thirdly, production occurs in consequence of the employment of "mechanical appliances." Fourthly, the businessmen obtain control of the said appliances, and hence of their use, by means of "ownership, and ownership [also] runs in terms of money." That is so because ownership is acquired ceremoniously, i.e., for the purpose of reaping monetary profits, by means of financial investment in productive equipment. Hence "industrial plants and processes are capitalized on the basis of their profit-yielding capacity" [1904, 51, 1, 85].[6]

"Progressively increasing efficiency of the processes in use is a pervading trait of the industrial situation" [Veblen 1904, 228]. Unfortunately for the businessman, it is a trait that plays havoc with the process of capitalization. Hence it provides them with an incentive to cause disturbances of the industrial system. Veblen's explanation of these phenomena may be summarized as follows.

Increasing efficiency is the result of inventions in the so-called capital goods industries. Consequently, the "cost of production of 'capital goods' is steadily and progressively lowered." In a "competitive market this is reflected . . . in the [reduced] prices of such capital goods to all buyers." The "lower scale of prices" appeals exclusively to "new investors" who either found "new industrial establishments" or make "extensions of the old." Because of its "lower scale of costs," each "new adventure or extension" has a competitive edge on "those that have gone before it" in the production and sale of a particular "line of staple goods" [Veblen 1904, 229]. Hence the newcomers will undersell "their predecessors" with the result that the "run of competitive prices is lowered" to the detriment of the latter because their "older establishments and processes will no longer yield returns commensurate with the old accepted capitalization." In other words, the price decline bred by the collusion of technological and pecuniary institutions occasions "a discrepancy between that nominal capitalization" which the owners of old equipments "have set their hearts upon through habituation," on the one hand, and "that actual capitalizable value of their property which its current earning-capacity will warrant," on the other [Veblen 1904, 230, 237].

This discrepancy, which Veblen viewed as "chronic," "discourages [the] business men." Consequently, they curtail their operations. Veblen was therefore convinced that "chronic depression"[7] is "normal to the industrial situation under the consummate regime of the machine, so long as competition is unchecked and no *deus ex machina* interposes" [Veblen, 1904, 234, 237, 255].

The business leaders seek to maintain the profitability of old investments which constitute the bulk of all investments. Hence a "remedy, to be efficacious, must restore profits [on past investments] to a 'reasonable' rate; which means, practically, that prices must be brought to the level on which the accepted capitalization has been made." Also, said Veblen, the remedy must be "sought in one or the other of two directions: (1) in an increased unproductive consumption of goods; or (2) in an elimination of that 'cutthroat' competition that keeps profits below the 'reasonable' level." The "'regulation' of prices and output" by means of "business coalitions" is an efficient way to accomplish the latter objective [1904, 241, 255, 255, 260]. By means of their cartel arrangements, the firms in question are enabled to replace unprofitable and competitive prices "by prices fixed on the basis of 'what the traffic will bear.' That is to say, prices are fixed by consideration of what scale of prices will bring the largest aggregate net earnings" from the sale of goods produced by old capital goods [Veblen 1904, 258].

Had the "'pooling [of] the interests' of the [former] competitors" resulted in lower prices, the outcome would have been "increasing sales." Given the fact, however, that "incomes continue to be distributed after the . . . scheme" of inequality, the higher prices, which actually followed upon the establishment of a fairly "secure monopoly," had the opposite effect. Hence a "surplus" of unsold goods materialized pursuant to the introduction of private price administration. In other words, "'overproduction'" or "'underconsumption'" became the rule of the day [Veblen 1904, 257-258, 260, 214]. Hence something had to be devised to "'take up the slack'." The aforementioned unproductive consumption, which Veblen identified with "conspicuous waste," was the means seized upon for this purpose [1966, 33].

From Veblen's point of view, conspicuous waste occurs in the creation of that part of the total output that comprises the "margin between production and productive consumption." By the latter, Veblen understood "necessary current consumption," i.e. items of consumption that "result in a net gain in comfort or in the fulness of life" [1966, 34; 1924, 100]. Such a gain occurs in the course of what he called the "life process." It is, therefore, a process that is cleansed of all traces of ceremony, including the "habit of making an invidious pecuniary comparison" [1942, 70; 1924, 100].[8]

No such life process exists in the industrial economy. On the contrary, said Veblen, pecuniary institutions assure that a "large proportion, perhaps the greater part, of what is included under the standard of living for any class . . . falls under the theoretical category of Conspicuous Waste." Thus he volunteered the opinion that the "margin of product disposable for wasteful consumption will always exceed fifty per cent of the current product" in industrial communities. And he surmised that this margin will "probably exceed seventy-five per cent of the whole" in the "more fortunate cases." It "takes thought, skill, and time" on the part of business to establish and maintain "a scheme of reputable standardised waste" of such a magnitude. "Advertising" is one of the principal "instrumentalities" used in an attempt to solve the problem of "surplus productivity" [Veblen 1966, 137, 35; 1942, 367, 369; 1966, 36]. To the extent that it is efficient, advertising, and other ceremonially generated emulation-spawning social pressures, work because they induce all classes, "rich and poor," to view a wasteful item of consumption as "a necessary of life." That is to say, the typical consumer feels compelled to acquire a wasteful article because of its apprehended "relative utility" [Veblen 1966, 137; 1924, 98-99].

In spite of the admitted massiveness of unproductive production, Veblen was of the opinion that "[p]rivate initiative cannot carry the waste of goods and services to nearly the point required by the business situation." Wasteful expenditures by governments on "[a]rmaments, public edifices, courtley and diplomatic establishments, and the like" are also of no avail because public waste is "altogether inadequate to offset [that part of] the surplus productivity" that the private sector fails to neutralize. Veblen concluded, therefore, that so long as "industry remains at its present level of efficiency, and especially so long as incomes continue to be distributed somewhat after the present scheme, waste cannot be expected to overtake production, and can therefore not check the untoward tendency toward depression" [Veblen 1904, 255-258].

Business managers strive to eliminate the depression of their firms' profits by means of "'SABOTAGE'" by which Veblen understood the "conscientious withdrawal of efficiency" [1944, 1].[9] The managers do not do so in order to "augment human discomfort." "But only by shortening the supply of things needed and so increasing privation to a critical point can they sufficiently increase their (nominal) earnings" [Veblen 1954, 220n]. It seems Veblen was of the opinion that businessmen were able to accomplish such a feat because their advertising campaigns and other forms of salesmanship had been effective in making the demand for their products highly inelastic over the relevant price range. As he put it, the managers keep past "capitalisation intact . . . by curtailing employment and output to such a point that the resulting smaller volume of output at the resulting increased price per unit will yield the requisite increased total price-return." As a consequence of the unemployment they have engineered collusively, the managers are able to "reduce wages" with a view to a further enhancement of profits [1954, 220].

In 1915, Veblen modified his concept of the dichotomy when he argued that "the industrial arts" and "pecuniary use and wont" actually live "in some sort of symbiosis" *within* a given economic institution [1966, 37]. He now maintained that each such institution performs *both* ceremonial and technological functions. By 1919, he was convinced that the pecuniary-ceremonial features of each major economic institution had overpowered, or, "encapsulated,"[10] the technological contents of the institution in question. In Veblen's opinion, the "Vested interests" of the business community had by then "sufficiently shown their unfitness to take care of the country's material welfare" [1944, 140]. As far as he was concerned, technology could wield its influence only if it were freed of the ceremonial shackles that held it back in each major economic institution. Veblen was convinced that the only social group that could bring about such a sea-change were "the technicians, the engineers and industrial experts" who constitute the "indispensable General Staff of . . . [the] industrial system." He proposed, therefore, that a select few among these specialists be constituted as "a Soviet of Technicians" with power "to act in matters of industrial administration" [1944, 135, 143].[11] Veblen stated his vision of the functions of the Soviet in the following manner:

> The duties and powers of the incoming directorate will . . . converge on those points . . . where the old order has most signally fallen short; that is to say, on the due allocation of resources and consequent full and reasonably proportioned employment of the available equipment and man power; on the avoidance of waste and duplication of work; and on an equitable and sufficient supply of goods and services to consumers [1944, 142].

It may be concluded that Veblen was a social critic who was committed to the task of contributing to an improvement of the human condition. The proposals that he advanced with that end in view were based on his institutionalist theory of the socioeconomic order. His theorizing, explanations, critique, and proposals for reform were tightly interwoven and undergirded by partly hidden value judgments. As Ayres once observed, "Veblen repeatedly declared that as a scientist he was passing no value judgments, thus seeming to align himself with the cultural relativists who put science and values on the opposite sides of an impenetrable wall." Yet, said Ayres, it "would be impossible for anyone now to read Veblen's first book,

The Theory of the Leisure Class, and to conclude that Veblen is really refraining from passing judgments" [1952, 26-27].

Ayres, who has been hailed as "the leading American institutional economist in the post-World War II era," [Breit and Culbertson 1976, 3] based to a large extent his own contributions on Veblen's work. As Ayres put it himself, he was "an avowed Veblenian" [1973, v].

AYRESIAN ARTICULATIONS

Ayres was not only a Veblenian, he was also a Deweyian. "My own ideas," said he, "have been chiefly formed . . . by reflections upon the work of John Dewey and Thorstein Veblen." From the former, Ayres acquired what "Dewey called the 'instrumental' process" of reasoning and valuation and as intimated above, he obtained the dichotomy from the latter [Ayres 1935, 27; 1961, 29]. Although he regarded "Dewey's 'instrumental' philosophy" and Veblen's "'institutional economics' . . . as almost identical expressions of . . . the trend of technology and science," Ayres was of the opinion that "neither Veblen nor Dewey ever gave us a clear and acceptable statement of the reason for . . . [the] fateful stand-off" between institutions and technology [1935, 27; 1967, 4]. Hence Ayres resolved to make a more clear-cut "differentiation of technological reality from ceremonial fantasy" than Veblen did and a more pungent separation of "real values from fancies, or pseudo values" than Dewey did [1961, 31].[12] In accordance with this programmatic statement, I shall first discuss Ayres's theory of the dichotomy and thereafter attempt to demonstrate that his value theory may be viewed as a bridge that connects his institutionalist theory to his policy recommendations.

Ayres emphasized that the dichotomy is one of two different kinds of "learned behavior" of which one is "technological" in nature and the other "ceremonial." According to Ayres, technology is "first and foremost a type, or form, or aspect, of human behavior" [1952, 51; 1944, 100]. As such, technology is not separate and distinct from those material artifacts that are conventionally identified with technology. That is so because in its behavioral mode, technology is "the tool-using aspect of human behavior," a behavior that Ayres identified with "skills." Consequently, he defined technology as "the sum of human skills" plus "the sum of [those] human tools" that humans employ so artfully [1961, 77; 1952, 52]. The requisite skills and tools include those employed by scientists. "Both science and industry are projections of . . . [the tool-using] process." The tools used by scientists are such things as scientific "journals," "cyclotrons and electronic microscopes" [Ayres 1973, vi; 1959, 5; 1953, 282]. There is some division of labor between science and industry. Ayres identified "science as the 'thinking' aspect of the tool-using process and technology [as mechanical arts] as the 'doing' aspect of the same process. Neither is possible or conceivable except as an aspect of the other" [1973, vi].

According to Ayres, the "technological process is continuously and progressively developmental." In short, "[t]echnology is dynamic" and it is so by virtue of the "dual character of the technological process." Technological advances occur because of interactions between the "ingenuity" of "bright and restless" people on the one hand, and existing tools, on the other [Ayres 1961, 111; 1952, 57, 59; 1962, xv, xvi]. Such interactions result in the creation of new tools and skills by means of invention. "All inventions and discoveries--in the mechanical arts, in pure science, and in the fine arts--result from the combination of previously existing tools, symbols, and devices so as to form new tools, symbols, and devices."[13] Inasmuch as "no one ever made a combination without there being something to combine," it follows that "the more tools, symbols, and devices there are in any given situation the more of a field day human ingenuity can have." Consequently, the "more likely inventions and discoveries become" [Ayres 1952, 56-57; 1962, xvi]. It is not just new tools that are created. New skills are spawned in the very same process of invention. This dynamic process may be curbed and in Veblenian terms, it is "ceremonialism that provides the curb." In Ayresian terms, ceremonialism is only one of several measures that join forces in an "institution" to halt technological advance [1962, xvi; 1952, 42]. These intramural measures are: (1) definition of rank, status, and social roles by the agency of "custom;" (2) establishment of rank, status, and social roles in accordance with the specifications of those existing "mores" that spawn customs; (3) selection of those "legends" from which mores are to emanate; (4) determination of the "ceremonial adequacy" of individuals for performing their assigned roles and tasks in the institution's affairs [Ayres 1952, 42-46]. Legends, mores, and customs are crucial features because they make institutions "inherently past-binding" and thereby programmed to "resist change" induced by present-day technology. Hence, said Ayres, "what we mean by an institution is a social pattern whose function is contributory to such resistance" [1963, 57; 1952, 50]. As this definition shows, Ayres conceived of an institution, "not [as] a structural category," but as a "functional category." Hence it has sole "reference to . . . a certain aspect of social behavior," namely that which follows from a propensity to be allergic to change [1952, 42].

Whereas technology "is dynamic," institutions "are static." What "happens to any society is [therefore] determined jointly by the forward urging of its technology and the backward pressure of its . . . [institutional] system." Although "we have no reason to suppose that either one will invariably prevail," Ayres was convinced that "modern Western civilization has been largely shaped, and is still being shaped, by science and the machine process." That is so because the "impact of technology upon the institutions of Western society" has been such that "all institutional ties and sanctions have been progressively weakened" in that society [Ayres, 1952, 59; 1962, xvii; 1951, 51; 1944, 185-186].

Although technology has subjected all institutions to a "process of dilution," such attenuation has been especially important and dramatic in the case of the "institution of property." This central economic institution was forced to *permit* changes in itself in consequence of a technological development that culminated in the emergence of large-scale units of production. It was "only in this permissive sense," said Ayres, that the "institution of property made modern industrial society possible" [1944, 188; 1952, 106]. He then continued in the following interesting vein:

> However, this means that the institution of property is a very remarkable affair. Perhaps we ought not to call it an institution at all now, except with careful reservations. It is a social structure in which *institutional functions* and *technological functions* are *blended*. Its institutional function is sufficiently attested by the fact that it has projected the feudal power system into the modern world, with consequences of the greatest importance. But it is also an organizational device of a unique degree of flexibility . . . [I]ts organizational adaptability, beginning with disposability, has extended in a number of directions and seems capable of virtually infinite modification. In this sense it is indeed characteristically modern, one of the outstanding technical achievements of the industrial revolution [1952, 106-107; emphasis added].

This declaration might be viewed as a logical inference from Ayres's long-held position that technological behavior and institutional behavior are "two aspects of what is still a single, continuous activity" [1944, 101]. Although he made no reference to Veblen at this point, Ayres's pronouncement might be viewed as an elaboration and extension of Veblen's statement that the "state of the industrial arts . . . lives in some sort of symbiosis . . . with pecuniary use and wont" [1966, 37]. In the late 1980s, Walter C. Neale echoed Ayres and Veblen when he remarked that "all institutional arrangements have ceremonial . . . aspects, but most, if not all, probably have technological aspects" also [1988, 247].[14]

It seems that it was this concept of symbiotic, or synthetic, institutions that Ayres had in mind when he formulated policy proposals designed to bring about "institutional adjustments" [1967, 3]; adjustments that might be brought about through a substitution of technological aspects for at least some of the ceremonial aspects of institutions.[15]

As far as Ayres was concerned, his institutionalist "interpretations [of the economic order] point toward certain policies" for this kind of adjustment. In order to serve as an "advocate" of such policies, he had to develop a "general *strategy*" for action together with its implemental "tactics" [Ayres 1952, ix; 1948, 225, 227]. As explained presently, Ayres obtained the relevant strategy and tactics from bodies of ideas that he viewed as "[c]omplementary" to institutionalism. The use of strategy and tactics presupposes a knowledge of the purpose for the achievement of which these tools are to be employed, however. Ayres formulated a "conception of value" as a means to gaining access to the requisite knowledge [1948, 225, 231]. When he developed this conception, Ayres acknowledged his "indebtedness" to Dewey [1961, 29].

"In all inquiry," said Dewey, "what is proposed as a conclusion (the end-in-view of that inquiry) is evaluated as to its worth on the ground of its ability to resolve the *problem* presented by the condition under investigation." Once arrived at, an end becomes the means for the attainment of a still further end-in-view. Values are therefore formed and applied in a process where "means . . . are constituents of ends attained and [in which] . . . ends . . . are useable as means to further ends" [Dewey 1939, 46-47, 50]. It was from this Deweyian proposition that Ayres "first learned . . . [the] way" human beings have "of knowing, clearly and consistently, what is good and what is not." It is a way that "Dewey called the 'instrumental' process" [1961, 29]. Hence, said Ayres, "true values," as distinguished from "the false values" of ceremony, "are made in terms of instruments and techniques." The process from which true values flow includes "a choice, a decision, and a judgment" [1966, 166; 1952, 26; 1944, 212]. Ayres illustrated this proposition by the following homely example:

> A mechanic reaches for a tool [and] . . . selects a wrench which he "judges" to be suitable. He "decides" which of two will more exactly fit his bolt and "chooses" that one. Clearly this issue is one of fact; that is, it is capable of being instrumentally verified. If both wrenches are actually tried, it can be established beyond argument which one fits the bolt and which does not [1944, 212].

According to Ayres, the sequence of judgment, choice, and verification is inherent in any technological process where it constitutes a continuum equivalent to Dewey's means-end continuum. It "is a logical continuum, a true progression each item of which implies succeeding items by the same process by which each has been itself derived from preceding items in the series" [Ayres 1943, 477]. "What we call truth is a function of this procedure. That is, it derives from the use of instruments, tools, and instrumentally manipulated materials." Consequently, it is "this technological continuum which is the locus of truth and value." In short, true "'Value' means continuity, literally; and that is its sole meaning." Unlike culture-specific false values, "[t]rue values are transcultural--they are the same for all" members of humankind [Ayres 1944, 221; 1943, 477; 1991, 167].

Being such a member, Ayres shared these values. He did so in an extraordinary degree because he was absorbed in what he called the "'thinking' aspects" of the science-technology complex [1973, vi]. The processes that Ayres found operational in the formation of true values among people in general were the very same processes in which his own values were shaped. His intellectual outputs were therefore not valueless precisely for the same reasons that "[s]cience and technology are not *wertfrei*." Hence he declared that "good and evil [do *not*] lie beyond the scope of scientific knowledge" and, in particular, they do *not* lie "beyond the grasp of [Ayres's own] trained intelligence" [1961, 15, 41].[16] As far as his contemporary society was concerned, it was Ayres's judgment "that the [existing] industrial way of life is *good*--and not only good: the best that man has ever known." Even the best is not good enough because society is marred by the *evils* of "poverty" and economic "instability" [1961, 15; 1952, 290, 274; emphasis added].

The institutionalism that Ayres inherited provided no solution to these twin problems. As intimated above, there was, fortunately, an extant body of "[c]omplementary ideas" that were "particularly strong" where "institutionalism is conspicuously weak." Ayres rubricated these exogenous ideas under the headings of "underconsumptionism" and "planning." The former could provide institutionalism with a "strategy" for economic stabilization and the latter could supply it with the "tactics" needed for such an enterprise [Ayres 1948, 225, 227].[17]

Taking some of his cues from J. M. Keynes [Ayres 1938, 73-76; 1952, 132-155], Ayres argued that existing institutions produce an "extreme discrepancy in the distribution of income." Maldistribution causes a "deficiency of mass purchasing power." This shortfall fosters "underconsumption" which, in its turn, generates "disemployment." Unemployment "still further reduces . . . consumer demand" and hence creates additional forced idleness, and so on. Thus there is a "multiplier" effect in a "downward direction" [1938, iv; 1948, 226; 1952, 146].

The "object of economic strategy must be a redistribution of income calculated to relieve . . . society from the burden of excess funds and to swell the mass of consumer purchasing power to the point where it absorbs the whole product of industry under full employment" [Ayres 1944, 272]. Strategic planning is the means to this end-in-view and it is to be effected through a careful orchestration of several institutional innovations. One method consists of deficit financing of "the outright issue of currency," or cash grants, to persons with low, or no, incomes. A permanent system of social security and unemployment compensation steers "the flow of income in [the direction of] small income-channels." The same objective is achievable by "public works programs" [Ayres 1944, 276; 1946b, 101, 89]. Ayres was emphatic that each of these programs must be "financed by direct progressive taxation" of "personal incomes" and "inheritances." If resort were taken to government borrowing, it "would not divert any funds from large-income channels" because most government bonds "are sold to banks which create the money with which to pay for them" [1946b, 114-115, 107]. Only if they are financed by progressive taxation, will the programs in question have maximum distributive effect.

In addition to cash grants, social-security and public-works programs, Ayres proposed the establishment of a "desperately need[ed] . . . new institution," namely that of a governmentally "guaranteed income" [1966, 167-168]. The institution is to be located in the Internal Revenue Service. Individuals and families "who have no income, or whose incomes are below the taxable minimum would receive a 'refund' check." Those whose "incomes are large enough to be taxable would receive their guaranteed income in the form of tax deductions, just as everybody . . . now receives tax deductions for dependents." Thus, said Ayres, "[u]niversal coverage removes the stigma of charity" at the same time as the program contributes to "stabilization of the economy" [1966, 170-171; 1952, 272-273].[18] Both humane and economic objectives are served.

CONCLUSION

It might be asked what all this has to do with international economic affairs. Veblen did not pay any attention to these affairs and Ayres couched his limited observations on the subject in terms of underconsumption. He argued that international economic rivalries and loans extended to developing countries by rich nations are caused by the latter's need to get rid of unconsumable surpluses without accepting unwanted imports in return [1938, 66-68, 85-88; 1952, 166-181]. There is "only one way out" of this dilemma, said Ayres, and that "way is by the [better] distribution of mass purchasing power." If "industry is to produce more and more both at home and abroad, then people will have to consume more and more both abroad and at home" [1938, 88].

The world economy and the position of the United States therein have changed dramatically since Ayres wrote these words. As Anne Mayhew observed in a different context, Ayres "did not address, and understandably so, the problems of the 1980s [and 1990s]. This should not prevent an . . . institutionalist from doing so today" [1981, 519]. Precisely! In addressing current problems in the international economic system, institutionalists would benefit from paying close attention to what Veblen and Ayres said in their texts *and* to what they said between the lines of these texts. In accordance therewith, the institutionalists in question should first of all state their value judgements "up front" and describe how they arrived at such judgments. Secondly, they should explain what they mean by institutions, select the relevant institutions for the problems at hand, and fill these institutions with contents derived from empirical studies. Thirdly, they should heed Veblen's (implicit) and Ayres's (explicit) admonition that economic "interpretations point to certain policies" [Ayres 1952, ix). In other words, institutionalist international economics must be policy-oriented. Fourthly, an institutionalist practitioner of international economics should pay close attention to the following observation by Ayres:

> Institutionalism . . . has suffered from a vital defect. In spite of its value as a general *theory*, it has never of itself produced any general *strategy* [emphasis in original]. . . . This defect, more than anything else, is responsible for the *insignificance* of the *influence* institutionalism has exerted hitherto [emphasis added]. If it stood alone, I fear that the theory would continue to be just a theory [1948, 225].

Ayres sought to make institutionalism operational, relevant, and influential by infusing it with the complementary ideas of underconsumptionism and planning. Warren J. Samuels seems to have been thinking along similar lines when he argued recently "that institutionalism, if it takes advantage of numerous sources of cognate research and analysis . . . may be on the threshold of a quantum change in level and sophistication of analysis." Thus like Ayres, Samuels averred that "insights and knowledge from one school can, with adequate formulae of translation, be carried over to other schools" to the benefit of the latter ones [1995, 581, 570n]. The chapters in this book show that some present-day institutionalist practitioners of international economics and its neighboring fields are establishing rapport with other paradigms. Ayres would have nodded his approval of such an endeavor.

ENDNOTES

1. For representative institutionalist work in development economics, see Adams [1993], Ayres [1960], Dietz [1992], Gordon [1982, 1984], Higgins [1960], Klein [1977], Street [1967, 1980, 1988], Street and James [1982].

2. For some recent institutionalist inquiries into international economic affairs, see Adams [1984, 1988, 1994a, 1994b], Harvey [1993], Lower [1994], Ramstad [1987], Scaperlanda [1992].

3. From the major works of Veblen, Marc R. Tool culled the following forms of what he called the "Veblenian distinction": "salesmanship--workmanship"; "business--industry"; "ceremonial--technological"; "ownership--production"; "free income--tangible performance"; "sabotage--community serviceability"; "pecuniary employment--industrial employment"; "invidious emulation--technological efficiency"; "consciencious [sic] withdrawal of efficiency--inordinately productive enterprise"; "competitive advertising--valuable information and guidance"; "business prosperity--industrial efficiency" [Tool 1953, 191-193].

4. As pointed out by Walter C. Neale [1988, 227], Veblen continued: "Its physiological counterpart would presumably be any one of those habitual additions that are now attracting the attention of experts in sobriety" [Veblen 1954, 101n].

5. Veblen used the term "invidious" in a "technical sense as describing a comparison of persons with a view to rating and grading them in respect of relative worth or value--in an aesthetic or moral sense. . . . An invidious comparison is a process of valuation of persons in respect of worth" [1924, 34].

6. In a Keynesesque manner, Veblen pointed out that "the value of capital is a function of its earning capacity, not of its prime cost or of its mechanical efficiency" [1904, 152-153]. Cf. John Maynard Keynes [1936, 135-137].

7. When Veblen used the term "depression," he had in mind depression of profits due to depressed prices, not depression of total output in the economy at large. For such a calamity, he used the term "'unemployment'" [Veblen 1966, 33].

8. As Veblen saw it, therefore, the life process is in the nature of a way of life that is molded entirely by science and technology. As he put it, "the matter-of-fact discipline" of science and technology "inculcates thinking in terms of opaque, impersonal cause and effect, to the neglect of those norms of validity that rests on [ceremonial] usage and on the conventional standards handed down by [such] usage"[1904, 360; 1947, 309-310]. Thus to paraphrase Ayres, the life process is an "antithesis" [1948, 36] of the "triumph of imbecile institutions over life and culture"[Veblen 1918, 25].

9. Veblen observed that sabotage is "a derivative of 'sabot,' which is French for wooden shoes. It means going slow, with a dragging . . . movement" [Veblen 1944, 1]. He pointed out that the definition of sabotage as "'A Conscientious Withdrawal of Efficiency . . . is said to have originated among the I. W. W." [Veblen 1954, 218n].

10. I have borrowed this phrase from Paul D. Bush [1988, 143].

11. Veblen was vague on details concerning the nature, organization, and methods of the structure of a Soviet of Technicians. For instance, he asserted that the "technicians may be said to represent the community at large" [Veblen 1944, 163], but he did not explain how they might be chosen for such a task.

12. It seems that it was under the influence of Walton H. Hamilton that Ayres's thinking veered toward institutionalism and that he decided to become a propagator of this brand of social science when Hamilton left economics in favor of the law. At this juncture, Ayres "made up his mind that his own mission would be to 'identify the philosophical parameters of Walton Hamilton's institutionalism'" [Breit and Culbertson 1976, 7]. For discussions of Hamilton's institutionalism and his influence on Ayres, see Ayres [1961, 27-28], John R. Sellers [1993], and William T. Waller [1982, 760-762].

13. Ayres emphasized that "there is no difference between 'mechanical' inventions and 'scientific' discovery. Scientific discoveries also result from the combination of previously existing devices, and materials, laboratory instruments, and techniques" [1944, 113].

14. Employing methods and arguments of which Neale did not approve, some followers of J. Fagg Foster, who claimed Ayres as his mentor, formulated the most frequently cited post-Ayresian synthesis. According to one of these post-Ayresians, Paul D. Bush, institutions are repositories of knowledge. In any institution, the relevant "knowledge is either 'embodied' in instrumentally [technologically] warranted patters of behavior or 'encapsulated' within ceremonially warranted patterns of behavior" [Bush 1983, 37]. The approach to institutionalism that has been chosen by Bush and his compatriots, in particular Marc R. Tool, has been criticized by Neale and his allies, especially Gordon and Anne Mayhew. For a discussion of the controversy in which these two groups have been embroiled, see Roland Hoksbergen [1994].

15. I use the term "ceremonial aspects" as a designation for that whole panoply of past-binding and condition-freezing features that Ayres associated with institutions: legends, mores, customs, status, rank, and ceremonial adequacy [Ayres 1952, 42-46].

16. Hence Ayres loathed the "moral agnosticism among the intellectual elite." He judged the prevalence of this "pestilence" to be paradoxical: "At this moment, when knowledge of the world and men has reached [unprecedented] levels," those who are "best informed have somehow persuaded themselves that good and evil lie beyond the scope of scientific knowledge and beyond the grasp of trained intelligence." The "doctrine of cultural relativism" is the "quintessence of moral agnosticism" and it exists because its adherents have failed to distinguish between transcultural true values and culture-specific false values [Ayres 1961, 41-42, 48].

17. By underconsumptionism, Ayres understood a conglomerate of carefully selected propositions from the works of J. A. Hobson, H. G. Moulton, and Waddill Catchings, but preeminently from the writings of John Maynard Keynes [Ayres 1952, 141, 1964a, 112-113, 114, 123-124]. According to Ayres, underconsumptionism was lacking in institutionalism because its founder, Veblen, "suffered from a fatal astigmatism. He failed to see the significance of underconsumptionism" [Ayres 1946a, 114]. Planning was an idea that sprouted in various quarters in the 1930s [Ayres 1943, 469-472].

18. For a thorough, but critical, analysis of Ayres's policy recommendations, see Donald A. Walker [1978].

REFERENCES

Adams, John. "Foreign Economic Policy: Challenges of the 1980s." *Journal of Economic Issues* 18 (March 1984): 275-294.

_____. "Trade and Payments as Instituted Process: The Institutional Theory of the External Sector." In Marc R. Tool, ed., *Institutional Theory and Policy*, Vol. 2 of *Evolutionary Economics*. Armonk, NY: M. E. Sharpe, 1988, pp. 421-442.

_____. "Institutions and Economic Development: Structure, Process, and Incentive." In Marc R. Tool, ed., *Institutional Economics: Theory, Method, Policy*. Boston: Kluwer Academic Publishers, 1993, pp. 245-269.

_____. "International Economic Relations." In Geoffrey M. Hodgson, Warren J. Samuels, and Marc R. Tool, eds., *The Elgar Companion to Institutional and Evolutionary Economics A-K*. Aldershot: Edward Elgar Publishing, 1994a, pp. 423-428.

_____. "Economy as Instituted Process: Change, Transformation, and Progress." *Journal of Economic Issues* 28 (June 1994b): 331-355.

Ayres, C. E. "The Gospel of Technology." In *American Philosophy Today and Tomorrow*, edited by Horace Kallen and Sidney Hook, pp. 24-42. New York: Lee Furman, 1935.

_____. *The Problem of the Economic Order*. Austin: University Co-Op, 1938.

_____. "The Significance of Economic Planning." In Seba Eldridge, ed., *Development of Collective Enterprise*. Lawrence: University of Kansas Press, 1943, pp. 469-481.

_____. *The Theory of Economic Progress*. Chapel Hill: The University of North Carolina Press, 1944.

_____. "The Impact of the Great Depression on Economic Thinking." *The American Economic Review: Papers and Proceedings* 36 (May 1946a): 112-125.

_____. *The Divine Right of Capital*. Boston: Houghton Mifflin and Co., 1946b.

_____. "The New Economics." *Southwest Review* 33 (Summer 1948): 223-232.

_____. "The Co-Ordinates of Institutionalism." *The American Economic Review: Papers and Proceedings* 41 (May 1951): 47-55.

_____. *The Industrial Economy*. Boston: Houghton Mifflin and Co., 1952.

_____. "The Role of Technology in Economic Theory." *The American Economic Review: Papers and Proceedings* 43 (May 1953): 279-287.

_____. "The Industrial Way of Life." *Texas Quarterly* 2 (Summer 1959): 1-19.

_____. "Veblen's Theory of Instincts Reconsidered." In Douglas F. Dowd, ed., *Thorstein Veblen: A Critical Reappraisal*. Ithaca, NY: Cornell University Press, 1958, pp. 25-37.

_____. "Institutionalism and Economic Development." *The Southwestern Social Science Quarterly* 41 (June 1960): 45-62.

_____. *Toward a Reasonable Society*. Austin: The University of Texas Press, 1961.

_____. "Foreword--1962." *The Theory of Economic Progress*, 3rd ed., pp. xiii-xxxiii. Kalamazoo: New Issues Press, Western Michigan University, 1978 [1944].

_____. "The Legacy of Thorstein Veblen." In Benjamin Aaron, ed., *Institutional Economics: Veblen, Commons, and Mitchell Reconsidered*. Berkeley and Los Angeles: University of California Press, 1963, pp. 45-62.

_____. "Guaranteed Income: An Institutionalist View." In Robert Theobald, ed., *The Guaranteed Income: Next Step in Economic Evolution?*. Garden City, NY: Doubleday and Co., 1966, pp. 161-174.

_____. "The Theory of Institutional Adjustment." In Carey C. Thompson, ed., *Institutional Adjustment*. Austin: The University of Texas Press, 1967, pp. 1-17.

_____. "Prolegomenon to Institutionalism." *Science the False Messiah [1927] & Holier than Thou: The Way of the Righteous [1929]*, pp. iii-xii. Clifton, NJ: Augustus M. Kelley, 1973.

Breit, William and William Patton Culbertson, Jr. "Clarence Edwin Ayres: An Intellectual Portrait." In William Breit and William Patton Culbertson, Jr., eds., *Science and Ceremony: The Institutional Economics of C. E. Ayres*. Austin: The University of Texas Press, 1976, pp. 3-22.

Bush, Paul D. "An Exploration of the Structural Characteristics of a Veblen-Ayres-Foster Defined Institutional Domain." *Journal of Economic Issues* 17 (March 1983): 35-66.

_____. "The Theory of Institutional Change." In Marc R. Tool, ed., *Foundations of Institutional Thought*, Vol. 1 of *Evolutionary Economics*. Armonk, NY: M. E. Sharpe, 1988, pp. 125-166.

Dewey, John. *Theory of Evaluation*. Vol. 2, No. 4 of the *International Encyclopaedia of Unified Science*. Chicago: University of Chicago Press, 1939.

Dietz, James L. "Overcoming Underdevelopment: What Has Been Learned from the East Asian and Latin American Experiences?" *Journal of Economic Issues* 26 (June 1992): 373-383.

Gordon, Wendell. *International Trade: Goods, People, and Ideas*. New York: Alfred A. Knopf, 1958.

_____. "Institutionalism and Dependency." *Journal of Economic Issues* 16 (June 1982): 569-575.

_____. "The Implementation of Economic Development." *Journal of Economic Issues* 18 (March 1984): 295-313.

Harvey, John T. "The Institution of Foreign Exchange Trading." *Journal of Economic Issues* 27 (September 1993): 679-698.

Higgins, Benjamin. "Some Introductory Remarks on Institutionalism and Economic Development." *The Southwestern Social Science Quarterly* 41 (June 1960): 15-21.

Hoksbergen, Roland. "Postmodernism and Institutionalism: Toward a Resolution of the Debate on Relativism." *Journal of Economic Issues* 28 (September 1994): 679-713.

Keynes, John Maynard. *The General Theory of Employment, Interest, and Money*. New York: Harcourt, Brace and Co. 1936.

Klein, Philip A. "An Institutionalist View of Development Economics." *Journal of Economic Issues* 11 (December 1977): 785-807.

_____. "The Institutionalist Challenge: Beyond Dissent." In Marc R. Tool, ed., *Institutional Economics: Theory, Method, Policy*. Boston: Kluwer Academic Publishers, 1993, pp. 13-47.

Lower, Milton D. "International Economic Policy." In Geoffrey M. Hodgson, Warren J. Samuels, and Marc R. Tool, eds., *The Elgar Companion to Institutional and Evolutionary Economics A-K*. Aldershot: Edward Elgar Publishing, 1994, pp. 419-423.

Mayhew, Anne. "Ayresian Technology, Technological Reasoning, and Doomsday." *Journal of Economic Issues* 15 (June 1981): 513-520.

Neale, Walter C. "Institutions." In Marc R. Tool, ed., *Foundations of Institutional Thought*, Vol. 1 of *Evolutionary Economics*. Armonk, NY: M. E. Sharpe, 1988, pp. 227-256.

Ramstad, Yngve. "Free Trade Versus Fair Trade: Import Barriers As a Problem of Reasonable Value." *Journal of Economic Issues* 21 (March 1987): 5-32.

Samuels, Warren J. "The Present State of Institutional Economics." *Cambridge Journal of Economics* 19 (August 1995): 569-590.

Scaperlanda, Anthony. "Direct Investment Controls and International Equilibrium: The U.S. Experience." *Eastern Economic Journal* 18 (Spring 1992): 157-170.

Sellers, John Robert. "The Institutional Economics of Walton Hale Hamilton: Sources, Nature, and Influence." Unpublished Doctoral Dissertation. Knoxville: The University of Tennessee at Knoxville, 1993.

Street, James H. "The Latin American 'Structuralists' and Institutionalists: Convergence in Development Theory." *Journal of Economic Issues* 1 (June 1967): 44-62.

_____. "A Holistic Approach to Underdevelopment." In John Adams, ed., *Institutional Economics Contributions to the Development of Holistic Economics: Essays in Honor of Allan G. Gruchy*. Boston: Nijhoff Publishing, 1980, pp. 239-249.

_____. "The Institutionalist Theory of Economic Development." In Marc R. Tool, ed., *Institutional Theory and Policy*, Vol. 2 of *Evolutionary Economics*. Armonk, NY: M. E. Sharpe, 1988, pp. 443-469.

Street, James H. and Dilmus D. James. "Institutionalism, Structuralism, and Dependency in Latin America." *Journal of Economic Issues* 16 (September 1982): 673-689.

Tool, Marc R. "The Philosophy of Neo-Institutionalism: Veblen, Dewey, and Ayres." Unpublished Doctoral Dissertation. Boulder: University of Colorado, 1953.

Veblen, Thorstein. *The Theory of Business Enterprise*. New York: Charles Scribner's Sons, 1904.

_____. *The Instinct of Workmanship and the State of the Industrial Arts*. New York: B. W. Huebsch, 1918 [1914].

_____. *The Theory of the Leisure Class*. New York: B. W. Huebsch, 1924 [1899].

_____. *The Place of Science in Modern Civilisation and Other Essays*. New York: The Viking Press, 1942 [1919].

_____. *The Engineers and the Price System*. New York: The Viking Press, 1944 [1921].

_____. *An Inquiry into the Nature of Peace and the Terms of its Perpetuation*. New York: The Viking Press, 1945 [1917].

_____. *What Veblen Taught: Selected Writings of Thorstein Veblen*, Wesley C. Mitchell, ed. New York: The Viking Press, 1947 [1936].

_____. *Absentee Ownership and Business Enterprise in Recent Times: The Case of America*. New York: The Viking Press, 1954 [1923].

_____. *The Higher Learning in America*. New York: Sagamore Press, 1957 [1918].

_____. *Imperial Germany and the Industrial Revolution*. Ann Arbor: Ann Arbor Paperbacks of the University of Michigan Press, 1966 [1915].

Walker, Donald A. "The Economic Policy Proposals of Clarence Ayres." *Southern Economic Journal* 44 (January 1978): 616-623.

Waller, William T., Jr. "The Evolution of the Veblenian Dichotomy: Veblen, Hamilton, Ayres, and Foster." *Journal of Economic Issues* 16 (September 1982): 757-771.

CHAPTER 2

FOREIGN INVESTMENT, ECONOMIC GROWTH, AND THEORIES OF VALUE: EVIDENCE FROM ECONOMIC HISTORY

Anne Mayhew
University of Tennessee

This chapter advances two propositions: (1) foreign investment is *not* needed for economic growth; and (2) foreign investment is wrongly thought of as a requirement for growth *because* of a deep confusion of machines and of financial claims on those machines. I begin by reexamining evidence for the first proposition and then try to explain why this evidence has not altered the view that monetary foreign investment is required for growth.

The failure to examine the relevant evidence about the relationship between foreign investment and economic growth and the theory of value that informs currently common wisdom has contributed to seriously flawed policies in the Third World. These policies rest on an assumed but fatuous relationship between foreign investment and economic growth that is supported neither by economic history nor by irrefutable logic. The assumption can itself, however, be explained by resort to the intellectual and practical history of financial capitalism.

The common wisdom is currently illustrated by the international response to the drastic decline in the value of the Mexican peso that led to the imposition of stringent conditions in exchange for loans and guarantees designed to regain at least part of that lost value. Conventional thinking holds that foreign investment can, and in many cases has, provided a powerful impetus to economic growth. The justification for the hardship imposed upon the citizens of Mexico by required policies that will reduce consumption and increase unemployment was the promise of growth to come.[1] It was widely accepted that this growth would be a consequence of the renewed inflow of investment funds that would follow the restoration of international faith in the peso.

FOREIGN INVESTMENT AND ECONOMIC GROWTH: THE HISTORICAL RECORD

That foreign investment is a fountain of growth is so widely accepted that to question it seems an act of insanity. Nevertheless, as examined by both Wendell Gordon and Douglass North, the records for the United States and for Latin America do not support that proposition. In 1961, Gordon noted the United Nations' commitment to the view that the capital required for planned growth in a poor country would exceed domestic savings. "[F]oreign investment thus acquired the role of a key residual, which had to materialize if the development plan was to be realized" [1961, 35]. This commitment, Gordon wrote, was consistent with the history of economists' thought about the relationships among foreign investment, the balance of trade, and economic growth that stretched from J. E. Cairnes through F. W. Taussig and on to W. Arthur Lewis. Indeed, the conventional viewpoint continues even more strongly in the present.[2]

The sequence whereby nations move from being immature debtors (with net borrowing and an import trade balance), to mature debtors (with net debt repayment and an export trade balance), to immature creditors (with net lending and an export trade balance), to mature creditors (receiving net debt repayment and running an import trade balance)--is deeply imbedded in economic thought and economic historiography. Gordon quotes Taussig's classic account about how the process was supposed to have been played out in the United States in the nineteenth century:

> The loan being made (in our assumed case) by British to Americans . . . an excess of exports develops in Great Britain. . . . In the United States an excess of imports gradually appears. . . . The people of Great Britain send merchandise to the United States, and add to the tangible equipment of the Americans, or to their consumable goods, giving up for the time being some of their own possessions and adding to those of the Americans [1961, 37; Taussig 1927].

Fortunately, data for the United States shed light on the accuracy of this account and show what actually happened. From the National Bureau of Economic Research, and the work of Matthew Simon and of Douglass C. North, estimates of total direct and portfolio, short- and long-term foreign investments from 1790 to 1900 are available, as are estimates of earnings on those investments. For the period after 1900 the Department of Commerce reports comparable statistics.

On the basis of the data compiled by Simon and North, and that made available by the Department of Commerce, Wendell Gordon put together two statistical series. One was net accumulating indebtedness (long-term and short-term, direct and portfolio) by year--in other words, a summation of foreign investment in the United States, year by year. The other series was net accumulating earnings of foreigners from those investments. From these two series, annual comparisons of inflows due to net new investment and outflows due to interest and dividends are possible.[3] In only 39 out of 84 years did the increase in indebtedness exceed net new debt service. That is, these were the years in which the relationship between the two series is what would have been expected in a country that was an immature debtor. Seventeen of these years were during the 1830s and 1850s; the others are scattered. Gordon observes that the significant fact is that "for the entire period 1790 to 1900 (or 1914) net earnings on foreign investments in the United States substantially exceeded the net increase in United States indebtedness. *And this relation prevailed generally during the whole 125-year period. Cumulative foreign income exceeded cumulative investment from the beginning of the process* (that is, at least, from 1790)" [1961, 45; italics in original]. The United States did *not* pass from the state of immature debtor to mature debtor in 1873 (as is often alleged); it was *never* an immature debtor at all.

Douglass North reached some of the same conclusions that Gordon did. Both wrote that the United States import trade balance of the first part of the nineteenth century was apparently financed through other means than borrowing, primarily shipping. North emphasizes funds brought in by immigrants as well [North 1961, 77; Gordon 1961, 45].

Shipping was a major source of funds to finance an import trade balance, as has been recognized in the extensive literature on the economic success of the American merchant marine during the nineteenth century. Textbooks are not, however, very consistent or rigorous in dealing with the relative importance of this source of funds compared to foreign investment. Their ambivalence illustrates the power of the assumption that foreign investment must always be the source of funds for early growth. One text notes that United States shipping earnings allowed imports of goods to exceed exports, but it is said in the same chapter that:

> the flow of foreign capital to the United States in the antebellum years was of great significance to the growth of the economy . . . loans from abroad allowed Americans to live beyond their current means while at the same time providing funds for enlarging those means in the future [Ratner, Soltow, and Sylla 1993, 209, 217].[4]

The evidence is that foreign long-term investment was offset by repayment of funds and that the flow of funds that allowed an import balance (or "living beyond their means") could be better explained by shipping and other sources of funds. Gordon wrote:

> I have not written this essay with any particular desire to prove that there is some kind of precise relation between debt service and new investment. . . . [For] the argument of this paper it probably does not make much difference whether debt service runs 110 percent of investment as a continuing proposition, . . . only 75 percent . . . or [at] no constant percentage. . . . Even if service ran 75 or 80 percent of investment . . . it might well be true that it would have been better judgement not to have incurred the debt but rather to have financed directly the purchase of such capital equipment as the capacity to import would permit instead of using those funds for debt service [1961, 52-53].

Gordon went on to draw a conclusion relevant to the present-day poor countries:

> Perhaps foreign investment is frequently merely a substitute for more effective domestic mobilization of resources . . . a little more healthy skepticism about the contribution that foreign investments make would be a good thing in some underdeveloped countries and on the part of some development planners [1961, 55-56].

Gordon's deep skepticism about the role of foreign investment did not stem from the United States data alone. Those data merely show that foreign investment as a source of growth in the United States is overrated and that the allegedly natural sequence of nations from immature debtor to mature creditor is misconceived. A region that did not enjoy the rates of the growth of the United States, Latin America, gave rise to the dark conclusions that Gordon has reached about the role of foreign investment in economic growth. In *The Political Economy of Latin America*, Gordon reported that:

> The International Monetary Fund balance of payments data for the Latin American countries indicate that, for the countries as a group in the sixteen years, 1946 through 1961, the foreign investment process (investment combined with debt service) financed a net outflow of resources from Latin America to the rest of the world in the amount of $4.2 billion. Net capital inflow into Latin America was $11.8 billion and

> net debt service transferred out was $16.0 billion for the period of years as a whole [1965, 240].

Gordon observes that even when foreign aid is added there was not a positive flow of funds to Latin America: "it would seem that the investment process combined with the grant process financed a net drainage of resources of $4.1 billion" [1965, 241]. In Latin America, moreover, there is considerable evidence that foreign investment mostly redistributed income in favor of the well-off rather than elevated growth; it is certainly true that it contributed to widespread unrest and xenophobia among the population [Gordon 1965, 232-236].

Doubt about the power of foreign investment to induce growth would seem to be required, yet skepticism is far from the prevailing attitude toward foreign investment. In Mexico and in many other places economic policy is driven by a desire for foreign investment, in spite of the fact that in the United States, where rates of economic growth were high during most of the nineteenth century, net foreign investment was not quantitatively important; and, in Latin America, where growth rates have been less satisfactory, a long-standing emphasis on foreign investment has not led to positive inflows.[5]

FOREIGN INVESTMENT AND CLAIMS TO A SHARE OF THE OUTPUT

The apparent reason why economists, politicians, and bankers stress the importance of foreign investment is made obvious in the popular press.[6] Economic growth requires capital; capital is in short supply in poor countries; if it were not in short supply the country would not be poor; therefore, the route to growth is to attract foreign investment. In an article in *The Economist*, Martin Feldstein put the matter bluntly: Mexico's domestic saving was too low to produce a satisfactory rate of growth, and "Mexico's low saving rate was a problem because of the limited international flow of capital" [1995, 72].[7]

The situation is not quite so simple. When economists, politicians, and bankers speak of foreign investment and its desirability they lump together several quite distinct processes. Foreign investment may be a purchase of shares in a going concern (portfolio investment) or a commitment of funds to undertake a new project (direct foreign investment). Portfolio investment may be for purposes of acquiring monopolistic power that can be exercised internationally. Profit rates may climb, but economic growth need not follow. Direct foreign investment is what most people envision when they say investment is necessary for growth, but it may comprise only a fraction of the total foreign investment that flows into a country.

The point here is to examine the strongest case that can be made for a positive role for foreign investment as an engine of growth, not to consider the differential effects of the various kinds of foreign investment. To that end let us assume, for purposes of argument, that all foreign investment is in fact direct and long-term. Is the theoretical case that such investment is vital for economic growth a strong one, and can the historical records of the United States and Latin America be dismissed as aberrations?

Consider the syllogism again: capital is required for economic growth. Capital is in short supply in poor countries; if it were not they would not be poor. Capital must be imported. In these simple sentences a powerful transformation of meaning occurs because of the adherence to a theory of value that has been fundamental to western economic thought for four centuries. This simple and powerful transformation, which is complex in origin, converts the obvious truth that poor countries need superior equipment to grow into a belief that an insufficiency of money is the problem. The policy that more money is the solution follows. It is now voguish to propose that the capital whose shortage requires foreign investment encompasses physical equipment as well as financial assets; the inappropriateness of this blurring is not now commonly understood. Fairly recently, the differences between physical and financial assets have been deliberately made trivial in economic analysis by the theory that efficient markets will ensure optimal production and investment decisions by firms as consequences of rational portfolio decisions. Put briefly, the argument is that "underinvestment" in physical capital would cause the yield on such assets to be greater and cause funds to flow to such uses. Systematic underinvestment could not occur, at least given the right assumptions. Among these are the easy availability of information, efficient markets for used physical equipment, and--not least--that Smith's invisible hand has become sufficiently bionic to make oligopolistic, multinational, multiproduct firms finely responsive to the interests of mankind.

The concept of hyperefficient markets has persuaded many economists that capital in its two meanings of physical capital (plant and equipment) and money *should* be used interchangeably, but most still know, and regard as important, that capital does have two meanings. Although drill presses, corporate bonds, and bank accounts can be arrayed on a spectrum of probable monetary yield, they differ in many other respects that are of economic consequence. Yet, confusion of the two meanings has persisted. In his article on "Capital" in *The Encyclopedia of the Social Sciences*, Frank A. Fetter wrote that the two concepts of capital "are so distinctive in essential thought and practical application that confusion inevitably resulted from the use of one word to designate both" [1931, 187]. Most of his article is given over to a discussion of the conflation of the two meanings. He concludes with a proposal to limit the use of the word capital to mean: "the market value expression of individual claims to incomes, whether they have their sources in the technical uses of wealth or elsewhere. This is essentially an individual acquisitive, financial, investment, ownership concept" [1931, 190].

In *The New Palgrave,* published in the more recent era when the dual meaning has come to be regarded as proper, in the entry, "Capital as a Factor of Production," K. H. Hennings spends several pages describing the confusion and the struggle that the two meanings have caused for economists from Smith onward. Hennings treats this obfuscation largely as a technical problem deriving from the juggling of the characteristics of capital as a factor of production and the use of a pecuniary valuation of that capital.

Writing much earlier, Fetter discussed at length the convoluted history whereby the word "capital," first used in commerce to mean "an interest bearing sum of money, came to be used as a synonym for the word "stock," which in the sixteenth century was the term for equipment [1931, 187-188]. He notes that Adam Smith used the two words interchangeably, and that "his treatment of capital as a whole manifests all the errors that have accompanied the use of this elusive term ever since. . . ." [188].

One should not follow Hennings in his faith that the coalescence of the two meanings is accidental. Neither is it simply a consequence of the economists' need for a numeraire nor a technical problem of purely intradisciplinary interest. Clarence Ayres [1944], building on Tawney and others, argued that the use of the word capital to mean two quite different things is not accidental.[8]

Increased commercialization in the centuries before Smith and Ricardo gave shape to modern economies requiring an increased use of money. Those who created bank money and bills of exchange played a visible but suspect role. Legitimation of their function involved the creation of an equation between "money" and "real" capital. This acceptance was built in part on the functional role that money-providers had in enabling traders to amass stocks of real goods and to command the ships in which to transport them. In a world of expanding markets, money conveyed the power to command. It is not surprising that money and the stocks of real goods so conveyed came to be equated and conflated in the minds of traders and money-providers. Money could beget goods and goods could beget money.

Remaining relatively well hidden within economics is the recognition that the money-goods equation carried with it an assumption about the role of money. The equation is commercially sensible and became part of the theory of value that has been the focus of so much economic analysis. This has remained obscured because, from David Ricardo onward, economists have focused on the distributive shares going to participants in production. Interest in the nature of the shares and the sources of their legitimacy has derived from efforts to judge the appropriateness of the size of those portions and their shares in determining costs. Very early in economic analysis, emphasis was put on the costs incurred in production and the difference between those costs and the sum that would be received by the seller. It was the margin over costs that so exercised Ricardo and Marx, though in different ways and for different reasons.

What was not emphasized by the founding fathers of classical and neoclassical economics was that the value of things is a consequence of socially legitimated claims on output. Ricardo certainly saw that landlords enjoyed increased incomes as the price of bread rose. Marx saw that capitalists reaped increasing surpluses above and beyond those to which they might be morally entitled, but neither Ricardo nor Marx (or Smith for that matter) considered that wages, rent, profits, and interest were equally socially evolving claims to shares of society's output--and that each in turn contributed to the costs and thus to the prices (or "values") of goods.

As both Thorstein Veblen [1990] and John A. Hobson [1969] pointed out, production is always joint, and relative contributions are unmeasurable.[9] Relative contributions can be abstractly conceptualized, but in reality all production involves complex interactions among people, nature, and tools, and the separation of relative contributions is always social and normative.[10] The works of R. H. Tawney, Clarence Ayres, and Karl Polanyi, among others, make it clear that it is sensible to see the values (that is, the prices) of things as the sum of the claims that are legitimately brought forward by participants in production rather than the sum of hypothetical productivities. These claims evolve and are, in Polanyi's phrasing, "instituted"--*not* by nature or by any natural mechanism, but as outcomes of long and on-going processes of conflict resolution.

All claims to a share of output, whether made by those who supply labor, by those who own land, by those who own drill presses, or those who provide money, are instituted and evolving. The deep roots of economic analysis in the natural law tradition have obscured this. Economists have analyzed value by developing "theories of value" that purport to explain product values as consequences of exchanges of products (the neoclassical approach) or of the characteristics of the products such as the amount of labor time put into each (Ricardo, Marx). A study of valuational processes should more properly focus on how it is that a society comes to assign *warranted* shares in the output to the activities that combine to produce output. Were this approach to be adopted, the role of those who provide money would be recognized, but the share of output earned would also be recognized for what it is and, *much more importantly,* for what it is not.

FOREIGN INVESTMENT AND ECONOMIC GROWTH REVISITED

The tragedy of the pressure currently being put on poor countries to constrict their economies so as to stabilize their currencies and attract new foreign investment is that the deflation is so unnecessary. Poor countries need plant and equipment, workers who can operate them, and public and private managers who can organize and oversee the work and the ensuing delivery processes. One way in which they can get equipment is by having foreigners build it, employing technology and skills not readily available in the poor country, and send it to them. When this happens, their inflowing foreign investment will register in the official accounts because some alien currency will be exchanged for claims valid in the recipient country.

This process has very little in common with foreign purchases of shares in ongoing companies, or with other international exchanges of monetary claims. Yet all are foreign investments by virtue of the history just told. That is, the exchange of money for property claims or interest-bearing assets is "provision of capital" and an "investment." Because of an accommodation reached long ago as money creators and lenders began to play increasingly important roles in Western and global society, Mexicans and Africans and Indians are today being made poorer.

ENDNOTES

1. For a description and analysis of the causes and consequences of the policies imposed on Mexico, see James Peach [1995].

2. The abiding faith of conventional economists in the importance of foreign inflows is revealed by a true story recounted by an economist who had attended a recent seminar sponsored by a Federal Reserve Bank. One of the participants apologized that he had been unable to specify his econometric model so as to show statistically that the "openness" of an economy was a significant variable in explaining growth. He reassured the audience that he would continue to work on his model. Both he and the audience, according to my informant, *knew* that openness to foreign investment and trade was a cause of growth; therefore, the problem must rest in the model.

3. The two series are constructed from items used by Simon and North in the process of estimating balance of payments for the nineteenth century. They are not themselves items that would normally be reported separately in a balance of payments statement.

4. British firms did provide short-term credit that facilitated United States (and other) international commerce during the nineteenth century. It is also clearly true that some British investors made long-term investments in canals and other infrastructure in the new United States, particularly during the 1830s. The evidence is skimpy for the proposition that foreign

investment "allowed Americans to live beyond their means . . . while at the same time providing funds for enlarging those means in the future." Or that, in the absence of foreign funds, growth in the United States would have been slower. Because the United States had a tumultuous banking history, and difficulty in providing a sufficiency of money that circulated both widely and at par, finance of purchases from abroad might have been more difficult in the absence of the financing arrangements provided by the House of Baring and other firms. Whether a smaller quantity of imports, or higher finance charges added to the price of imports, would have altered the rate of internal growth is unclear.

5. In this paper I limit my survey of the historical record to the United States and Latin America. The history of economic growth in Russia (1930-60) and Japan from the 1880s to the present is well-known and supports the argument that I make in this section that foreign investment is not a prerequisite to growth. A review of the literature on the economic growth of England, France, and Germany in the nineteenth century will also support the proposition. It is certainly true that technology borrowing and technical assistance have been important in the growth of Japan, Russia, and Germany but investment, *not* diffusion of technology, is the issue being considered here.

6. It has been suggested to me that officials may seek foreign investment for the foreign currency itself. That is, foreign investment--whether portfolio or direct--involves an exchange of the foreign currency (let us say dollars) for the domestic currency (let us say rupees or pesos). This exchange helps to bid up the price of the rupees or pesos and this--rather than the investment itself--may be the goal of public officials. If so, this would mean that the usual assumption that the goal of an increased price of the peso is to increase foreign investment should be turned upside down: the goal of foreign investment is to raise the price of the peso. I have no evidence that this is correct, but it is possible.

7. I deal not with the reasonable, and in my view valid, Keynesian response that the level of saving is more a consequence than cause of the level of investment.

8. Thorstein Veblen wrote two essays "On the Nature of Capital" [1908] that explore the causes and consequences of the intertwined meanings. They are highly recommended.

9. See Hobson's Appendix to chapter V, "Marginal Productivity as Basis of Distribution," in *The Industrial System* [1969] for an especially powerful critique of the theoretical and practical validity of the theory that marginal products determine distribution.

10. Veblen said it this way: It is "assumed that the product which results from any given industrial process or operation is, in some sense or in some unspecified respect, the equivalent of the expenditure of forces, or of the effort, or what not, that has gone into the process out of which the product emerges. This theorem of equivalence is the postulate which lies at the root of the classical theory of distribution, but it manifestly does not admit of proof--or of disproof either, for that matter; since neither the economic forces which go into the process nor the product which emerges are, in the economic respect, of such a tangible character as to admit of quantitative determination. They are in fact incommensurable magnitudes" [1990, 281].

REFERENCES

Ayres, Clarence E. *The Theory of Economic Progress*. Chapel Hill, NC: The University of North Carolina Press, 1944.

Buck, Norman Sydney. *The Development of the Organisation of Anglo-American Trade 1800-1850*. New Haven: Yale University Press, 1925.

Feldstein, Martin. "Global Capital Flows: Too Little, Not Too Much." *The Economist*, June 24, 1995: 72-73.

Fetter, Frank. "Capital." *Encyclopedia of the Social Sciences*. New York, NY: The Macmillan Co., 1931, 187-190.

Gordon, Wendell. "The Contribution of Foreign Investments: A Case Study of United States Foreign Investment History." *Inter-American Economic Affairs* 14 (Spring 1961): 35-36.

———. *The Political Economy of Latin America*. New York: Columbia University Press, 1965.

Hennings, K. H. "Capital as a Factor of Production." *The New Palgrave*. London: The Macmillan Press, Ltd., 1987, pp. 327-333.

Hobson, John A. *The Industrial System: An Inquiry Into Earned and Unearned Income*. New York, NY: Augustus Kelley, 1969. [Original published in London by Longmans, Green & Co., 1909].

North, Douglass C. *The Economic Growth of the United States, 1790 to 1860*. Englewood Cliffs, NJ: Prentice-Hall, Inc., 1961.

———. "The United States Balance of Payments, 1790-1860." *Trends in the American Economy in the Nineteenth Century*, Vol. 24 of *Studies in Income and Wealth*. Princeton, NJ: Princeton University Press, 1960.

Peach, James. "NAFTA and Mexico's Current Economic Crisis: Short-run and Long-run Perspectives." *Social Science Journal* 32 (October 1995): 375-378.

Polanyi, Karl. *The Great Transformation*. Boston, MA: Beacon Press, 1944.

Ratner, Sidney, James H. Soltow, and Richard Sylla. *The Evolution of The American Economy: Growth, Welfare, and Decision Making*. New York, NY: Basic Books, Inc., 1979.

Simon, Matthew. "The United States Balance of Payments, 1861-1900." *Trends in the American Economy in the Nineteenth Century*, Vol. 24 of *Studies in Income and Wealth*. Princeton, NJ: Princeton University Press, 1960.

Taussig, Frank W. *International Trade*. New York: Macmillan, 1927.

Tawney, R. H. *Religion and the Rise of Capitalism: An Historical Study*. London: John Murray, 1926.

Veblen, Thorstein, "On the Nature of Capital I and II." *The Quarterly Journal of Economics* XXII (August and November 1908). Reprinted in *The Place of Science in Modern Civilization*. New Brunswick, NJ: Transaction Press, 1990 [the collection was originally published in New York by Viking Press, 1919].

———. "Industrial and Pecuniary Employments." *Publications of the American Economic Association*, Series 3, 1901, pp. 190-235. Reprinted in *The Place of Science in Modern Civilization*.

CHAPTER 3

THEORY AND PRAXIS OF THE EMERGING GLOBAL ECONOMY

Milton D. Lower
Senior Staff Economist, U.S. House of Representatives

Important developments in the history of economic thought, said Leo Rogin, "first emerge (and persist, often in a changed role) in the concealed or unconcealed guise of arguments in the realm of social reform" [1956, xiv]. The meaning of an economic theory is best explored "by relating interesting contexts of controversy in economic theory to the respectively contemporaneous areas of controversy in the field of economic policy" [Rogin 1956, xiv]. Finally: "It is not until this relation has been established, not until the practical objective of the theorist has been discovered, that the issue of the validity of a particular theory or concept can usefully be raised" [Rogin 1956, xiv-xv].

ADAM SMITH AND FREE TRADE

As is well known, the distinct body of mainstream economic thought often called *the* theory of international trade has its origins in Adam Smith's *Wealth of Nations* [1776]. As is equally well known, the central policy correlate of Smith's theory on that head--the key argument that persists in mainstream trade doctrine down to the present--is "free trade." Yet, as Leo Rogin's careful reading of Smith revealed many years ago, Smith's "practical objective" in developing the argument--i.e., the "meaning" of free trade for Smith--differed from that of his successors in the classical and neoclassical tradition. The *Wealth of Nations* was a reformist response to a pressing issue of international economic policy in historical context. The work was a fact-based attack on wrongheaded mercantilist doctrines that, in context, boded to reduce the sum of economic interchange between England and France to smuggling. The same commercial doctrines supported a corrupt and exploitative British colonial policy whose flaws were "self-evident" to those who made the American Revolution in the same year Smith's book was published [Rogin 1956, 51-109].

What Adam Smith sought, then, was "a theoretical instrument which is destructive of mercantilistic doctrine and policy. The crux of Smith's theory is found in the elaboration of such an instrument" [Rogin 1956, 55]. This instrument, central to Smith's entire theory of economic development--or the "causes of improvement in the wealth of nations"--was his theory of the relative productivity of capital in different employments. From this Smith derived a hierarchy of the uses of capital in the employment of productive labor, which "sets the mercantilistic hiearchy of productivity on its head. The employment of capital is more productive in agriculture than in industry, in industry than in commerce, in domestic commerce than in foreign trade" [Rogin 1956, 55].

As Rogin observed, Smith's theory "appears to lead to the absurd conclusion that a country should *abstain from foreign trade*, or even that it should limit its economic enterprise to agriculture" [1956, 76, emphasis added]. Rogin concluded, however, that Smith's heavy emphases on the internal and external economies of occupational differentiation, and on the productive interplay of economic sectors, "place such an interpretation outside the range of plausibility" [1956, 76]. One must nevertheless conclude that for Adam Smith, international trade--while certainly better "free" than in the hands of government-sponsored monopolies--was something of a last resort for increasing the wealth of nations. More precisely, absent the *artificial* stimulus to foreign trade under mercantilism, the nation "would be led to" exploit the more productive domestic employments of capital, "before proceeding to large investment of capital in those less productive" [Rogin 1956, 76].

How--by what motive or mechanism--would this result be assured under free markets and free trade? The pursuit of private gain would spur productive effort, but given Smith's theory of relative productivity it would not be sufficient to ensure the identity of private and national interests under his "obvious and simple system of liberty." For in a free economy the *gains* of the citizen can be redeployed as *capital* overseas, thereby increasing productive work and wealth not at home but abroad. Smith thought the answer to this question so important that he enshrined it along with--indeed, ahead of--the motive of gain in his famous passage on the invisible hand.

What this most famous--but not well known--passage in the literature of economics says is that the individual under the competitive economy will endeavor "both to employ his capital in the support of domestic industry, and so to direct that industry that its produce may be of the greatest value" [Smith 1776, 423]. As to motives, Smith continued:

> By preferring the support of domestic to that of foreign industry, he intends only his own *security*; and by directing that industry [to produce] the greatest value, he intends only his own *gain*, and he is in this, as in many other cases, led by an invisible hand to promote an end which was no part of his intention [1776, 423, emphasis added].

By "security," Adam Smith meant no more than the common sense of his day implied: the "uneasiness" that the merchant feels "at being separated so far from his capital," or the fact that he "will always be glad, upon equal or nearly equal profits, to sell as great a part of [his goods] at home as he can" [1776, 422]. Thus, said Smith:

> Home is in this manner the center, if I may say so, round which the capitals of the inhabitants of every country are continually circulating, and towards which they are always tending, though by particular causes they may sometimes be driven off and repelled from it towards more distant employments [1776, 422].

Adam Smith's assumption that the insecurity of doing business abroad would suffice to keep capital at home might seem a quaint prejudice to the CEO of the average European or American multinational corporation today. But Smith's common sense was hardly so far-fetched in his own day. More broadly, the positive but limited role thereby accorded to international trade in Smith's theory of development was probably near the policy mark for a market economy about to take the lead in the early stages of industrialization. Moreover, by framing his argument in terms of the domestic and foreign uses of capital--however inadequate the theory of capital accumulation may seem as a theory of development today--Smith, in contrast to many who have followed him, brought the trade sector under a common analytical and policy umbrella with domestic economic activity.

THE MAINSTREAM THEORY

The mainstream of classical and neoclassical economics transformed Adam Smith's contextual argument for free trade in a developing market economy into a closed, deductive model of the ideal international economy. While this transformation preserved and extended the policy argument for free trade--which in Rogin's phrase above has tended to "persist, often in a changed role"--the *meaning*, hence certainly the *validity*, of the whole exercise has often been in doubt. While this may have been equally true of the mainstream (especially the neoclassical) theory of the domestic economy, it has largely been a case of "separate but equal." For the development of the two mainstream theories--one for the domestic self-regulating market, one for the international economy--became increasingly divergent enterprises after Adam Smith, and certainly after Ricardo.

In effect, the seamless economy in which Adam Smith sought a practical meaning has been divided into distinct international and closed economy models. By the very premises that allowed this, however, the international trade theory that traces its pedigree to Smith's free trade policy has been cut off from two centuries of evolving global reality. Recognizing only the market mode in which economies can be instituted in society, and holding constant the forces of technology and organization that have reshaped cultures and nations toward a global industrial system, mainstream theory has denied the dominant facts a theoretical place.

These omissions rendered the theory incompetent to encompass or assess national or regional policies for technological and institutional change, except in their static bearing on trade. Hence, policy options having any international bearing--including every dynamic undertaking from national technology policy to the formation of a customs union in the Third World--were perforce reduced to polarized classes: "free trade" or "protectionism." Such terms, employed as shibboleths, pro and con, during the long reign of the theory of international trade, have more often obscured the broader meaning of practical theoretical endeavors than they have illuminated it. Within the mainstream, resistance to facts not encompassed by the theory has substantially compromised the theory's claims to scientific validity as well as policy usefulness.

The scientific response to Adam Smith's having, in retrospect, gotten (at a minimum) half of the invisible hand mechanism wrong, would have been to correct his error. As experience proved his assessment of the security motive to be overdrawn, later theorists needed to come to terms with some far-reaching implications--including, among other things, the need for a theory of foreign investment at the center of the theory of the international economy.

For if home is not where the heart is, but one wishes to retain Smith's free trade policy--indeed, extend it to free investment--then one requires a larger theory that integrates the newly emerged practical issues of human importance. These included, early on, virtually all problems and issues--but especially technology transfer--affecting the economic development and international relations of the latecomers to the industrial revolution.

In the mainstream international trade theory, this enlargement of scope did not occur. Instead, Adam Smith's commonsense observation that capital resists moving abroad or into the foreign commerce was generalized, and reified, by the formal axiom that in international trade, by contrast with the domestic economy, the factors of production--including, of course, capital--are immobile. As John Adams has noted: "In such a system in which factors of production are immobile, but goods are mobile, the only issue to be resolved is where production will be sited" [1987, 1840].

Despite subsequent tinkering, orthodox trade theory remains today largely a theory of the location of production--or in its more vulgar forms an ex post justification for whatever choices are made in this regard by private agents--based on the alleged quasi-natural comparative advantage (or factor proportions) of particular nations in given lines of production. While the mobility of capital (if not labor) was acknowledged as a fact of life, limited theoretical efforts to explain capital movements--including the pattern and direction of direct investment--have been a gloss on mainstream trade theory. That theory, while failing to integrate the foreign investment process into its core, nonetheless assumed--given only free trade and then free investment--that sufficient capital would automatically flow to latecomer countries (incidentally carrying technical knowledge) as to bring them up to the level of the industrial leaders.

Given this ideology, it is little wonder that workmanlike orthodox studies of the foreign investment process, from the nineteenth century on, were destined to fall by the wayside. In a sense these efforts were the true legacy of Adam Smith, for they generally sought to explain foreign investment on Smith's motive of gain, incorporating the reality that such gain might be pursued abroad as well as at home. Such theorizing neither found a place in the grand design of orthodox trade theory, nor--since it proceeded under Smith's theory of capital accumulation--did it contribute to an emerging evolutionary economics directly encompassing technological change and technology transfer in a global setting [Gordon 1962].

THE GLOBAL ECONOMY

In recent years the defects of the mainstream theory and approach have become ever more apparent, in the face of a dramatic surge in global economic integration, both technological and financial. The linked causes are a revolution in computer-based telecommunications and other technologies, explosive growth of financial and direct investment, and the ascendance of the multinational or stateless corporation. Events have literally stood Adam Smith on his head, as the favored approach to selling in a foreign market is, increasingly, to establish a manufacturing subsidiary, not to produce and export from home. In the real world, capital mobility has become an alternative mechanism and explanation for the location of production, not a passive current account item to offset trade. This can be so, as everyone is now coming to realize, because comparative advantage is a technological, not a natural, creation.

Even as the theory of international trade has for two centuries failed to account even remotely for the varieties of "intersocial economic exchange" as instituted under widely varying cultural arrangements [Adams 1987], it is now missing the transformation of the "inter-national" economy into a global one. The mainstream, as Adams notes, always "assumed that a system of international markets exists; there is, in short, a global system of shared rules governing exchange to which exporters and importers adhere" [1987, 1840]. In the post-Cold War world, though publicists hail the belated arrival of this worldwide self-regulating economy, details like Bosnia leave us skeptical. Beyond all of this, it must be recognized that economic integration, both national and global, has always been driven primarily by technology, not markets.

Thirty years ago, Simon Kuznets wrote: ". . . the nineteenth-century theory of international division of labor, with its promise of the inevitable and rapid spread of the benefits of modern economic civilization to all corners of the earth, is hardly tenable" [1965, 7]. This recognition, Kuznets said, explained the growing emphasis on economic growth and development as an explicit theoretical and policy concern.

Yet since the mid-1960s, those Third-World countries that have experienced the most rapid growth have done so neither through the "natural" workings of the market nor by enlightened policy. Rather, the movements of goods, people, and especially technology to and from such countries have been in the main and increasingly "intra-corporate" movements between affiliated multinational entities. These can only technically be called "inter-national" trade and investment and are distinctly non-market relationships. Such a pattern of integration poses wholly new and global questions for international economic theory and policy.

Confronting the new realities, industrial country economic policies touting free-market aims, such as Reaganomics in the 1980s, in fact produce cumulative and destabilizing global impacts on exchange rates, trade balances, investment flows and debt, international competitiveness, and the standard of living [Lower 1986]. The espousal of free trade ideology in such chaotic circumstances is no guarantor of results. Thus, the conservative Cato Institute felt compelled to say in 1988: "Ronald Reagan by his actions has become the most protectionist president since Herbert Hoover, the heavyweight champion of protectionists" [Japan Economic Institute 1988, 13].

Meanwhile, nations not under the sway of obsolete economic doctrines have pursued coordinated trade and industrial policies, achieving rapid industrial development and global competitive strength--if also by flaunting the trade rules, and by paying their own domestic price.

Japan expert Chalmers Johnson has shrewdly observed that: "The inadequacy of Western theory to explain the most advanced industrial economy that ever existed means that the study of the Japanese economy is today itself an exercise in theorizing" [Johnson 1988, 83]. Indeed! In ways that fit the Leo Rogin mold, "controversies in the field of economic policy" that attend the Japanese case--and the industrial policy model it may offer to others--have even begun to produce theoretical controversy within the mainstream citadel.

Although some of the leading contributors to the new trade theory display an on-again-off-again attitude regarding their discovery that comparative advantage can be created by technology policy, at least one holder of the Nobel-named prize in economics seems convinced. "For [Robert] Solow, the eye-opener came when he realized how the electronic age has yanked the rug out from under a basic tenet of economic theory. Because of information technology and global telecommunications, Solow now concludes that the theory known as comparative advantage has 'forever changed'" [*Business Week* 1989, 174].

EVOLUTIONARY ECONOMIC THEORY

It is sometimes said that evolutionary and institutional economists have neglected international economics, and this is in some respects true. If the allegation were that evolutionary economics has neglected the substance of international economics, that would be quite wrong. Unless one has grasped the ideas in *The Theory of Business Enterprise* and in *Imperial Germany and the Industrial Revolution*--two of Thorstein Veblen's books--one has no clue what the international economy of the nineteenth century was about, or what the next century's global economy may *mean*. Karl Polanyi's *Great Transformation* is at least equally essential to both of these aims. The list could be extended with other works, none of which would be classified under "international trade" in the Dewey decimal system.

Evolutionary economists have for the most part pursued an integrated approach to what the mainstream has treated as distinct problems of national economic development and international relations. The method has been to research holistic problems of going concerns along technological and institutional dimensions of change. The core problem has been seen by most, through the epoch of corporate capitalism, as national economic development--always in conditions of global interdependence--because the nation, or even the national corporation, was the dominant going concern.

Substantively, international trade, foreign investment, technological borrowing--any contextually relevant international movements of goods, people, and ideas--have played important roles in this analysis of national change. This tendency is if anything stronger for those who specialize in the economic development of less developed countries.

The charge of neglect is in another sense misplaced. It is clearly the mainstream that was neglectful, for example, in failing to incorporate Thorstein Veblen's theory of technological borrowing (warts and all) from *Imperial Germany* [1915a]. They failed to do so because Veblen presented a very substantial truth about the international transfer of technology that was utterly at odds with prevailing orthodoxy. Veblen explained how, in catching up economically with Britain, the imperial German dynasty had succeeded in "gaining usufruct" of the machine process directly--only partially and incidentally by trade, and without foreign investment.

Veblen's book, published in 1915, was anything but pro-Kaiser, though that charge was leveled by some. Rather, it further established the universality of technological change as the dynamic of economic development, and now asserted the primacy of direct transfer of technology and knowledge over pecuniary investment as the key to this process in latecomer countries.

The Germans had gotten a foretaste of Veblen's theory of technological change from their own Friedrich List in the 1840s. List's inchoate evolutionism took the form of a stages model, based on the "theory of the productive powers," with policy in one stage employing an infant-industry tariff [List 1885]. Had List's exception to free trade been endorsed by some global arbiter at that time, it is interesting to speculate whether relations between the free-trading industrial leader, Britain, and the aggrieved latecomer, Germany, might not have gone smoother, with German dynastic impulses, nationalistic fervor, and protectionist excesses forestalled or weakened.

On the charge of neglect, what it is fair to say is that too few evolutionary economists in recent times have consciously combined the relevant international insights from the classic formulations with their own and others' research, and dared against prevailing orthodoxy to call this international economic theory and policy. That of course is exactly what Wendell Gordon proceeded to do early in his career, and it is that liberating legacy and promise that is celebrated in this volume. Now, as may be judged from his most recent book, *The United Nations at the Crossroads of Reform* [1994], Gordon has moved beyond international economics to world institution-building, as the critical requisite for strengthening and improving global economic, environmental, and security policy for the future.

TOWARD A GLOBAL THEORY AND POLICY

Gordon's ambitious goal is clearly a "practical objective," in Rogin's sense, that should inform all efforts today to construct a global economic theory that would meaningfully encompass and help resolve the mounting policy dilemmas of a world in fundamental change. The global economy of the multinational corporations is simply not the mainstream's self-equilibrating system of market trade between *nations* (or between *nationals* of different countries). Nor is it a system in which the nation *state* can have the long-run expectation of maintaining effective control over its own domestic process of development, production, distribution--nor indeed of its intersocial exchanges with others.

In these circumstances, none of the historic models for national or "inter-national" economic policies that consistently or automatically serve human purposes any longer holds. The critical context of meaningful economic problem-solving is suddenly the world community as a whole. What is needed now is a shift in theoretical focus to the "global going concern," which is already quite far along as a "concatenation of industrial processes" in Veblen's phrase [1904, 15]. Such theory must then be directed explicitly to the making of institutional adjustments ("policy" in the evolutionary economist's definition) at this global level.

As Wendell Gordon [1994] makes clear, one reform essential to all this is a substantial, generally-agreed-upon transfer of sovereignty from the national to the global level. In today's world political climate, such institutional adjustments may--but perhaps may not--be a long time in coming. All that makes this daunting task practical is that the alternative--Veblen would call it the "main drift"--is demonstrably failing all concerned, which is to say all people in all countries. Gordon's proposals for reform have more to do with needed governmental, environmental, and peacemaking responses by a world authority than with economic policy per se. I agree with Gordon that until such institution-building is accomplished, the dilemmas of the global main drift cannot be wholly resolved. Such reforms are of a piece with the development of a meaningful theory and policy for the global going concern. Notably in his most recent book [1994], Gordon elaborates upon proposals he has made before, to gain some public control--now possible only at the global level--over the multinational corporations.

These proposals will play a crucial role in any serious attempt to develop new mechanisms of public accountability for business enterprise in a global economy, and in restoring order and progress to the home economies.

In moving toward a global economic theory and policy, the classic formulations of evolutionary economics are directly applicable, in no small part because virtually all were developed consciously within holistic frameworks. Neither the level nor the changing technological and institutional content of the processes studied is a priori, let alone reified forever within a closed system of logical relations. Policy as institutional adjustment can likewise be conducted at any level, but it must be a comparably open-ended quest for solutions to problems at the level of the going concern in question.

It was granted earlier that too few evolutionary economists in recent times have undertaken to elevate key theoretical constructs from other contexts, to confront directly the issues of global economic theory and policy. It was also alleged, however, that any of the classic works of evolutionary economics would yield deep insights into global problems if this effort were undertaken. As an example of this, and perhaps as a model to encourage more such efforts, let us consider Thorstein Veblen's "Theory of Multinational Business Enterprise."

THE THEORY OF MULTINATIONAL BUSINESS ENTERPRISE

It is of course not strictly true that Veblen offered such a theory. He called his opus *The Theory of Business Enterprise* [1904]. It has somehow always seemed enough to point out that in this work, Veblen invented a new economics in order to make sense of the corporate industrialism that had emerged in late nineteenth-century America. This was, indeed, the practical interest that gave meaning to his theoretical effort. From this and later works by Veblen, it has seemed enough to say, everything known about the corporation as an economic institution, and hence about public policy to make it accountable, has flowed.

It has appeared sufficient to note that when Veblen described the modern industrial system that superseded Adam Smith's division of labor as a "concatenation of industrial processes," this was not merely the first concept of technology useful for economic theory. It also involved a rather clear embodiment of the fundamental ideas of input-output analysis [Janeway 1989, 61]. This is not to mention the dichotomous tension between "business" and "industry" that Veblen exposed at the heart of the postcompetitive economy and its business cycle--which became the central theoretical instrument of the old institutionalism. Yet, there is nothing whatsoever in Veblen's treatment of any of these theoretical issues--except the particular institutional facts adduced in evidence--that limits the analysis to the U.S. economy or to a national economy per se. It is merely that an evolutionist does not speculate about a divergent line until it has diverged.

Now the multinational corporation *has* diverged from the industrial corporation that Veblen discovered--itself a product of the union between Adam Smith's competitive commerce and modern industry. Yet, with respect to the global integration of far-flung industrial processes, connected by computer command, under the aegis of multinational corporations having operations in perhaps dozens of countries, outsourcing from some, exporting capital goods and technical services to others, one can hardly improve upon the following description.

> The whole concert of industrial operations is to be taken as a machine process, made up of interlocking detail processes, rather than as a multiplicity of mechanical appliances each doing its particular work in severalty. This comprehensive industrial process draws into its scope and turns to account all branches of knowledge that have to do with the material sciences, and the whole makes a more or less delicately balanced complex of sub-processes [Veblen 1904, 7].

Thus, under Veblen's theory of multinational business enterprise, the decisive basis for the existence of the going concern is a global process of technological expansion, which at any given moment has the corporation engaged, sometimes with its affiliates, sometimes with other industrial concerns, in producing output that employs human and other resources, and finally gets counted as gross national product in one or more nations' accounts. For the corporation, the nationality, let alone domesticity of inputs and outputs is inconsequential. For wherever it may be chartered, the multinational enterprise has no home. What directs the going concern is the "corporationality" of profits.

This was the other side of Veblen's global theory of business enterprise. While the theory of the competitive firm had since Adam Smith asserted an identity of interest between profit-seeking business and the public, Veblen showed that such an identity--indeed, any coincidence of aims even between business and a technologically-based industry--would at best be occasional and incidental. Veblen recognized that some superintendence of the industrial process was indeed required by the very character he had ascribed to it. The sheer comprehensiveness and balance of the machine process poses a constant "requirement of interstitial adjustment" [1904, 16] between processes and branches of industry. It is this "strategic management of the interstitial relations of the system" [Veblen 1904, 29] that the larger industrial corporation undertakes for pecuniary gain.

Because business proceeds in terms of pecuniary advantage rather than industrial efficacy, it is as likely that the differential advantage will come, as Veblen would have put it, from "derangement" of the system, by financial machinations, monopolistic combinations and takeovers, curtailment of output, plant closures, and the like--as from adjustments that keep the machines running. For the corporate "captain of industry," as Veblen put it:

> This work of keeping and of disturbing the interstitial adjustments does not look immediately to the output of goods as its source of gain, but to *the alterations of values* involved in disturbances of the balance. . . . It is directed to the acquisition of gain through taking advantage of those conjuctures of business that arise out of the concatenation of processes in the industrial system [1904, 49, emphasis added].

Today this work of the captain is made more complicated by the increase in the economic role of national governments since Veblen's time. For the multinational corporation, there is not only the task of comparing the prices of the human and material inputs in many different countries, and of making this calculus against the expected returns on output in terms of numerous fluctuating national currencies, but there is the need to take whatever action will minimize the net payment of taxes and escape the cost of social, economic, and environmental regulations enacted in benefit of the various underlying populations.

Nor was the work of the captain of multinational industry ever limited to the pecuniary oversight of production in place or its expansion through real investment. Rather, the "traffic in vendible capital is the pivotal and dominant factor in the modern situation of business and industry" [Veblen 1904, 168]. In this category are included all financial machinations of the corporation--from the capitalization of intangible business assets in the stock market to a possible leveraged buyout (which Veblen described without naming) in which the intangibles are converted to cash by the dealmakers.

Today, the speed with which pecuniary deals can be done in global markets, including not only mergers and traditional securities investments, but choices from an ever expanding menu of casino plays, overwhelms the real economic process. By far the largest market remaining in the global economy is the foreign exchange market, which as long ago as mid-1991 easily exceeded $700 billion per day in trades [*Houston Chronicle* July 7, 1991]. Global speculation in this market now threatens uncontrollable panics in response to untoward news from any developed or developing country in the world, and can only be brought under control by new global financial arrangements.

The strategic decisions of the captain--involving the siting of the branches of industry, employment levels in the several countries, rates of economic growth and development, distribution of benefits and burdens, livelihood--were once believed to be made either by the automatic workings of the international division of labor or by national governments. To some extent, for now, they are; however, long before they went multinational, the industrial corporations had become masters at tempering the effects of market competition. This was, for Veblen, a defining point:

> So long as related industrial units are under different business managements, they are, by the nature of the case, at cross-purposes, and business consolidation remedies this untoward feature of the industrial system by *eliminating the pecuniary element* from the interstices of the system as far as may be [1904, 48, emphasis added].

In other words, the corporation has always sought, by combination or any other means, to *remove from the market* and make internal to the corporation as many as possible of the input-output conjunctures it must on technological grounds share with potential or actual business competitors. The salient global form of this today is the intracorporate trade and investment relations between parent multinationals and their overseas affiliates.

Increasingly, the most consequential "inter-national" trade and investment transactions have come to be *internal* affairs of multinationals, conducted outside the market at transfer prices. This particular "alteration of values"--in Veblen's sense and the literal sense--not only removes all transparency of costs and other pecuniary data from the scrutiny of potential competitors in international markets, but it allows taxes and other imposts to be paid in the national jurisdiction of choice.

In magnitude, intracorporate trade is now widely estimated to account for something over half of "inter-national" trade. In the total trade between the United States and Japan, the two largest national economies, trade accounted for by each country's multinational parents and their affiliates--which would include but exceed purely intracorporate trade--has in recent years approached or exceeded 90 percent, according to data regularly presented in the *Survey of Current Business*.

TOWARD A GLOBAL RULE OF LAW

It is time, as Wendell Gordon has repeatedly argued, for a United Nations agency to be given powers of international incorporation and of global income taxation over multinational business enterprises [1994, 112-113,

124-26, 218-19]. Grants from these revenues to developing countries, replacing bilateral aid, could finance national development policies and enlarge the scope of local control over the direction of development in Third-World countries where multinationals are a dominant economic factor.

The less developed country-foreign investor relationship could thus be globalized, with dispute settlement procedures in the International Court of Justice replacing the historically rancorous--and often mutually costly--relations between debtor countries and the corporations (and governments) of more powerful nations. As Gordon says: "If corporations can obtain the rule of law in exchange for the international corporate income tax, they will have struck a good bargain" [1994, 126].

Bringing the multinationals under the rule of law would ease an enormous number of policy dilemmas facing the global economy today. By doing so it would also put in the place of Adam Smith's and the mainstream's flawed arguments, a new *contextual* and *constructive* basis for freer trade. So long as "free trade" can be taken to mean the absence of any controls over that growing portion of world trade that is intracorporate trade, protectionist responses will be in vogue, and rightly so. The issue here is not merely free trade but absence of accountability for whatever the multinationals choose to do with the technological heritage and the livelihoods of what Veblen called the "underlying population."

Under the global rule of law, legitimate protective responses of national governments on behalf of their citizens--in industrial as well as developing countries--could be debated, negotiated, arbitrated, or adjudicated in a higher council. This would surely broaden the scope for general efforts to devise and implement the kinds of contextually crafted policies that Wendell Gordon has called "constructive free trade" [1958, ch. 6].

HOME AGAIN

Consistent with the emergence of a global economy, what is the nature and role of Adam Smith's home economy, today the social economy, within which people will continue to live their lives? What measure of democratic control and what range of economic policies for the domestic economy articulate with a global authority, a less sovereign national government, and the multinational form of corporate organization?

In the foreseeable future, the global economy will remain a business economy, in which Adam Smith's commerce still must validate Veblen's industrial progress before the latter can go forward. This essential characteristic has not changed since Veblen wrote of Japan:

> It is only by way of commerce and a commercialized industry that Japan can get a footing among the commercial nations of the West. . . . Japan must in all essential respects accept the scheme as it is already in force. . . . Incompetent, or even puerile, as this commercial enterprise may seem when seen in the large and taken as a means of the international coordination of industry, it still affords the sole method available for the purpose under the given conditions, because it is one of the chief of the given conditions [1915b, 260].

This was the long-term prognosis; the immediate focus of Veblen's article, "The Opportunity of Japan," was the brief window of opportunity for Japanese dynastic politics to seize--on the imperial German model--full usufruct of modern technology for anachronistic, warlike purposes. Veblen concluded on this score that: "Japan must strike, if at all, within the effective lifetime of the generation that is now coming to maturity" [1915b, 266].

In the aftermath of World War II, Japan was still, in Veblen's earlier phrase "not yet mature enough in the secondary effects of the industrial revolution" [1915b, 263] to be considered fully assimilated to the world order. The most obvious of these secondary effects--still ahead for Japan before and after the war--was "what might be called the "sabotage" of capitalism--the competitive working at cross purposes of rival business concerns and the control of industrial processes by considerations of net gain to the managers rather than of material serviceability" [Veblen 1915b, 263].

In due time, said Veblen, Japan would grow into these ways, and like the West, would also come to "competitive spending as the legitimate counterfoil of competitive gain as the legitimate end of endeavor" [1915b, 264]. Whence, Japan, too, would evolve a "ubiquitous system of 'conspicuous waste'" [Veblen 1915b, 264]. Whether this last prediction is already coming true, is difficult to discern. It may be that the wish of Japan's trading partners and of influential circles in Japan--for surcease from the nation's inordinate productivity--is seen as reality. There *is* consumerism in the wind.

Veblen's analysis might seem to contradict the idea that the Japanese model is unique, or that it offers policy guidance to others. Certainly, Veblen was right that Japan will not escape indefinitely from the global system of business enterprise. Indeed, in order to realize its trade surpluses, and then to vent the proceeds, Japan has been required to employ "multinational" trading companies and, increasingly, to invest in "multinational" production abroad. Nonetheless, in a way that is no longer true for others, home is where the Japanese executive's heart is.

So perhaps the way the Japanese economy relates through trade is less important than the domestic economic model they have evolved. Were the Japanese model literally "mercantilist," per capita gross domestic product might still be at about the level of eighteenth century England (ignoring gold). The difference is technology, and its diffusion throughout the culture--what Veblen (also in the *Theory of Business Enterprise*) called "the cultural incidence of the machine process" [1904, ch. 9]. In the worldwide trade of this "product," technical knowledge, the Japanese have been net importers with a vengeance.

In the global economy under the rule of law, the lead focus of domestic economic policy should remain--or become--technology policy in the broadest sense: research and development, education and training, and industrial policies to create and strengthen dynamic linkages among productive sectors. Public-private partnerships and research consortia in each nation should include foreign-owned firms that have strong technological and employment linkages to strategic domestic sectors. Perhaps there is even room for "sunsetted" tariffs (or subsidies) for "sunrise" industries. In short, comparative advantage should be created, but not necessarily on the model of rent-seeking preferred by the new trade theory. The broader aim should be, in each country, the *dynamic advantage* that arises from the diffusion of knowledge and skills.

Over time, as each nation pursues these broad developmental aims--at times in competition and conflict with each other, and perhaps with the stateless corporations--the real basis for a healthy expansion of all intersocial exchange would be improved, not limited. At the global level, the role of the global authority as an economic arbiter, coordinator, and planner could expand as desired under democratic procedures.

CONCLUSION

Obviously, this exploration of some key theoretical considerations for global economic policy does not touch all issues, or even the range of specific policy dilemmas that were adumbrated in the earlier sections of the essay. The presentation of Veblen's "theory of the multinational corporation" must be followed by a similar modernization of Karl Polanyi's *The Great Transformation* [1944]. This would explore how the world's habitat, humanity, and purchasing power came to be--since the collapse of the market economy--subject to multinational commodity fictions. The policy issues need then to be taken up as the evolving elements of a global social contract, by means of which the commercial thralldom of land, labor, and capital might be broken anew. Polanyi's institutionalism, coming later than Veblen's and after nineteenth-century civilization collapsed, to be replaced by the welfare state, is in many ways better suited to the issues of reconstructing domestic livelihood under rampant globalism. Possibly, some young evolutionary economist will take up this challenge.

Having begun by quoting Leo Rogin, I close with another quotation from Rogin--which also seems to embody the constructive spirit that Wendell Gordon has brought to the field of international theory and policy. Rogin said of his approach to the history of economic thought:

> By raising to selfconsciousness the relation of theory to policy, misdirection of theory to policy . . . may be decreased. What is more important, it may serve to specify and narrow the range of disagreement among those who in this critical age should be united in their fight against the retreat from reasonableness in human affairs [1956, xv].

REFERENCES

Adams, John. "Trade and Payments as Instituted Process." *Journal of Economic Issues* 21 (December 1987): 1839-60.

Business Week. "Innovation 1989." Special issue (n.d.).

Gordon, Wendell C. *International Trade: Goods, People, and Ideas*. New York: Alfred A. Knopf, 1958.

———. "Foreign Investments." *University of Houston Business Review* 9 (Fall 1962): entire issue.

———. *The United Nations at the Crossroads of Reform*. Armonk, NY: M. E. Sharpe, 1994.

Janeway, Eliot. *The Economics of Chaos: On Revitalizing the American Economy*. New York: E. P. Dutton, 1989.

Japan Economic Institute. "President Reagan's Trade Record." *JEI Report* 25B (June 1988): 13.

Johnson, Chalmers. "The Japanese Political Economy: A Crisis in Theory." *Ethics and International Affairs* 2 (March 1988): 79-97.

Kuznets, Simon. *Economic Growth and Structure: Selected Essays*. New York: W. W. Norton, 1965.

List, Friedrich. *National System of Political Economy*. Reprint. London: Longmans, Green, and Co., 1904 [1885].

Lower, Milton D. "The Industrial Economy and International Price Shocks." *Journal of Economic Issues* 20 (June 1986): 297-312.

Polanyi, Karl. *The Great Transformation*. Boston: Beacon Press, 1957 [1944].

Rogin, Leo. *The Meaning and Validity of Economic Theory*. New York: Harper and Brothers, 1956.

Smith, Adam. *The Wealth of Nations*. New York: The Modern Library, 1937 [1776].

United States Department of Commerce. *Survey of Current Business*. Annual Articles of foreign direct investment (FDI) in the United States and United States FDI abroad. Various publication dates, usually May-July.

Veblen, Thorstein. *The Theory of Business Enterprise*. New York: Charles Scribner's Sons, 1936 [1904].

———. *Imperial Germany and the Industrial Revolution*. New York: The Viking Press, 1954 [1915a].

———. "The Opportunity of Japan." In Leon Ardzrooni, ed., *Essays in Our Changing Order*. New York: The Viking Press, 1954 [1915b].

II. INTERNATIONAL TRADE AND FOREIGN INVESTMENT

CHAPTER 4

INSTITUTIONAL COORDINATION, TRANSACTIONS COSTS, AND WORLD TRADE[1]

John Adams
Northeastern University

Institutional arrangements and the transactions costs associated with them are a primary determinant of the level and composition of world exchange. An impressive number of strong theoretical conjectures may be derived from this proposition. These can be fleshed out by judicious use of historical evidence and by looking at features of contemporary trading relationships. The institutional theory of intersocial transactions does not dislodge the standard, widely-held comparative advantage theory. Rather, the conventional model remains a special and rather uninteresting boundary case, where there are no institutional frictions associated with crossborder exchanges and transactions costs equal zero. Adams [1987] presents the institutional theory at length. Adams [1984] adumbrates institutional international economic policies. The paramount thrust here is to proffer a thorough menu of international transactions costs. A subsidiary but crucial intention is to make an initial bid to estimate the scale of intersocial transfer costs, to examine how their impact has changed over time, and to assess the consequences for a set of modern bilateral trade flows.

THE THEORY OF INTERSOCIAL EXCHANGE

International economics has stood apart as a subfield of the discipline since its origins. One need only conjure the shades of the Mercantilists, Adam Smith, David Ricardo, and Alfred Marshall to make this claim self-evident. The dichotomy between the domestic and foreign sectors is long-standing and has implications for theory, concepts of value, and policy. It is worth asking why external transactions have invited special inspection by great economists and yielded such remarkable insights into the process of exchanging. The answer is that trade within the boundaries of a particular society raises no unusual issues. There are rules that those engaged know they should follow, the gains and losses are more-or-less anticipated and shared by all, and information and enforcement costs are comparatively low. A stable and known institutional context may be taken for granted, in which to analyze actors' behavior. In vivid contrast, when exchanges occur across social and national borders none of these conditions may be presumed.

Differing social and economic regimes incorporate inconsonant institutions or rules of the game. Examples include variations in business codes, judicial procedures, relations between state and market, and stances towards market agents. Languages, weights and measures, coinages, and normative judgements about dealings in selected products will diverge. Each of these myriad dimensions of variety adds to the information, transactions, and enforcement costs associated with effecting acts of intersocial exchange. From the 1400s on, the consolidation of the mercantile nation-states of Europe was achieved by numberless collectively and privately engineered measures to reduce domestic exchange or transfer costs. During the late nineteenth and early twentieth centuries, technological changes lowered shipping and communications expenses, as railways, steam shipping, and telegraphy spread. After Bretton Woods, international organizations, trade negotiations, and regional trading arrangements have achieved pronounced decrements in the costs and risks of moving products from one country's jurisdiction to another.

The standard comparative cost model assumes transactions costs are zero. The conventional textbook treatments sometimes mention transportation charges, insurance rates, and banking fees, all of which are monetized, but do not integrate them into the discussion. This extreme simplification has the effect of reducing the entire analysis of exchange merely to a determination of the location of production. It obviates any discussion of the institutionalization of exchange, of broadly defined transactions costs, and of culturally defined consumption imperatives. All trading parties are presumed to follow identical commercial practices. One effect of ignoring institutional gaps and frictions in the exchange process is that the gains of trade are substantially overstated. The orthodox model, with zero transfer costs, yields a best-case, maximum volume of trade. One could as realistically make the obverse assumption that transactions costs are infinite, in which instance there would be no trade; all goods would be untradeables. Clearly, in the transsocial exchange process all public and private actors function in a variety of institutional realms, possess only flawed prognoses about outcomes, and are subject to a vitiating level of combined monetary and non-monetized transaction expenses. There is not sufficient wisdom at this point to propose more than that these transfer costs are higher than generally thought in comparison to supply costs and that, over time, the ratio of the two has fallen substantially because of technological improvements and institutional refinements.

Conventional theory employs partial and general equilibrium models to determine prices and quantities before and after trade, and to identify the gains from trade, or the losses from a feckless departure from free trade. The simplest partial equilibrium model treats only one traded commodity in one economy. If the product in figure 4.1 is designated product R, without trade the home price and quantity in a small country, A, are represented by point **Z** where the supply and demand schedules intersect. In open-economy trade with a large nation, B, when there are no transactions costs, A will export **ab** at B's higher price, $\mathbf{P}_{\mathbf{ab}}$, consume less of R at home, and produce more. If there is some level of transactions costs such that the autarkic home price plus the transactions costs are less than $\mathbf{P}_{\mathbf{ab}}$, then exports will be reduced to **cd**, at a net price, $\mathbf{P}_{\mathbf{cd}}$. If transactions costs are greater than the difference of $\mathbf{P}_{\mathbf{ab}}$ and $\mathbf{P}_{\mathbf{z}}$, then no trade will occur.

Two things are evident: trade is higher, the smaller are transfer expenses; and, the zero-cost case is a limiting boundary outcome. Transactions costs, and the institutions that determine them, matter, and the only issue is how much. Devising an institutional theory of trade that is consistent with the comparative cost model must confront the wide gulf between heterodox and orthodox thinking about economic behavior. This can be expressed as a divide between those who favor a cultural or structural stance and those who rely upon an agency or individual-action construct. Most orthodox economists now accept the principle that theorizing about individually motivated transactions requires an appreciation of a concrete institutional context; in other words, a pure model of independent rational agents is inadequate in and of itself. This premise has long been held in economic history and is reaffirmed in the current surge of enthusiasm for game theoretics. Institutional economists have consistently appreciated the roles of beliefs, habits, and culture play in framing human choices in a situation of complex personal interdependencies. Formidable barriers remain at very deep levels in attempting to foment a full synthesis of the orthodox approach that stresses individual action and the institutional approach that emphasizes social patternings, although there is mounting optimism that a reconciliation or synthesis may be feasible [Rutherford 1994]. Minimally, a long-overdue dialogue is in order.

A potentially unifying concept is process, taken to signify an irreversible time path of interaction between individual human calculations and deeds and the encompassing web of ideas, values, and cultural constraints and opportunities involved in a particular social moment, conveniently called a situation or transaction [Adams 1994]. International trade is an archetypical case of an instituted process and its differentiation from run-of-the-mill domestic transactions renders in high relief the crucial character of the institutional milieu and the special burdens that are in effect when individual actors seek to cross cultural boundaries. Domestic exchange is embedded in a more-or-less coherent and shared matrix of institutions, values, language, and concepts, while dealings with outsiders, to the extent they are tolerated by a society at all, are burdened with the baggage of differences in trading customs, standards of valuation, concepts, and languages.

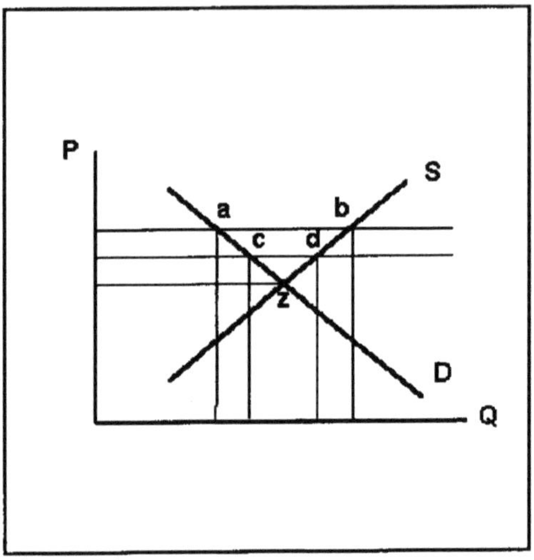

Figure 4.1

A's Trade in R With and Without Transactions Costs

In view of the apparently high expenses, burdens, and risks associated with intersocial transactions, it may well be asked why such exchange historically has been so important. The response is that external bargains, particularly in long-distance trade, are likely to afford exceptional benefits to the engaged parties. As a general postulate, because climatic and technological variations rise with distance, ancient international trade transmitted into the domestic realm items of rarity and value, predicated on local considerations of need or status. Typical early trade goods include salt, gemstones, spices, furs, weapons and metal articles, textiles, and previously unknown psychoactive substances. Wide divergences between domestic availabilities and costs and those to be obtained in trading provoke compulsive incentives to seek out the most rewarding and viable channels of exchange. In this ongoing comparison of values, and the ensuing puissant incentives to realize the gains of intersocial transacting, one can perceive the nucleus of the deterministic, classical theories of absolute and comparative advantage. Yet, the challenges and rewards of intersocial exchange are everywhere amenable to human intervention and it is this that must be analyzed rather than, ostrich-like, assumed away. Intersocial exchange is the outcome of cogent action in a particular institutional context. Even in the face of steep transactions costs and indeterminate risks, it behooves agents to seek zealously to engage in transborder commerce. Such agents are by no means limited to classes of private market dealers or legions of itinerant peddlers. Perhaps most frequently in precapitalist times, long-distance trade was steered by instituted compacts and was regulated and overseen by branches of city or state governments. As in Venice and the Italian city-states, congeries of elite families may have been instrumental. By the sixteenth century, that novel institution, the chartered merchant trading company, forerunner of today's transnational corporation, moved toward center stage as an instrument of exchange management.

Conceiving intersocial trade as entailing varying forms of instituted process yields several robust principles [Adams 1987].

- Transactions costs will be higher, and volumes of exchange lower, the more disparate are the institutions of the two societies involved, subject to the usual ceteris paribus caveat.
- To put this axiom the other way 'round, trade will be greater the more similar are two societies' institutions, such as modes of exchange, forms of governance, juridical methods, and property rights, because transactions costs and risks will be lower.
- Trade within spheres where there is growing institutional convergence, arising through imperial expansion or cooperative negotiation, will expand more rapidly than in a highly segmented setting.
- A traditional society, or a modern nation, may unilaterally adopt policies to bring its practices into conformity with those of a larger component of the global system, and thereby reap the benefits of diminished transfer burdens.

Because it is very costly over the long term for any society, even a large imperial state, to try to go it alone, states and private actors will devote considerable energy, alone and in concert, to the reduction of barriers to intersocial exchange. The modern instances of the Soviet Union and China are compellingly illustrative. Isolation from Euro-Asian channels of exchange condemned Sub-Saharan Africa and the uncolonized Americas to technological, military, economic, and immunological backwardness. In contrast, adaptive trading peoples, even those with relatively small numbers, have secured economic and even military supremacy over large closed societies in recent centuries [i.e., the Netherlands (Netherlands Indies), Great Britain (India), and Japan (East Asia)]. None of this denies the reality that under particular conditions a high degree of isolation may be desirable, at least for a time. The arguments for an infant-industry tariff, or subsidy, are compelling. Closing the city gate to bearers of the plague makes sense. The aloofness of the Swiss or the Tibetans' Shangri-La proclivity may have temporary merit. Nonetheless, over the reach of time, there are very large and cumulative material and non-material sacrifices incurred by remaining outside global trade and intellectual flows.

INTERNATIONAL TRANSACTIONS COSTS

The potential costs of intersocial exchange involve out-of-pocket monetary payments, the commitment of real resources, the forgoing of immediate consumption, and intangibles such as time, bother, and risk. From the point of view of the people involved, or potentially involved, these costs are normally viewed as multiplicative rather than simply additive. In other cases, resolving all problems but one, such as getting insurance or bank credit or meeting the demands of a single bandit king, is still fatal to consummation of a deal. More likely, though, transfer costs will decline sharply because of economies of scale and scope. An initial transaction for a commodity will pave the way for future like exchanges; similarly, penetration of an alien trading domain in one dimension will ease the path in others.

A catalog of intersocial transactions costs with adduced commentaries on avenues to their reduction suggests their considerable range and magnitude. No distinction is drawn between monetized and non-monetized costs because the line between the two varies from case to case and time to time. Although the point cannot be developed here, it is instructive to notice how many of the efforts to lower the costs of transacting require the provision of public goods, of which the lighthouse has long served as the prototype. How public goods get provided in a world in which there is no overarching political authority is itself a conundrum to unravel, one that is becoming ever more necessary to resolve as the burgeoning population of the planet faces continuing environmental, water, security, and basic-needs challenges.

Transport charges and risks

Production costs are those entailed in the manufacture or provision of a good or service. Subsequently, transfer expenses related to locational change begin to accumulate. These embrace packaging, storage, and inventory costs, which may encompass actual cash outlays or opportunity costs. Shipping involves loading a conveyance such as a camel, diesel truck, barge, or train car; the expenses of moving the product, including actual or imputed interest; transloading to other modes, such as a freight vessel; offloading and storage; and, finally, movement to a final place of use. Along the way, shipments will be lost or damaged; there will be pilferage and spoilage. Allowances must be made for losses of cargoes to storms and, in early times particularly, to pirates or to bandits. The nature of a good affects the influence of each of these types of transport charge and risk. The conventional differentiation is between bulky goods and those of low weight and high value. This hardly does justice to the many distinctions that may be drawn. Shipping the identical weight of grain or wine necessitates different methods and costs, and the same applies to saffron and diamonds.

Many variables affect the level of transport expenses. Technological advances lower costs and are among the most striking features of economic history. Improvements in sailing ships and navigational skills have occurred in many settings and diffused to others. The extension of road systems, canals, railways, and port facilities manifests the function of infrastructure in reducing shipment expenses. Risk-pooling by merchant families and the rise of insurance agencies lower individual agents' jeopardies. Societies with dominant naval and land power could suppress such hazards as thievery or buccaneering, ofttimes conveying public-good benefits to weaker, free-rider states. In the Mercantilist era, shipping in foreign vessels was frequently barred, effectively establishing an infinite price. An added element in determining exactly what charges a merchant faces, in more modern times, is the existence of extremely complex freight-rate conventions governing many modes of transport, which may or may not be discounted from their nominal quotations, and may or may not have official sanction.

Tolls, tariffs, customs charges, non-tariff barriers

Most political authorities, of whatever legitimacy, have sought to raise revenue by imposing charges on imports, exports, or transit trade. These tolls, tariffs, imposts, permits, customs charges, and taxes have been so common, and their negative bearing on exchange so thoroughly probed, that not much needs to be said about them. Quotas, prohibitions, and non-tariff barriers are equally well comprehended. In fact, the only important question to raise is why this type of transfer cost has attracted so much attention compared to others. Perhaps the answer is that these instruments are official policies that impede trade and merchant profit. Unlike many of the other obstructions to exchange, these can be immediately applied or removed in response to political forces. The evasion of high imposts or absolute barriers by smuggling and bribery has always been a by-product of trade charges and controls.

A good deal of the world's political history has involved contests among jurisdictional leaderships for command of the revenues, or spoils, from trade excises. Such taxes have been widely adopted because it is easy to collect them at ports, bridges, or city gates; and, there may have been the naive but not wholly inaccurate belief that foreigners were paying the fees. During the Mercantile epoch, the rise of nation states simultaneously stripped local authorities of much of their power to assess charges on domestic trade, while controlling and garnering the revenues from international commerce for the central government. From the 1700s on, national tariffs have moved up and down in concert with political forces, beggar-thy-neighbor attitudes, and business-cycle pressures. After World War II, a great range of bilateral agreements, customs unions, and regional trading blocs have come upon the scene. In combination with the negotiating rounds of the General Agreement on Tariffs and Trade, now the World Trade Organization, these institutional initiatives have cantilevered trade barriers downwards in dramatic fashion.

Financial charges and risks

Excepting cases of pure barter or gifting, which are a rare but continuing component of intersocial exchange relations, all transactions in goods have financial complements. These add other costs and uncertainties to any bargain. There are fees associated with changing coins, handling bullion, and acquiring foreign exchange. Money changers are never figures of popular esteem because they take visible slices out of others' directly useful and productive trades. The emergence of paper instruments, such as bills of exchange, greatly facilitated the financial clearings that underpinned merchandise commerce, but brought other forms of charges and discounts. Today, banking, interest, and currency charges are a component of any transaction. Many forms of risk travel along on the financial bypaths of international dealings. In a metallic money system, these include debasement, the theft or loss of coins or bullion, and malfeasance in exchange, possibly attributable to asymmetric information about rates. Non-payments or delayed payments are hazards. Embezzlement of funds is generally easier and more lucrative than diversion of physical cargoes. Realizing an expected profit in any monetary regime depends on accurately forecasting money costs and money revenues. Inaccurate knowledge of purchase and sales prices and of the monetary costs of production, such as wages, inputs, or supplies, may lead to disappointing results.

The financial and reputational facets of long-distance trade have presented a daunting barrier to exchange. From early times to the present, social relationships have served as conduits of commerce because of the advantages they afford in coping with these transactional handicaps. First prior to, and now alongside, the multinational company, families, kinship alliances, and clan networks have functioned to lower transfer costs and overcome information voids and deficiencies in reputational knowledge [Adams 1993; Greif 1989, 1993]. Recently, in more formally organized ways, many corrective developments have abated or controlled international financial costs and risks. These include innovations in banking and financial intermediation and the rise of new forms of payment, today including telegraphic and electronic transfers. To some degree, bank certification of the contractual adequacy of importers substitutes for a lack of experience with and knowledge of the reputations on the part of remote exporters. Fuller information about prices and exchange rates, and its rapid dissemination, have been facilitated by newspapers, the mails, semaphores, the telegraph, and the telephone. In the absence of a true world currency or unit of account, national monies have been compelled to serve as media of commerce and standards of accountancy. Exchange-rate instabilities have been countered by such fixed-rate systems as the gold standard and the postwar IMF gold-dollar arrangement. In the contemporary world's predominantly flexible-rate paradigm, forward hedging is a means for private agents to control their exposures.

Information and search costs

Accomplishing intersocial trade across wide distances requires acquiring vast reservoirs of information. From the exporting side, there is the need to identify those persons who are interested in acting on the other side of the transaction. In a market setting, these are customers or clients; in a non-market pattern, they may be agents of a government or delegates of an elite. How does an itinerant peddler or the captain of a merchantman know that a long journey will lead to sufficient sales to make the venture worthwhile? Rumors, good guesses, and repeated visits help. Conversely, how does the importer as an active agent locate sources of supply for needed grains, metals, perfumes, or luxury cloths? Information and conjectures about how prices and exchange ratios differ across space must be in mind before trading ventures can be launched and realized.

In all cases, except those that are serendipitous, time, effort, and the devotion of wealth are needed to secure useful, accurate facts about exchange opportunities. Explorations, prospecting, and voyages of discovery are means of learning about foreign supplies, needs and tastes. Trade missions, fairs, and embassies are institutions that facilitate and concentrate information flows. Economic historians are quite aware that the loci of market transactions shift with mutations in search and information costs. S. R. H. Jones [1994] has investigated the transition from reliance on periodic markets (fairs) to personal or diffused trade in England from about 1350 through the 1700s. In the middle of the fourteenth century there were at least 1,750 weekly public markets operating in the countryside. Jones believes that the ever more abundant commercial intelligence flowing from London, as that metropolis achieved economic ascendancy, "lowered information costs to transactors throughout the provinces, who were no longer obliged to search local markets" [5]. London's generally higher prices rewarded those merchants and provincial suppliers willing to devote time and resources to search for price differences and pursue arbitrage opportunities. Travelling traders became more specialized and knowledgeable. Increasingly numerous urban inns provided not only lodgings, meals, and trade gossip but warehousing and auction spaces [27]. Although Jones's account pertains to England, its lessons readily extend to exchange patterns in global space.

Weights, measures, standards

The devising and extensive adoption of conventional measures of physical quantities has profound public-good consequences for networks of traders in a select set of commodities. Any culture devises ways of counting and measuring dimensions and weights. For an intersocial transaction to occur, there must be some way of establishing a translation or numeraire to align disparate gauges. A traditional South Asian measure of grain is the *seer*, which varies from village to village but is roughly two pounds. How many *seers* are there in a ton? is an unanswerable question, and not only because of the ambiguity over the weight of a *seer*. There is culpability in the West as well. What exactly is a ton? A long ton is 2240 pounds; a short ton is 2000 pounds; a metric ton is 1000 kilograms. As for measures of length, a Biblical cubit was 21.8 inches; a Greek cubit was 18.3 inches; a Roman cubit was 17.5 inches. What size of European woman fits into an American size 10 dress? Parallel questions can be asked about the purity of drugs or chemicals, about tolerable levels of pesticides on crop shipments, about the threshold octane rating of aviation fuel, and about tolerances on machine tools. Different trackage gauges confront French and British trainmen at each end of the Chunnel. A constricting obstruction of the sales of American automobiles in Japan has been the crudest type of standard: the difference between leftside and rightside steering wheels. The United States has thus far been unwilling to bear the real and psychic losses of effecting a full conversion to the metric system.

It is hard even to imagine procuring a satisfactory estimate of the degree of braking of transcultural exchanges attributable to incommensurable weights, measures, and standards. What is evident is that enormous resources are being devoted to creating universal criteria. Even as one set of issues is resolved, others spring up as new technologies emerge, examples being found in such product lines as VCRs, software, and high-definition television broadcasts and receivers. One of the most difficult tasks faced by the European Union is hammering out acceptable standards, amidst existing regional diversity. The problem is exemplified as well as anything by the unharmonious electrical currents and sockets a traveller encounters. In any field, adoption of a standard imposes disproportionate burdens on one or the other country, producer, or consumer. As fresh technologies come on line, selection of one variant over another will yield huge rent gains to one set of innovators and render the others extinct or maintaining marginal positions.

Property rights and contract enforcement

Resolving a transaction from start to finish involves negotiations within a stable customary or formal legal framework. It is not always correct to call this "reaching a contract" since that is only one form of commitment, but the term can suffice if broadly read. Prerequisite to transfer is ownership or control. Any society has a set of property rights and one or more ways of regularizing the shift of use or ownership from one person, or collective entity, to another. The capture and moving of a good include appropriational and locational adjustments. One of the most meaningful ways, if not the most consequential, in which peoples differ is in their institutionalized management of appropriational and locational movements of resources and products and their associated rights. Because intersocial exchange must bridge at least two incompatible realms, special provisions must evolve. These could be worked out spontaneously by the trading agents or be put in place by prenegotiation between appropriate authorities. In either case, resources must be committed and costs incurred. The inevitably remaining ambiguities impose hardships on future agents of trade.

Defaults on contracts and other matters of dispute must be resolvable in a timely and orderly way, if exchange is not to be impeded or riven with uncertainties. European fairs had associated courts or arbitrators that tried to resolve contracting and performance conflicts. The classical Athenians sponsored merchant courts in Piraeus. The European colonial empires sometimes worked with local authorities to resolve differences with native dealers and suppliers, and on other occasions unleashed naked force to impose solutions to their liking. A contemporary issue that was very incompletely resolved during the final, Uruguay round of GATT was controversy over intellectual property rights, which stems from rampant pirating of books, patents, and entertainment media in some nations.

Languages and communications

Economists underestimate the significance of language and communication in framing market and exchange behavior. Speaking is prerequisite to almost any type of human interaction. In his famous passage on the propensity to truck, barter, and exchange, Adam Smith denied that this human tendency was innate to human nature and said is was more likely a " . . . consequence of the faculties of reason and speech" [quoted in McCloskey 1994, 32]. To learn, to be trusted, to persuade, to negotiate and to reconcile, all these depend upon speech and are features of an exchange compact. As McCloskey justly says, " . . . markets live on people's tongues" [37]. To go further: in a lively African or Middle Eastern marketplace, the talk may be more valued than the petty commerce that is effected.

If markets live on people's tongues, how then can intersocial exchanges occur when languages differ? There are several possibilities and each incorporates the devotion of time and resources and imposes hindering transfer obstacles. A merchant must learn one or more foreign languages. A multilingual translator can be hired. In a colonial system, an imported language such as English, French, or Spanish was imposed, or material necessity and invidious pride drove its spread among the indigenous population. The unplanned rise of a trading language, such as Swahili or pidgin English, can ease communications. The use of common symbols, abbreviations, and number systems can transcend verbal differences. Sign language was used in the early North American fur trade, a practice that continues with a different alphabet and grammar in the pits of the Chicago Board of Trade.

MEASURING INTERNATIONAL TRANSACTIONS COSTS AND THEIR TREND[2]

Surprisingly, despite the increasing use of the idea of transactions costs, efforts to define them operationally and then measure them are rare. As with a number of other economic concepts (such as risk), transactions costs are often treated as a residual differential rather than independently measured. Their presence is inferred from something that does not happen when it should, in this case an exchange that would yield gains to parties on both sides of the transaction. Much of the empirical work on transactions costs has centered on such microlevel topics as business organization and contracting and little has been done concerning foreign trade or the behavior of multinational corporations [Klein and Shelanski 1994]. Wallis and North [1986] estimated that the transactions sector in the U.S. economy has come to absorb as much as 40 percent of GDP, but this conveys little information about what is happening to transfer costs per unit of output or per episode of exchange in different areas at different historical moments.

It is only from the latter part of the nineteenth century that constructions of world trade and income have much validity. Figure 2 [Maddison 1982] shows the rise in world exports from 1880 to 1913. Value and volume more than doubled in these three decades. Supply and demand factors, including rising productivity and incomes and the opening of new markets, certainly shared responsibility for this extraordinary growth. Institutional changes, the emergence of a freer-trade climate, breakthroughs in transportation and communications led to falling transactions costs and were undoubtedly of consequence. Fomenting trade growth is only one effect of reductions in hindrances to exchange. It may be proposed that when international transactions expenses fall more rapidly than equivalent domestic costs, then the growth of world exports will exceed the growth in world output. Another way of stating this hypothesis, is that a reduction in transboundary costs increases the range and volumes of tradeables versus non-tradeables. In a universe with zero transactions costs, everything is tradeable and moves towards those who value it most.

Confirmation of these suspicions is provided by figure 3 [Maddison 1982] which documents a sharp uptick in the world's export/GDP ratio from the mid-1890s through 1913. The traffic in many categories of goods benefited from the spread of a market system, from comparatively tranquil international relations, from the stability of the gold standard, and from radical improvements in transport and communications technologies. Trade in bulky items such as sugar, coffee, oils and oilseeds, hides, cotton, rice, meat, coal, iron, and steel shows strong gains. Among the most crucial of the institutional changes associated with the diffusion of the market system

Figure 4.2
World Exports, 1880-1913

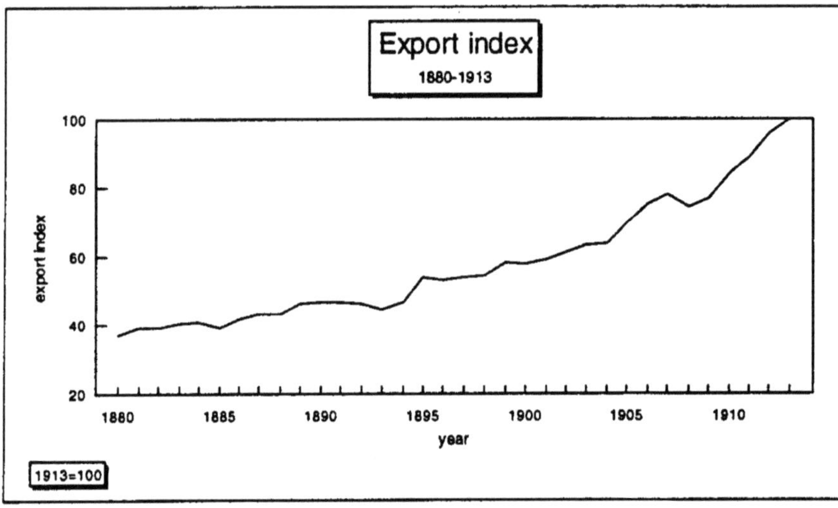

Figure 4.3
World Export/GDP Ratio, 1850-1910

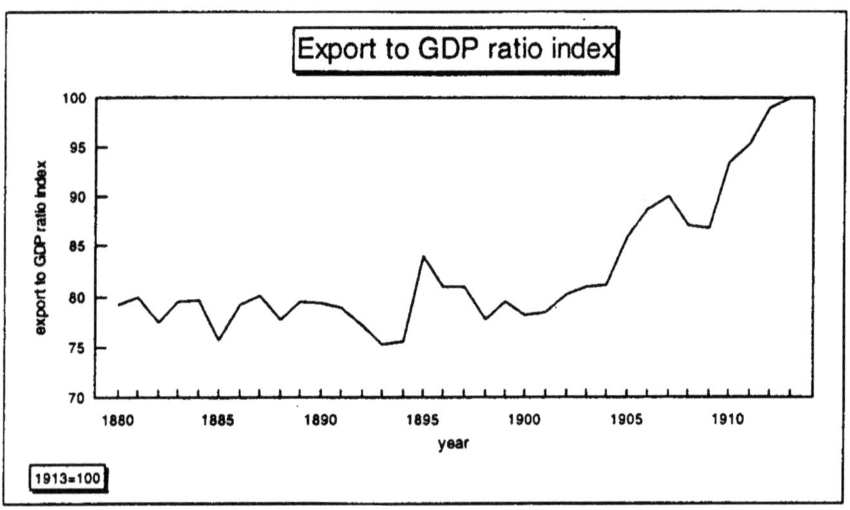

on a broader scale than had been previously known in the Americas, Asia, and Africa was the assertion of the European vision of property rights and their disposition. Farmlands, mineral rights, trading concessions, and commercial factories were putatively purchased or extracted, often in circumstances where the non-Europeans acting on the other side of transactions had no indigenous authority or customary or legal basis for their representations. This one-sided establishment of novel property regimens eased the appropriational dimensions of goods transfers just as the improvements in physical infrastructure facilitated locational activities.

Not all international transactions costs are readily calculable, the difficulties of language translation being one example. The inferential evidence of figures 2 and 3 bolsters the proposition that appropriational and locational bonds on global traffic rapidly loosened between 1850 and 1910. There remain essentially two questions to answer. First, what was the ratio between transactions costs and the values of exports; or, restated, how important were transactions costs? Second, what was the trend in transactions costs after 1850?

Table 4.1 offers rough estimates of six types of trade costs, expressed as a percentage of merchandise trade on a decadal basis. The far right-hand column shows the sum of these fractions. In the absence of tariff data for the 1850s and 1860s, only four decades' totals are calculated. These categories of expenses comprised about 23 percent of export value in the 1870s but declined to some 16 percent in the 1900s. Looking at the columns, freight charges rose into the 1870s then fell rapidly; losses at sea show a similar path. Meltage, cargo shrinkage from theft or spoilage, does not show a trend. Average tariffs decline and there are dramatic drops in communications charges, first in postage in the 1880s, then in telegraph and telephone fees in the 1890s and 1900s. Factorage, or foreign representation, expenses are taken to remain constant even though there was a transition from use of agents to reliance on internal sales subsidiaries in many commercial businesses.[3]

Table 4.1
International Transactions Costs, 1850-1910
(% merchandise trade value)

Decade	Freight	Losses at Sea	Meltage	Tariffs	Communi-cation	Factor-age	Total
1850s	7.80	1.00	3.00	n/a	2.00	1.00	n/a
1860s	8.82	1.00	3.00	n/a	2.00	1.00	n/a
1870s	10.17	1.74	3.00	6.26	0.67	1.00	22.84
1880s	6.62	1.89	3.00	7.58	0.21	1.00	20.30
1890s	6.21	1.29	3.00	6.66	0.12	1.00	18.28
1900s	3.79	1.06	3.00	6.66	0.04	1.00	15.55

Source: Bowen [1995].

Of course, the figures reported in table 4.1 do not encompass all transfer hindrances. Omitted are such categories as information, search, enforcement, and contracting costs. Let us make the heroic assumption that the counted costs are one-half of the total; this would suggest that total exchange costs added at least 50 percent to production costs, on average, in the 1870s, and no less than 35 percent in the 1910. Most of these favorable trends were reversed by the wars and tariff walls of the 1920s, '30s, and '40s, and the world's ratio of exports to GDP moved downwards.

INSTITUTIONS AND BILATERAL TRADE

It is feasible to examine whether patterns of bilateral trade are sensitive to institutional factors. Transactions costs, or some component of them, may be measured directly, or proxies representing country features may be used to hint where frictions are low or high. Information on bilateral trade flows and country characteristics may then be combined into explanatory statistical models. Joint work with F. Shah and S. Alam of Northeastern University [Shah 1995] has yielded preliminary but intriguing suggestions of the importance of institutional frictions and transactions cost factors in shaping bilateral trade relations.

Consider the following index of export intensity:

$$XI_{ij} = (X_{ij}/X_i)/[(M_j - M_{ji})/(M_W - M_{ij})], \qquad (1)$$

where X_{ij} = exports from country i to country j, X_i = exports of country i, M_j = imports of country j, M_{ji} = imports of j from i, M_W = world imports, and M_{ij} = imports of i from j. The plan is to examine the ratio of i's exports to j in comparison to j's imports from the world. When the intensity index is greater than 1, j is importing relatively more from i, than from the remainder of the world. When it is less than 1, the reverse is true.

The bilateral trade flows and export intensity indexes are regressed on 9 independent variables. The aim is to explain bilateral trade flows among 12 Asian and 14 industrialized countries. The Asian exporting and importing countries are: Bangladesh, Hong Kong, India, Indonesia, Japan, Korea, Malaysia, Pakistan, The Philippines, Singapore, Sri Lanka, and Thailand. The industrialized importing countries are: Australia, Belgium, Canada, Denmark, France, Germany, Italy, New Zealand, The Netherlands, Spain, Sweden, Switzerland, the United Kingdom, and the United States. Over the period 1975 to 1989, the total data set numbers 4,500 observations (12 x 25 x 15). The export coverage for the sample of Asian countries falls from 90 to 70 percent of total Asian trade during this period and amounts to

15 percent of world trade, as of 1989. The explanatory variables are the national incomes and per capita incomes of the two partners, variables representing factor proportions, the distance apart of the pairs, and dummies for adjacency (common borders), former colonial ties, and membership in ASEAN.

The equation for trade flows is

$$LX_{ij} = -22.71 + 0.73LY_i + 0.67LY_j + 1.43Ly_i + 0.78Ly_j + 0.09LHO - 1.05LD_{ij} + 0.47CAD + 0.92COL + 1.03ASEAN \quad (2)$$

and that for trade intensity is

$$LXI_{ij} = 3.35 + 0.14LY_i + 0.10LY_j + 0.24Ly_i - 0.06Ly_j + 0.14LHO - 1.19LD_{ij} + 0.40CAD + 0.65COL + 0.11ASEAN. \quad (3)$$

The adjusted R^2 for (2) is 0.68 and for (3) is 0.39.[4] In (2), all coefficients are significant at the 0.001 level or higher and have the correct signs. Both countries' GDPs (Y's) and per capita GDPs (y's) are positively related to the volume of bilateral trade. Disparities in K/L ratios (LHO) stimulate trade as the factor proportions theory predicts. Considering the same variables in the intensity version (3), all are significant and with the correct sign, with the exception of y_i. Broadly speaking, the larger are the sizes of two national economies and the higher their per capita incomes, the wider and proportionately more intensive will be their exchanges. Beyond this gravity model, the conventional factor proportions divergence offers explanatory leverage.

The remaining four variables in the two equations are distance (LD_{ij}), adjacency (CAD), previous colonial relationship (COL), and membership in the chief regional trading bloc (ASEAN).[5] In addition to the obvious interpretation that can be put on each of these, they may be taken to represent the unmeasured influence of institutional and transaction-cost elements. Distance registers not only transport costs but other communications and information handicaps; adjacency does much the same. The lasting importance of a colonial connection strongly implies that four or five decades of independence does not sever important commercial ties, mutual knowledge, the role of immigrant communities in transactional networking, and shared cultural, linguistic, and legal trappings. Lastly, the comity implied by membership in ASEAN does foster trade, and certainly not only by tariff reductions. All four of these variables are significant and appropriately signed in (2) and all but ASEAN are significant in (3).

CONVERGENCES IN THOUGHT AND DIRECTIONS OF INQUIRY

The two equations taken together vigorously reinforce the viewpoint that a fully satisfactory explanation of global trade patterns and growth most grow from examination of supply and demand variables, factor proportions, and a large set of institutional and transactions-cost parameters. Underrepresented in the discussion in this chapter are technological and human-capital sources of advantage as well as other institutional conditions such as forms of business organization, the nature of private-public sector synergies, and public infrastructures. Institutions do matter in shaping the pattern and growth of world trade. Institution-building and transaction-cost reductions have had a key function in the expansion of trade, in specific modern regions or earlier contexts, such as that fostered in the eastern Mediterranean by the thalassocracy of ancient Athens [Adams 1994] or by the British Empire.

Economists have used the phrase "the law of one price" to highlight the impact of free trade on national markets, but one may with equal vigor advance "the law of one rule" as a foundation injunction for sharing the advantages of trade. In the modern world, there are mighty autochthonous pressures working to achieve convergence in operating principles and accomplish reductions in transactions costs. There is nothing preordained or teleological about the processes at work; they are under the control of various forms of individual and collective, private and public, action. As history has so far played itself out, the adoption of common rules appears to have led to convergence towards a private-property, mixed-capitalist market system. This is far too simplistic and deterministic a conclusion. The open-ended roles of national governments and international organizations, operating increasingly in conjunction with councils of participatory democracies, have been and will continue to be voluntaristically directive in shaping workable global institutions. What matters most is that one set of rules for transsocial enterprise be soon established, not that the rules be optimal, efficient, or just. The climax of our conjoint history lies well over the horizon.

ENDNOTES

1. A version of this chapter was presented as part of the panel, Why and How Institutions Matter, American Economic Association, Washington, DC, 6 January 1995.

2. This section draws heavily on a paper done by a graduate student at Northeastern University under my supervision [Bowen, 1995]. Her industrious and skilled contribution is appreciated and hereby acknowledged.

3. The estimates in table 1 should be regarded as first passes and as the outgrowth of work in progress. As North [1958, 1968] and Harley [1988] have demonstrated, even getting a clear handle on movements in average shipping costs is fraught with peril. Important caveats that apply to table 1 should be voiced. The freight factor is based on North [1958] as extended by Bowen [1995] and applies to American wheat as a leading staple of the period. Losses at sea are based on trends in U.S. tonnage and value losses, less growth in exports (losses fall even as traffic rises). Spoilage may have declined, but pilferage was probably increasing, so meltage is taken as a constant. The average tariff rate is based on a trade-weighted average of the rates for Austria, Belgium, France, Italy, The Netherlands, Sweden, the United Kingdom, and the United States. Postal rate tendencies are judged by the price of the cheapest first-class letter in the United States. Telegraph and telephone fees are approximated by trends in British rates.

4. Equation (2) is corrected for heteroskedasticity. It is impossible to rectify simultaneously both heteroskedasticity and autocorrelation. Correction for the latter condition yields very much the same coefficients. Equation (3) is corrected for first-order autocorrelation and is an OLS model, which may not be the ideal specification [Shah, 125]. For (3), n = 4200 after adjustments for non-normalcy of the intensity index.

5. Distance is measured by water routes and land paths to the economic centers of gravity of the countries. Adjacency means sharing a common border, which generally facilitates trade, but in a case such as India-Pakistan may capture an antagonistic embargo. Japan and Thailand are the only two countries that did not have a colonial overlord. Membership in ASEAN is a clear marker, but including SAARC in earlier equations did not yield any result, which is not surprising inasmuch as it has not become an effective trade bloc and is marred by the aforementioned rivalry on the subcontinent, a reprehensible disjunction in a converging world.

REFERENCES

Adams, John. "Foreign Economic Policy: Challenges of the 1980s." *Journal of Economic Issues* 18 (March 1984): 275-294.

———. "Trade and Payments as Instituted Process: The Institutional Theory of the External Sector." *Journal of Economic Issues* 21 (December 1987): 1839-1860.

———. "The Family and Management of the Firm: An Institutional Theory." Presented at the Association for Institutional Thought Meetings, Corpus Christi, Texas, April 1993.

———. "Economy as Instituted Process: Change, Transformation, and Progress," Presidential Address, Association for Evolutionary Economics. *Journal of Economic Issues* 28 (June 1994): 331-355.

———. "The Institutional Theory of Trade and the Organization of Intersocial Commerce in Ancient Athens." In Colin A. M. Duncan and David W. Tandy, eds., *From*

Political Economy to Anthropology: Situating Economic Life in Past Societies. Montrèal: Black Rose Books, 1994, pp. 80-104.

Bowen, Frances. "Transactions Costs and International Trade, 1850-1914." Photocopy manuscript, Northeastern University, August 1995.

Federico, Giovanni. "A 'Textbook' Example of Market Integration: The Raw Silk Market, 1894-1913." Presented at the 11th International Economic History Congress, Milan, Italy, September 1994.

Greif, Avner. "Reputation and Coalitions in Medieval Trade: Evidence on the Maghrebi Traders." *Journal of Economic History* 49 (December 1989): 857-882.

———. "Contract Enforceability and Economic Institutions in Early Trade: The Maghribi Traders Coalition." *American Economic Review* 83 (June 1993): 525-548.

Harley, C. Knick. "Ocean Freight Rates and Productivity, 1740-1913." *Journal of Economic History* 47 (December 1988): 851-876.

Jones, S. R. H. 1994. "Search Costs and the Transition from Pitched Periodic Markets to Private Trade in English Economic History." Presented at the 11th International Economic History Congress, Milan, Italy, September.

Klein, Peter G. and Howard A. Shelanski. "Empirical Research in Transaction Cost Economics: A Survey and Assessment." A Ph.D. Student Paper in Business & Public Policy, Walter A. Haas School of Business, University of California, Berkeley, 1994.

Maddison, Angus. *Phases of Capitalist Development*. Oxford, Oxford University Press, 1982.

McCloskey, D. N. "The Extent of the Market and the Faculty of Speech." Presented at the 11th International Economic History Congress, Milan, Italy, September 1994.

North, Douglass C. "Ocean Freight Rates and Economic Development, 1750-1913." *Journal of Economic History* 18 (December 1958): 537-555.

———. "Sources of Productivity Change in Ocean Shipping, 1600-1850." *Journal of Economic History* 76 (September 1968): 953-970.

Persson, Karl Gunnar. "Integration and Deregulation of European Grain Markets, 1500-1900." Discussion Paper 94-07, Institute of Economics, University of Copenhagen, 1994.

Rutherford, Malcolm. *Institutions in Economics: The Old and the New Institutionalism*. Cambridge, Cambridge University Press, 1994.

Shah, A. K. Fazlul H. *Determinants of Bilateral Trade*. An unpublished dissertation, Department of Economics, Northeastern University, Boston, Massachusetts, June 1995.

Wallis, John J. and Douglass North. "Measuring the Transaction Sector in the American Economy, 1870-1970." In S. L. Engerman and R. E. Galman, eds., *Long-Term Factors in American Economic Growth*. Chicago, University of Chicago Press, 1986.

CHAPTER 5

TRADE AND THE ROLE OF CITIES: WHAT DOES INSTITUTIONALISM HAVE TO OFFER US?

Peter Karl Kresl
Bucknell University

There is a rough temporal concordance in the first writing on political economy, the evolution of the organization of production and distribution into the capitalist mode, and the rise of mercantilism. The state was the primary decision-maker in the Western economy of the seventeenth century and mercantilist writings stressed the role of the nation in organizing economic affairs. During the centuries that followed, economists kept their eyes focused on the nation. Adam Smith [1937] wrote of the wealth of nations, Friedrich List [1965] of the national system of political economy, and, most recently, Michael Porter [1990] of the competitive advantage of nations. Indeed the classic texts of the current century, those by such writers as Gottfried Haberler [1936], Jacob Viner [1937], Carl Iversen [1935], and James Meade [1951], all proclaim in their titles a focus on international trade or international capital movements.

In his major contribution to this literature, *International Trade*, Wendell Gordon justifies this focus on the nation by noting that:

> In studying international economic relations we are dealing with a topic which influences mightily, for good or ill, the destiny of the human race. Nations have fought wars for outlets to markets or for sources of raw materials. Confusion in international finance can affect the national income of countries, however much those countries would like to stay

> aloof from the troubles of others. Restrictions on the free movement of goods, people, and ideas from country to country should be a matter of concern to all of us. They affect our whole way of life whether we approve them or not [1958, 3].

In other words, just as Willy Sutton robbed banks because "that is where the money is," economists, of whatever ideological, philosophical, or methodological bent, studied the trade and financial relations among nations because that is where the action was.

Reality frequently has an impact on theory, and the fact that labor was limited in its mobility by often insurmountable barriers (such as linguistic differences; attachment to place, family, and culture; and discriminatory hiring practices) was soon translated into the assumption that at least one factor of production was immobile. The effect of this assumption was to make it necessary to limit attention to the movements of goods among and between political entities according to comparative advantage, rather than to allow for the movement of all factors. Under both mechanisms, the resulting theory concluded that movement would occur until factor prices had become equalized. The existence of nations complemented this approach since nations can be seen as entities that both respond to and exacerbate the cultural, ethnic, and religious distinctions among peoples that reinforced their immobility.

One dissenter among the pre-World War II classic theorists is the Swedish economist Bertil Ohlin, whose alternative view is suggested by the title of his major work, *Interregional and International Trade* [1933]. Ohlin tells us:

> the general theory of pricing is almost exclusively a *one-market* theory, wherein the idea of space, i.e., different local markets, hardly figures at all . . . As a matter of fact, the geographical distribution of productive factors is important. Industrial activity must be adapted to the varying supply of such factors in different places, for only a limited extent can the supply itself be adapted to the demands of various industries . . . A theory of *international* trade alone is inadequate, for location is relevant to pricing within countries also. Thus, the theory of pricing must be extended to include *a number of more or less closely related local markets* [1967, 1-2].

It is, one can add without doing damage to Ohlin's original intention, in the subnational regions and in urban economies that comparative advantage and the basis for exchange are powerfully created.

Ohlin's emphasis on the importance of subnational entities was soon ignored by the mainstream of economic analysis, while pieces of it were picked up by urbanologists, regional scientists, and geographers, little of whose analysis was incorporated in the international trade literature.

Recently, Paul Krugman [1991] has made an effort, in his small book, *Geography and Trade* (actually a series of lectures given on the safe territory of the Catholic University of Leuven, Belgium), to bridge the gap between economic geography and regional science, on the one hand, and international economics or international trade theory on the other. The titles of the three lectures in the book make Krugman's intentions clear: "Center and Periphery," "Localization," and "Regions and Nations." Bringing Ohlin's voice back to us after sixty years, Krugman admonishes us "to think about the geographical structure of production, [and] not treat countries as natural units of analysis" [87]. The thrust of his argument makes it clear that purposeful intervention at the local level of governance "can tip the balance in one region's favor" [90].

INSTITUTIONALISM AND THE ROLE OF CITIES

Institutionalist economists have not written much at all on the role of cities in economic development and in international economic relations, at least in the Veblen-Commons-Ayres-Gruchy line of thinking, but there are a few citations that give one access to an institutional approach to the issue. Clarence Ayres stresses, when discussing governance, that "in democracy considerations of operational efficiency are paramount" [284]. This is not a startling observation, but it does enable one to raise the question as to whether cities can have a positive, or operationally efficient, role to play. Gordon himself, writing with John Adams [1989, 218], suggests that the nation is primarily a source of conflict and war and in a world in which the United Nations, or a similar organization, could effectively reduce and arbitrate international conflict there would be a greatly diminished need for the national level of government [1995, 17-19]. Writing by himself, Gordon is more specific: "the general rule should apply that says: Governmental control should be administrated at the lowest level of government which can usefully administer that activity. Many problems can better be dealt with by a hands-on approach at the level of quite small governmental units" [1995, 10-11]. This view approximates the notion of "subsidiarity" that is so prominent today in discussions within the European Union, that is, that responsibilities for policy action ought to be allocated to the lowest level of government that can implement and administer that policy, with dispute resolution between units of governance being arbitrated at a higher level. Gordon and Adams are fairly explicit about the role of local decision-making:

> If we recognize the principle that the next higher level of government resolves conflicts, and if the spoiled child (nation or ruler) is not allowed to impose its views on others, it may well turn out that relatively few problems actually have to be resolved at the level of the world authority. Much more good-citizen type local decision-making might then naturally occur and the whole atmosphere be more pleasant [1989, 218].

It would perhaps not be inappropriate to amend that conclusion to read "more pleasant and operationally efficient."

Gordon takes us a bit closer to the central thesis of this chapter when he discusses the role of institutions in economic development and especially in the adaptation of an economy to new technologies: "The institutions into which society is organized adjust slowly and reluctantly to assimilate and use new technology and to accommodate and adjust their own structure the better to utilize the new technology" [1973, 5]. This is a high-stakes game, as Gordon and Adams argue persuasively:

> We do have to have institutions (social organizations and rules) in order to avoid chaos, in order to have civilization. The problem is to fix things so that we are masters of the rules instead of the rules (tradition and force of habit) being our masters. The society that is flexibly, continually, objectively, and intelligently reevaluating its rules and norms is going to assimilate technology more readily and offer a higher standard of living to its members and be a more pleasant place in which to live, than is the society which is rigidly frozen in its ways [1989, 16].

While Ayres and Gordon and Adams do not in any way throw the mantle of policy formulation, implementation, and administration regarding economic development and continental and intercontinental economic interaction on the shoulders of cities and other subnational governments, they do leave us with the following questions:

- Which level of government, local or national, can perform in this area of policy with the greatest degree of operational efficiency?
- Which level of government is likely to be most flexible and adaptive and, therefore, most able to take advantage of technological change?
- Which level of government will be most responsive to the needs of its constituencies? and,
- What developments in the context in which economic development and economic interaction take place suggest a reevaluation of the appropriate allocation of policy responsibilities among the various levels of government?

The principle of subsidiarity would suggest that the answer to the first three questions is that in a contest between the national and the city government, the latter should be chosen. This is by no means to deny that the national government has a powerful role to play, but a stronger argument can be made that economic development planning decisions and efforts to create comparative advantage in an intercontinental division of labor are best made when they emanate from local authorities and institutions; and that it is these decisions that should guide the national government in much of its policy implementation. Furthermore, it has always been the case that some of the most important elements in the development of an urban economy, such as K-12 education, local infrastructure, mobilization of local energies and institutions, and development of a civic spirit, are already the responsibilities of local government [Kresl 1995].

It is the fourth question that makes this a policy issue for which the primary concerns of institutionalism have special relevance. The relative importance, or operational efficiency, of national and city governments in economic development and economic interaction has been powerfully affected by events in the global context during the past decades. The most powerful of these forces of change, for this area of public policy, have been: (1) changes in the technologies of production, transportation, and communication; and (2) trade liberalization on the global and the regional level. Although technological change has been a primary concern of institutionalists from the outset, beginning with Veblen, it is clear that trade liberalization, especially during the past decade, has had an equally powerful impact on the role of cities in the global economy. The remainder of this chapter will examine how these changes have affected cities and what some cities have done in response.

THE IMPACTS OF TECHNOLOGICAL CHANGE AND TRADE LIBERALIZATION ON CITIES

The situation of cities has been changed during the past two or three decades because of two fundamental structural discontinuities that have altered dramatically the roles and capabilities of all governmental entities. In this section I examine the importance of these two structural discontinuities: technological change and trade liberalization.

Technological Change

When economists began to focus their attention on the national economy, nations were isolated from each other. Land transportation in the eighteenth and nineteenth centuries was slow and costly, and shipping was subject to a variety of risks, from piracy to gales. Communication was subject to the same limitations since it, too, was confined to ship and coach. Railroads and telegraphy in the second half of the nineteenth century reduced the cost-distancing that had limited international interaction, but only in the twentieth century was speedy and secure transportation of goods and communications assured. The pace of technological change in both of these areas has reduced exponentially the economic consequences of long distances. The spatial organization of economic activity appropriate for the transportation and communication technologies of the nineteenth century has scant relevance for a world of air and high-speed rail travel, and satellite and fibre optic telecommunication.

Similarly, technological change has transformed the spatial location of production activities. The legacy of the nineteenth century is huge complexes of production both in the sense of single large factories and of clusterings of many producers in the same line of work. Pittsburgh, Detroit, and the mill towns of New England were only the most obvious examples of this phenomenon. The economic rationale for these complexes included the needs to gain economies of scale, to capture agglomeration economies, to minimize transportation costs, and to utilize some common factor or resource. Production today is marked by mini-mills, global product mandates, outsourcing, and precise coordination by computer of widely dispersed production facilities. The consequences of this are a liberation from constraints of the nineteenth-century system of production and the related possibility of a complete rethinking of what should be produced and where it should be produced. In what many refer to as a post-Fordist economy, production sites can now be scattered throughout economic space according to a logic that is governed by a dramatically new economic rationale.

These changes in the technologies of transportation, communication, and production call for a reconsideration of economic space and of how production units relate to each other. The degree of interaction that was possible a century ago for, say, Chicago and Milwaukee (90 miles apart) is now feasible for Chicago and Atlanta or Toronto. The latter international linkage has been limited to a mere potentiality by the powers of national governments to control the degree to which cities or regions separated by national borders may establish direct linkages and a functioning economic interaction. Trade liberalization has had the effect of making this potential into a reality, and it is to this that we must now turn our attention.

Trade Liberalization

During the past decade international trade liberalization has advanced on both the global and the regional levels. The members of GATT have just concluded their eighth round of liberalization, the Uruguay Round, in which many previously formidable barriers to trade in goods have been lowered to the point of insignificance. Some progress has been made to extend this process to previously excluded sectors such as agriculture and services. The World Trade Organization has been established to provide greater powers of enforcement and dispute resolution. On the regional level, Europe has more or less completed the "1992 process" of completing its internal market and has taken the next step towards economic integration by adopting the Maastricht Treaty, in which the member nations have agreed to attempt to put into place by the end of the century an economic and monetary union. In North America, Canada and the United States introduced their free trade agreement in 1989, and have extended that agreement to include Mexico in the North American Free Trade Agreement. The participation of other countries in the hemisphere is being considered.

In all of these agreements, national governments have imposed on themselves constraints on their ability to intervene in their own economies. Tariffs have been reduced to minimal levels, limitations on the use of non-tariff barriers have been accepted, efforts have been undertaken to define more precisely subsidies and dumping, and measures to counter these practices, including contingency protection, have become subject to international supervision and sanction. Finally, and perhaps most importantly, nations have subjected themselves to impartial dispute resolution mechanisms which, if effective, severely limit unilateral action. National governments still retain a wide array of powerful tools, such as tax, competition, labor market, and interest rate policies, but at the margin nations have become less significant as economic actors. Concomitantly, as changes in technology and trade liberalization have redefined economic space and as national governments have imposed constraints on their capacity to intervene, subnational economies have become increasingly exposed to competition from, and to the actions of, economic entities from which they had previously been shielded by cost-distance and international barriers. States or provinces are worthy of study in this regard, but their objectives are almost always complicated by competing pressures for attention from rural and urban interests. Often state and provincial governments are disproportionately controlled by rural constituencies because of rural biases in districting. Hence, for a clear and consistent set of economic development objectives, we are better off focusing on the planning and initiatives of cities, and it is to this that the next section of this chapter is devoted.

WHAT CITIES HAVE DONE AS ECONOMIC ACTORS IN THE GLOBAL ECONOMY

The changes in the economic environment detailed in the previous section suggest strongly that there has been a potentially powerful change in the roles that ought to be assigned to the national and city levels of governance and in their capacities to intervene in a positive manner in economic processes and decision-making. In addition, there are several other structural changes that have made it urgent for cities to become more actively engaged in shaping their economic futures:

- *Global restructuring* of production has allowed manufacturing to grow rapidly in economies that were previously limited to raw material and highly labor intensive, low-level activities. This has meant that all markets have become subject to more intense competition.
- *Deindustrialization* in many mature manufacturing centers has caused regional decline. This is in part due to an institutional inflexibility that has both made it difficult to modernize the existing activities and made the region unattractive to pursuing new activities, such as a transition to a service-based economy.
- *The state is under attack*, in most developed economies, as the public mood has swung toward unleashing the private sector. The link between development activities at the national level and local producers is often not obvious and is more likely to be seen as meddling and cost increasing rather than as efficiency or competitiveness enhancing; thus national governments are less able to intervene.
- *Capital has become more mobile than ever* so the potential that corporations have for restructuring their activities can be realized beyond the wildest dreams their CEO's had just a few years ago.

The consequence of these structural changes is that all regional and urban economies are, on the one hand, more vulnerable to forces of economic dislocation and disruption and, on the other hand, able more than ever to create their comparative advantage or, to use Porter's term, competitive advantage,[1] rather than taking it as given by its factor endowment, location, class structure, or entrepreneurial energy. These more general structural factors, when combined with technological change and trade liberalization, usher in a new world of opportunities for cities to take command of, or at least powerfully influence, their economic futures.

Although the mainstream economic literature has not made great strides in the direction of recognizing the impact these changes have had on the appropriate role of cities, two of its widely known writers have pointed us, with varying degrees of conviction, toward such a recognition. Michael Porter, in *The Competitive Advantage of Nations*, presents a four-faceted structure of elements required for national competitiveness: factor conditions, firm strategy, demand conditions, and related and supporting industries [ch. 3]. Two of these elements, the first and the last, are most directly affected by actions by the local level of government. Indeed, Porter himself argues: "Internationally successful industries and industry clusters frequently concentrate in a city or region, and the bases for advantage are often intensely local. . . . While the national government has a role in upgrading industry, the role of state and local government is potentially as great or greater" [622].

Jane Jacobs has long been an analyst of the economics of cities and a quarter century after Gordon wrote *International Economics* she took the sense of his reference to nations, quoted above, in her own direction, one which is close to the central theme of this chapter:

> Nations are political and military entities, and so are blocs of nations. But it doesn't follow from this that they are also the basic, salient entities of economic life or that they are particularly useful for probing the mysteries of economic structure, the reasons for rise and decline of wealth. . . . The all-important function of import replacing or import-substitution is in real life specifically a city function [1985, 31, 35].

In her context the term "import substitution" should be taken as a reference to the need to stimulate the level of economic activity, rather than the economist's less attractive reference to the restructuring of domestic activity by restricting imports. For her, only the city can generate the five forces needed for a sustained economic development: markets, jobs, transplants (inward investment), technology, and capital [44].

In many cities municipal decision-makers have recognized the opportunities and challenges inherent in the new competitive context and have initiated actions to improve their city's position relative to other cities. In the discussion that follows two possibilities for city action will be examined: 1) strategic planning; and 2) interurban networking, with examples taken primarily from the experiences of cities in Europe. United States cities could have been used but the use of European cities will probably be more informative to a United States audience.

STRATEGIC PLANNING

Planning is essentially the forward-looking, managed allocation of resources over time, and is practiced by virtually all economic entities whether or not the word is used. Cities have planned for centuries, especially given the nature of the goods and services they provide. Urban infrastructure projects, such as transportation and port facilities, are large scale, long-lived initiatives which require considerable financing and long-term thinking. What has changed with the discontinuities introduced as a consequence of technological change and trade liberalization is the recognition on the part of cities that they now have the additional responsibility of planning for the evolution of their economic structures and for their roles in an economic space which embraces the entire globe [Logan and Swanstrom 1990, 3-24].

Rather than concentrate only on planning for new highways and airports, city governments must also plan the development of their financial and business services sectors. They must facilitate the restructuring of manufacturing from traditional products to cleaner or more technology-intensive products. They must consider their place in the urban hierarchy and the way in which they want to relate to other cities. This can all be done through:

- encouragement of firms of a certain size,
- development of an educational system with specific characteristics,
- promotion of a research complex with strength in desired areas,
- improvement of such urban amenities as cultural facilities, historic districts, sports and recreation, and restaurant and shopping districts,
- encouragement of development of a housing stock appropriate to the labor force the city wishes to attract and hold, and,
- achievement of a desired status in transportation, as a headquarters for major enterprises or for general decision-making activities, and as an international presence.

Examination of the planning activities of European cities during the past five years shows that major cities have been very actively planning in this new way, and that there are a limited number of distinct strategies that are available to them.[2] As is illustrated in table 5.1, their first task is that of deciding between two goals: #1, "quantitative change" and #2, "qualitative restructuring." While the former entails building directly on the past strength of the city's economy and essentially doing more of the same thing, the latter requires that the city consciously give up a past advantage, presumably being subjected now to intense competition from another city that has only recently become part of its economic space, and instead develop new economic activities in which it has the potential to become competitive.

The basic strategies from which a city can choose are numerous, but for purposes of illustration we can note that:

Goal #1 strategies include:

- export promotion by industries in which it has traditionally had an advantage,
- enhancement of the city's role as a bridge city,
- development as a regional center, and
- strengthening of the city as a national headquarters center.

Goal #2 strategies include:

- becoming a point-of-access city,
- developing niches in new sectors,
- building strength as a research and development center, and
- enhancing the city's status as an international headquarters center.

The difference between the two goals can be made clear if we consider the concept "gateway city." A gateway city can be either a "bridge" city or a "point-of-access" city. Bridge cities have as their primary asset a location that enables them to link two distinct economies; thus, when a city adopts the strategy of becoming a bridge city it is simply promoting what it has always had. Examples are Lyon and Hamburg. Lyon has always been a link between the Mediterranean and northern European economies and today the city is using new methods, such as high speed rail lines, to achieve this traditional goal under modern conditions. Hamburg advertises itself as a "Drehscheibe," or turn-table, city linking the European Union with: (1) the Nordic countries, (2) the Baltic states, (3) the city's traditional Elbe hinterland, and (4) central and eastern Europe.

Table 5.1

A Model of Urban Economic Strategic Planning Options

Ultimate Objective: **ECONOMIC VITALITY IN AN INCREASINGLY INTERNATIONALIZED ENVIRONMENT**

	Quantitative expansion				Qualitative restructuring			
Basic Goal Strategies	Export Promotion	Bridge City	Regional Center	Headquarters: National	Develop Niches	Access Point City	R & D Center	Headquarters: International
Means								
I	X				X		X	
II	X		X	X				
III					X		X	
IV	X					X		
V				X	X	X	X	X
VI		X		X		X		X
VII	X	X	X		X			
VIII								

I = Development and support of small and medium sized firms
II = Development of alliances with other cities
III = Establishment of effective links between firms and universities and research centers
IV = Establishment and expansion of international linkages
V = Construction of Infrastructure: housing and urban amenities
VI = Construction of Infrastructure: transportation
VII = Construction of Infrastructure: communication
VIII = Develop adequate specialized business services

A point-of-access city seeks to attract regional headquarters and decision-making centers of firms from other continents. Some cities, such as London, Frankfurt, and Paris, have had this role because of such factors as the strength of their national economy and their central role in it. Other cities have recently decided to gain contemporary acceptance in this capacity. Copenhagen and Amsterdam are two cities that have explicitly made this decision. In each instance the city had to rethink its relations to the economy of Europe and then try to create something it had lacked, at least in recent history. Having no locational or other characteristic that would give either a natural advantage over other cities, Amsterdam and Copenhagen must consider qualitatively restructuring their economies, as Goal #2 cities, while Hamburg is quantitatively expanding its existing activities.

Barcelona is in the Goal #1 category with Hamburg, but for different reasons. Although it does not seek to be a bridge city, at least to the degree that is true of Hamburg, Barcelona has two quantitative-expanding strategies that dominate its economic planning: 1) it seeks to increase its status as the dominant center of an ethnic region, in this case, Catalonia; and 2) it is attempting to revitalize its traditional manufacturing sector, rather than to restructure into new activities.

Cities can, of course, combine elements of both goals, rather than being a pure Goal #1 or Goal #2 city. Copenhagen and Amsterdam share with Barcelona the strategy of enhancing a city's status as the center of a national economy, with all three pressing for a restructuring of priorities for public expenditures away from rural development and agriculture toward urban infrastructure; at the same time, the two northern cities are presenting themselves as point-of-access cities. Lyon combines the Goal #1 strategy of promoting itself in its historic role as a bridge city between the Mediterranean and northern European economies with the Goal #2 strategy of developing niches in new industries, in this case pharmaceuticals and financial services for smaller firms.

Whatever strategy or set of strategies is chosen, a city must be certain that its approach is based in a realistic appraisal of its assets and its ability to implement and to realize a strategic thrust based on them. The choice will entail a set of specific claims on public funds for investment in appropriate housing, cultural facilities, historic district renewal, transportation and communication facilities, and subsidies to desired economic activities. Of course, the city must be prepared to approach other levels of government for their financial participation, and other cities for their assistance in lobbying higher levels of government for projects that benefit more than one city or urban region.

INTERURBAN NETWORKING

Linkages and contacts among European cities have received considerable interest during the past five years, most comprehensively in a double issue of the journal *Ekistics* [1991; 1992]. The relationship among the cities may be of two different types:

- the vertical, dominant city model, or
- the horizontal, equal cities model.

The networks which have been established with Lyon, Turin, and Hamburg and smaller cities in their larger urban regions are examples of the dominant city model. The large city in each network has a continental, even international, status that the smaller cities lack, as well as large-scale financial and manufacturing production and decision-making enterprises. The smaller cities have specialized capabilities in labor skills and narrowly focused interactions between universities and corporate research facilities. The symbiotic characteristic of the interaction between the large and smaller cities creates benefits for all participants that keeps them in the network, in spite of differing local ambitions and a fear on the part of the smaller cities of being dominated .

The equal city model of networking may be composed of several large and small cities, but the structure must be such that no single large city dominates the others. Examples include:

- the network of cities in the Ruhr District of Germany in which four large cities, Dortmund, Essen, Bochum, and Duisburg cooperate with several smaller cities,
- the Euro-Cities Movement, composed of 40 cities located throughout of Europe,
- the North of the Souths linkage of Lyon, Barcelona, and Turin, and
- local trans-national networks such as that of Copenhagen (Denmark) and Malmö (Sweden), or Maastricht (Netherlands), Aachen (Germany), and Liége (Belgium).

The impetus to formation of an inter-urban network may be that of:

- meeting a common problem, such as regional industrial decline, or environmental contamination,
- cooperation in the planning of a major infrastructure initiative,

- capturing the positive externalities that may be inherent in cooperation,
- cooperation among cities in the same industry, or
- enhancing the degree of specialization of cities in proximity to each other.

City networking has elicited much unfavorable comment in North America because of the unsatisfactory experiences many cities have had with the personality- or cultural-based Sister Cities linkages [Kresl 1993-94, 13-29].[3] Often limited to foreign trips for the mayors or exchanges of high school groups, these initiatives have brought little if any economic benefit. The common feature of all of the European networks listed above is that they are problem- or initiative-directed. Thus, although networking is rather advanced in Europe, North American cities have been very slow to see the advantages of contact with other cities, other than acting in such all-encompassing politically focused groupings as the National League of Cities, the Federation of Canadian Municipalities, and the Conference of U.S. Mayors.

Here is an area in which there is still much that can be accomplished. Trans-Atlantic inter-urban networking among cities in Europe and North America would meet some real needs of all participants. Cities are often reluctant to discuss their problems and strategic plans with neighboring cities because of the competitive aspect that must always be part of their relationship with each other. Firms and international agencies will locate large facilities in one city rather than another, major sporting events will be gained by one city and lost by another, and high-speed rail lines and airport expansion will favor one city and another will lose out. In spite of the globalization of economic activity, this competitive aspect generally does not exist for cities on different continents.

In structuring trans-Atlantic city networking, a solid basis for interaction can be found in the economic strategies the individual cities are pursuing. This will build on the experience European cities have had with common problem- or initiative-based networks, and avoid the negative experiences North American cities have had with Sister Cities efforts. A review of the strategic planning initiatives of cities on both continents is summarized in tables 5.2 and 5.3; it suggests the following as examples of the potential for trans-Atlantic networking:

- Toronto and Vancouver share with Copenhagen and Amsterdam the aspiration of becoming point-of-access cities,
- Chicago and Barcelona seek to revitalize their traditional manufacturing sectors through exports,

- Buffalo, Detroit, Lyon, and Hamburg are all enhancing their position as bridge cities,
- Seattle-Vancouver and Toronto-Buffalo are emerging cross-border metropolitan regions, as are Copenhagen-Malmö,
- Seattle, Vancouver, Toronto, Stuttgart, and Munich are faced with the need to control or manage economic growth because of its negative consequences on labor markets, quality of life, and the environment,
- Buffalo, Detroit, Barcelona, Hamburg, and Lyon are subject to regional free trade agreements that will provide the primary stimulus to growth in the near future, and
- Calgary, Montreal, Cleveland, Copenhagen, Manchester, and Seville share the challenges of locations on the periphery of large, dynamic economic spaces.

If the potential benefits of functional trans-Atlantic inter-urban networking are to be realized a structure will have to be created through which European and North American cities can share experiences, solve problems together, and cooperate to ensure that cities capture the gains inherent in trade liberalization and technological change, in the Ayresian sense of becoming more "operationally efficient." While Euro-Cities is the natural participant on the European side, work needs to be done to create a similar entity in North America. Some initial steps have been taken, both at the city practitioner and academic researcher levels, but as yet a NorAm-Cities Movement does not exist.

CONCLUDING COMMENTS

The environment in which all economic actors must operate is evolving exponentially as structural changes, such as the technological change and trade liberalization increase their vulnerability to new threats, challenges, and opportunities. This has been especially true for the importance in economic planning and decision-making of the various levels of government. In this chapter I have argued that, in this period of dramatic structural change, cities have emerged as increasingly important economic actors. The consequences of this for such policy actions as strategic planning, inter-urban networking, and enhanced competitiveness, have been demonstrated through examination of the experiences of several major European cities. From this the reader should gain some appreciation for the variety of actions, now available to cities, that influence the economic development and economic functions of urban economies.

Table 5.2

**CLUSTERS FOR COMPARISON:
NORTH AMERICA AND THE EUROPEAN UNION**

1) Cities which are asserting themselves in an environment in which there is a dominant city
   - North America
     - Chicago (New York), Toronto (New York), Montreal (New York)
   - European Union
     - Turin (Milan), Lyon (Paris), Barcelona (Madrid)

2) Cities with full employment that focus on restructuring and growth management
   - North America
     - Seattle, Toronto, Vancouver
   - European Union
     - Munich, Stuttgart

3) Cities positioning themselves in a region of other cities
   - North America
     - Cleveland, Detroit, Montreal
   - European Union
     - Amsterdam, Barcelona, Copenhagen

4) Cities peripheral to the area of main activity
   - North America
     - Calgary, Cleveland, Montreal
   - European Union
     - Copenhagen, Hamburg, Seville

5) Cities for which a continental trade liberalization agreement is a key to their economic future
   - North America
     - Buffalo, Detroit
   - European Union
     - Barcelona, Hamburg, Lyon

Table 5.3

Figure 3

City Comparisons: North America and the European Union

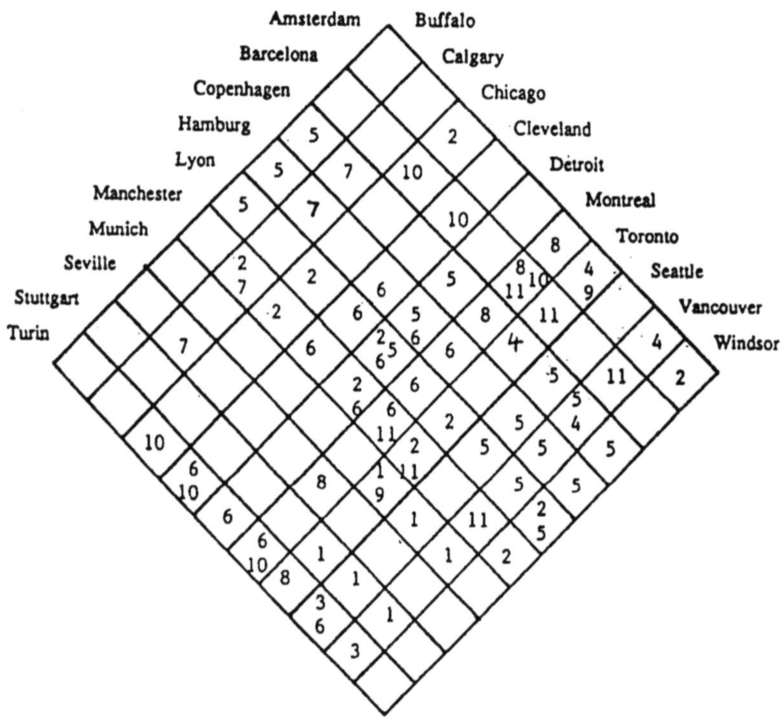

Strategic Challenges:

1. Growth management
2. Finding a niche
3. Research and technology linkages
4. Point-of-access gateway
5. Bridge city gateway
6. City networking
7. Coping with periphery status
8. City as center of "nation"
9. Head office city
10. Vitality of manufacturing
11. Effective governance

While institutionalist writers did not explicitly focus their attention on the role of cities, we see that in the writings of Ayres and Gordon there is much that is amenable to reconsidering the way we think about government and the allocation of policy responsibilities to its various levels. Ayres and Gordon advise us, in effect, to mistrust the nation as a way of organizing human society; nations have potentially enormous destructive capacity and often become vehicles for the expression of destructive human characteristics. Second, Ayres and Gordon manifest a desire to examine what works in organizing society and implementing policy. Mind-freezing ideology has no beneficial role to play here, nor does that which seeks to render sacred the unfettered market and/or central planning. Third, Ayres and Gordon give primacy to changes in the context in which we live and in which, therefore, our social institutions must function.

While in institutionalist writings there are few if any specific guides to us in policy formulation in the subject area of this chapter, there certainly is a general presumption that we ought to be ready to scrap the habitual way of thinking about it and to try to develop an analysis that places a higher priority on being in harmony with reality rather than on conformity with orthodox thinking. Those of us who received our training as economists in an institutionalist environment may not always actively try to fit our subsequent research into that mold, but our instincts are nevertheless influenced by institutionalist predilections.

ENDNOTES

1. The Ricardian term comparative advantage always has the suggestion that the world consists of two national economies, each of which is in a comparative relationship with the other. Porter's competitive advantage can be interpreted as being more appropriate to a multinational context in which one's trade is not mirrored by that of another. To say that an economic entity (national, regional, or urban) has a competitive advantage in some activity by no means implies that its trade, even in the long run, must balance or that that entity cannot have an advantage in a vast array of things that will result in a long-run trade surplus. This is particularly true if the economy is sufficiently attractive as a place to produce goods and services that it experiences a long-term capital inflow.
2. This section is based on Kresl [1992].
3. Some of the above has been applied to the situation in Quebec.

REFERENCES

Ayres, Clarence. *Toward a Reasonable Society*. Austin: The University of Texas Press, 1961.

Gordon, Wendell C. "A World of Nations and the United Nations." Presented at meetings of the Eastern Economic Association, 18 March 1995.

———. *Economics from an Institutional Viewpoint.* Austin: University Stores, Inc., 1973.

———. *International Trade.* New York: Alfred A. Knopf, 1958.

Gordon, Wendell C. and John Adams. *Economics as Social Science: An Evolutionary Approach.* Riverdale, MD: The Riverdale Company, 1989.

Haberler, Gottfried. *Theory of International Trade.* London: William Hodge and Company, 1936.

Iversen, Carl. 1967. *International Capital Movements.* New York: Augustus M. Kelley, 1967 [1935].

Jacobs, Jane. *Cities and the Wealth of Nations.* New York: Vintage Books, 1985.

Kresl, Peter Karl. "Restructuring in Response to the Canada-U.S. Free Trade Agreement: The Case of Québec Cities. *Québec Studies* 17 (Fall 1993-Winter 1994): 13-29.

———. *The Urban Economy and Regional Trade Liberalization.* New York: Praeger, 1992.

———. "The Determinants of the Economic Competitiveness of Cities: A Survey." In Peter Karl Kresl and Gary Gappert eds., *North American Cities and the Global Economy.* Thousand Oaks, CA: Sage Publications, Urban Affairs Annual Review Series, 1995.

Krugman, Paul. *Geography and Trade.* Cambridge: MIT Press, 1991.

List, Friedrich. *The National System of Political Economy.* New York: Augustus M. Kelley, 1965 [1841].

Logan, John R. and Todd Swanstrom. "Urban Restructuring: A Critical View." In John R. Logan and Todd Swanstrom, eds., *Beyond the City Limits: Urban Policy and Economic Restructuring in Comparative Perspective.* Philadelphia: Temple University Press, 1990.

Meade, James E. *The Theory of International Economic Policy.* London: Oxford University Press, 1951.

Ohlin, Bertil. *Interregional and International Trade.* Cambridge: Harvard University Press, 1967 [1933].

Porter, Michael. *The Competitive Advantage of Nations.* New York: The Free Press, 1990.

Smith, Adam. *An Inquiry in to the Nature and Causes of the Wealth of Nations.* New York: The Modern Library, 1937 [1776].

"Urban Networking in Europe, I and II," *Ekistics: The Problems and Science of Human Settlements* 58, no. 350-351, 1991, and 59, no. 352-353, 1992.

Viner, Jacob. *Studies in the Theory of International Trade.* New York: Augustus M. Kelley, 1965 [1937].

CHAPTER 6

MULTINATIONAL ENTERPRISE EXPANSION FROM AN INSTITUTIONALIST PERSPECTIVE

Anthony Scaperlanda
Northern Illinois University

As World War II was coming to an end and institutions like the International Monetary Fund (IMF) and the General Agreement on Tariffs and Trade (GATT) were being organized, a theory of multinational enterprise (MNE) expansion was indistinguishable from the general theory of international capital flows. The neoclassical paradigm, which held that differential interest and profit rates were the sole determinants of FDI flows, reigned supreme. Differential profit rates remained the orthodox explanation for foreign direct investment flows at least as late as 1958, as evidenced by Wendell C. Gordon's description of the prevailing theory as he evaluated FDI's contribution to economic development [Gordon 1958, 514-32]. As Gordon succinctly put it in 1962, "the generally accepted proposition has been that investments flow from the more developed countries, where the rate of return is relatively low to the less developed countries where the rate of return is higher" [Gordon 1962, 7]. A theory of foreign direct investment (FDI), a theory emphasizing the parent firm's actual equity in its foreign affiliates plus any liabilities that the foreign affiliates have to the parent through which the parent firm controls its affiliates, was in its infancy in the early 1960s.

Scholarship such as Gordon's, Steven Hymer's doctoral dissertation [1960], and G. D. A. MacDougall's "The Benefits and Costs of Private

Investment from Abroad: A Theoretical Approach" [1960] signal that a more sophisticated understanding of the motivation for MNE expansion was emerging in the late 1950s and early 1960s. During the last three decades the steadily increasing economic and political importance of MNEs has motivated these more sophisticated theoretical developments. Total equity (FDI) in the foreign subsidiaries of firms that have operations, other than trade, outside their home country increased more than 11 times to 1,284 billion SDR in the last quarter century [Rutter 1992, appendix table 2], and the relative importance of home and host countries has changed [Scaperlanda 1993, 606]. In general, the rapid growth of MNEs and the dramatic shifts in the importance of home and host countries have stimulated the search for a better understanding of the determinants of MNE expansion and heightened the call for an oversight organization for MNEs (an OMNE).

I first focus on contemporary understandings of the factors that motivate MNE expansion, placing primary emphasis on factors internal to an MNE. Emphasizing a technological approach to "internalization theory" of MNE expansion, I discuss a strategy for developing an OMNE, and conclude that an OMNE stands to benefit both MNEs and the general public of the countries in which MNEs operate.

THEORIES OF MNE EXPANSION

The theory of MNE expansion via FDI can be cast in at least three perspectives. One perspective emphasizes the influence of factors external to an MNE such as the size and growth of the host country market and government policies like tariffs, domestic taxes, and labor laws on the MNE's expansion decision. A second perspective on theoretical developments places factors internal to a firm at the center of the inquiry. A third perspective is John Dunning's "eclectic" approach that combines consideration of external and internal influences on MNE expansion [1988, 69-70]. The question: Why does the parent firm not export to the host country or license its product or process to a host country firm? provides a useful basis for judging the interrelationship between the external and internal categories of determinants of MNE expansion. Effectively the "export" portion of the question places emphasis on the external category and the "license" portion on the internal.

Underlying the question: Why not export? is the more fundamental question: What is the theoretical relationship between trade and FDI? This question does not admit of a general answer because an answer requires knowledge of industry-specific and timing considerations. The range of orthodox theoretical possibilities includes trade and FDI as substitutes

[Mundell 1957], complements [Helmberger and Schmitz 1970], or substitutes for one another over the life cycle of the product being traded or invested in [Vernon 1966]. The FDI-substitutes-for-trade hypothesis is predicated on the existence of natural or created obstacles to trade that prompt FDI. The latter two hypotheses have technological underpinnings. The "complements" hypothesis explains the case where the export of equipment or intermediate products is necessary to effect FDI. The product-life-cycle hypothesis explicitly posits FDI as a function of the technical stage of a product's development.

Because trade barriers are a necessary condition if FDI is to substitute for trade and because the modification of trade barriers is observable and often measurable, empirical tests of the external factors influencing the MNE expansion decision have usually tested the hypothesis that trade and FDI are substitutes. The complex theoretical relationship between trade and FDI, however, results in empirical support for the substitution hypothesis often being elusive, although some support has been found [Scaperlanda and Balough 1983, 381]. In addition to a proxy for trade barriers, empirical tests of the determinants of MNE expansion that are external to the firm have included proxies for the size of the host country market, the growth of that market, the existing stock of FDI, and disequilibrium exchange rates, among others. Thought to be a measure of the extent to which technologically-driven FDI could profit in the host country, the size of the market has consistently been found to be very important in these empirical studies. The growth of the market is also sometimes found to be significant, as has been the pre-existing stock of foreign investment when incorporated into empirical tests. Insofar as FDI "flows," as defined by the U.S. Department of Commerce, include reinvested earnings as well as outflows from the U.S., this finding supports Wendell Gordon's hypothesis that growth in the stock of foreign investment is importantly influenced by accretion [1962, 20]. Generally, empirical tests of the role of home-country characteristics and of differences between home and host country characteristics have been less statistically successful than studies that emphasize host country characteristics. It seems clear, then, that external factors exert influence on the decision to make new FDI and thereby expand MNEs.

Forces internal to the firm comprise a second category of FDI determinants and complement the external factors [Rugman 1980 and 1985]. This second category of theoretical inquiry into the motivation of MNE expansion is based on the assumption that FDI, or an extra-trade international economic link, is needed either to circumvent actual or anticipated [Bhagwati 1987] trade barriers or to service foreign markets more effectively and efficiently than is possible by exporting. According to the conventional hypothesis, instead of franchising its organization or distribution expertise or licensing its production technology, a firm chooses FDI in order to insure quality and to capture the maximum rents to be derived from its global operations. Frequently these motives are cast as minimizing the transactions costs of extra-trade servicing of foreign markets. In other words, many different transactions are said to be handled more efficiently intrafirm compared to the option of out-sourcing them to agents in the market place. Consequently, FDI is chosen as the means of international expansion because this channel minimizes a firm's transactions costs [Williamson 1991, 85]. This so-called "internalization theory" has been extensively refined by analyzing all manner of transactions that could be handled intrafirm or through extrafirm agents [Ethier 1986].

An institutionalist and evolutionary version of internalization theory is a more general, alternative explanation of the motivation for a firm internalizing its overseas expansion than is the transactions cost explanation. First developed by Wendell Gordon as part of his critique of the contemporary theory of the 1950s, this theory posits that the motivation to undertake FDI rather than use alternative channels is centered on the technology utilized by the parent firm. More recently Brent McClintock has proposed an institutionalist approach to a theory of FDI that emphasizes a culture-based methodology [1988 and 1989], but in this chapter, I emphasize the technology-based approach pioneered by Gordon.

The FDI work of Gordon is relatively absent from contemporary, mainstream theorizing about the determinants of MNE expansion for three reasons. First, his work was done before the term "MNE" was coined. Second, it was focused on FDI's contribution to economic development instead of on the theory of MNE expansion.[1] Third, only in the 1990s has a technology-centered theoretical model begun to emerge in the literature that is central to the MNE-expansion discussion. It seems clear that the MNE-expansion discussion will remain incomplete unless the institutionalist perspective provided by Gordon is more explicitly incorporated. Although Gordon explored other motives for MNE expansion such as spreading risk and adopting altruism toward underdeveloped countries, three of the motives that Gordon discussed are especially important: the "Before-and-After Profit Rates" motive, the "Relative-State-of-Development" motive, and the "Agglomeration Effects" motive [1962, 12].

The Before-and-After Profit Rates motive holds that at any moment in time a firm (in a developed country) is committed to the use of a particular technology. When expansion is contemplated, the range of opportunities is threefold: domestic expansion using the same technology, foreign expansion using that technology, or expansion into another domestic industry that would require a modified or different technology. Gordon assumed that when the domestic market becomes "saturated" with a firm's primary product, the first alternative becomes much less attractive. Of the remaining two, foreign expansion is the more attractive because using the same technology in an additional location involves the least "transactions" cost [Gordon 1962, 13-14]. Gordon's second technology driven motive for MNE expansion, the "Relative-State-of Development" motive, is related to the first. He observes that, because advanced technology is abundant in the most developed countries, firms headquartered there will find many opportunities to extend the technology in developing countries as long as the conditions in the host country's market are hospitable [Gordon 1962, 14-16]. With his third technology-related motive, the "Agglomeration Effects" motive, Gordon anticipated some of the current thinking of Paul Krugman [1991], among others. Gordon hypothesized, in this instance, that a firm that is expanding internationally will locate near other, similar firms in order to minimize costs [Gordon 1962, 16-17]. In my judgement, Gordon's concluding evaluation of the "Before-and-After Profit Rates" motive for MNE expansion applies to all three motives. He said: "the argument does introduce a new element, the state of technology in the company considering the investment" [1962, 14].

In the 1990s, Gordon's institutionalist explanation of the forces internal to a firm that encourage FDI has been echoed in the work of Alfred Chandler [1992]. Chandler's analysis of the evolution of industrial firms has led him to conclude that central to understanding the motivation for MNE expansion "is the firm and its specific physical and human assets" [Chandler 1992, 86]. Recognizing that Gordon's concept of technology incorporates both the physical equipment and processes and the knowledge necessary to use it (human assets), it is fair to say that Chandler's work parallels Gordon's, as does Chandler's observation that the international expansion of a technology in use is easier and more profitable than is domestic expansion into ventures that require new physical and human technologies [Chandler 1992, 94].

In general, the Gordon-Chandler technology-centered internalization theory of MNE expansion holds that a firm will extend its global reach through FDI instead of exporting its output or licensing its processes or products if three conditions exist. In Chandler's ordering, they are: (1) A firm must be sufficiently capital-intensive to require substantial skills and extensive expertise for its success, (2) the minimum efficient plant size must be small enough to obviate all cost advantages of a single production site, and (3) the host country's market must be of sufficient size to accommodate and be otherwise favorable to a plant of at least minimum efficient size [Chandler 1992, 89].[2] If these three conditions are accompanied by high barriers to trade in the potential host country, FDI will substitute for trade [Mundell 1957].

The Gordon-Chandler hypothesis that technological factors are vital to most MNE expansion is more comprehensive and has more explanatory power than the transactions cost version of internalization theory. It provides more general answers to three basic, relevant questions that have been synthesized by Thomas Brewer: (1) Why does a firm use FDI and become an MNE instead of using exporting or licensing to serve foreign markets?, (2) How can a foreign firm, taking into account the extra costs it incurs, compete with host-country firms?, (3) Why do MNEs acquire supplies intrafirm rather than from unrelated firms? [Brewer 1992, 113]. The theory permits an analyst to deal with these questions effectively, and moreover, even if market forces led to an equalization of internal and arms-length external transactions costs, a firm's technical endowment may continue to favor expansion internationally in the form of an MNE.

Assuming that technologically-centered forces internal to a firm will continue to drive the expansion of MNEs, the evolution of national or international public policy toward MNEs is inevitable. The favorable conditions that the GATT, the IMF, and the World Bank have created in the last half century will, of course, continue to shape MNE expansion. Other international influences may develop in the future, and non-governmental interest groups or national governments will continue to have an interest in the plans, the behavior, and the production and revenues of the MNEs with which they have some working relationship. Although contemporary restrictions on the activities of a multinational enterprise are country-specific, an MNE's costs are inflated as a result of coping with a multiplicity of regulations. If one assumes that each nation state is attempting to insure that its citizens get a fair share of an MNE's rents, then country-specific attempts to accomplish this end are destined to be inefficient and ineffective because each nation state does not exert enough control over MNEs operating within it to achieve the goal. Although the diversity of cultures around the globe will limit the extent to which harmonization can be achieved, the harmonization of national policies toward MNEs or the development of a supranational organization, an OMNE, that would supplant national governments as the principal governmental entity interacting with an MNE in non-domestic affairs could increase the efficiency of both the MNE and of public policy toward MNEs.

Offering a slightly different perspective, John Dunning has argued that:

> The debate should not be centered on whether governments should intervene more or less in the macro-organization of economic activity, in the light of FDI, but rather what kind of governance changes such

> investment requires. Even if all structural market distortions were removed, the role of government as a systemic or individual market facilitating force would still be a critical one. . . . [1992, 10-11].

The basic question is what changes can be made that simultaneously insure fair treatment of an MNE and encourage the development of MNE policy that is useful and fair to the citizens of the various nations affected by the MNE. These welfare implications are my next topic.

MNES AND THE GENERAL WELFARE

The welfare implications of MNE expansion are complex and will vary over time. As we have recently heard in the NAFTA debate, some citizens of an MNE's home country, and sometimes the government, may view the outflow of foreign investment as a threat to domestic living standards. Likewise, the government of a host country, and sometimes its citizens, may view the arrival of an MNE on its territory as a threat to the general welfare of its citizens.[3] An MNE will view any governmental act that inflates costs or restricts the firm's actions as an infringement on its prerogatives. Although Edward Graham [1994, 3], among others, has noted that many host countries have liberalized their policies toward incoming MNEs, absolute threats to the investment of MNEs continue in some host countries. A recent example developed in mid-1995, when, despite a solid commitment from the previous state administration, the new government of the Indian state of Maharashtra challenged the terms of a $2.8 billion power plant investment that was being undertaken by the U.S. firm, Enron [*The Economist,* August 12, 1995, 12]. Not only did Enron stand to lose the $300 million thus far expended and future earnings from completing construction and operating the plant, but all other MNEs operating in that state, and possibly in the whole of India, had new, cost-inflating uncertainties introduced into their profit calculations.

Institutions are more established to deal with disputes between home country government and an MNE or between the MNE's home and host governments and therefore likely to be more satisfactory to both parties than is the case when a dispute arises between an MNE and a host country. Because different welfare expectations and calculations by MNEs and by host countries have been the basis for the greatest contention and dispute, I concentrate on the welfare implications for these two entities.

One set of welfare implications rests on the benefits that an MNE brings to a host country in addition to financing new investment. Graham has enumerated some of these benefits. They include an "inward transfer of technology and management know-how, both of which tend to permeate the general economy. Transnational corporations also have in place international networks that facilitate the marketing of exports of host countries in which these firms operate." Graham notes that MNE trade is "characteristically two-way" so that home country exports are stimulated as the host country obtains machinery and materials necessary for development [1994, 4]. In addition to the technology transfer, a host country may expect an MNE to provide remuneration of workers and indigenous managers commensurate with technology-stimulated increases in productivity. MNE coverage of social costs resulting from the new investment and tax payments that bear a relationship to the value-added in the host country may be expected by the host country government, as well. As the *Financial Times* [July 17, 1995, 1] reported recently "[i]nternational tax authorities are becoming increasingly aggressive over the way in which they claim multinationals transfer profits between countries to reduce tax. . . . as many jurisdictions simultaneously demand their 'fair share' of the global revenue." In general, the host country government will aim to retain for its citizens what it considers as a fair share of the rents generated by an MNE operating within its territory.

Another set of welfare implications rests on the fact that from the moment of its conception, an MNE is intended to provide a sufficient return to its investors to keep them from investing elsewhere. It follows that a larger return only enhances the perceived welfare of the investors, and happy investors will be supportive of increased remuneration for the MNE management, a further increase in perceived welfare. That is, MNE welfare is directly tied to the size of profits, at least in the minds of those who count most, its managers and investors. Since MNEs sell in the global marketplace, host country actions affect MNE profits primarily on the cost side. Within a context of trying to minimize cost, what would a typical MNE want from a host country? Fundamentally, most MNEs prefer to be completely unfettered in their entry into a country and in their operations.

It is unrealistic to expect that any responsible government will give any firm, domestic or MNE, completely free rein to operate as it pleases. Richard Robinson [1976] records examples of the restrictions that selected host, developing countries place on MNEs. Edward Safarian [1993] does the same for 15 industrial host countries. Safarian says that of the ten European countries he considered, "France has had the most highly-developed policies toward inward FDI" [1993, 208]. Generally the French government has tried to retain a distinct French ownership presence in industry sectors like aerospace and telephone systems, "sometimes by easing out U.S.-owned firms as French capacities increased" [Safarian 1993, 222]. The French government has also prohibited the sale of a firm or industry that is considered part of the national heritage, for example the prestigious Chateau-Margaux vineyards, to a non-French MNE [Safarian 1993, 223]. Safarian thinks that Japan's more complicated and more comprehensive "administrative guidance" to incoming FDI could weaken, but notes that the head start Japan has given its own industries can be expected to have long-term effects [1993, 282].

What host country treatment is likely to optimize the welfare of an MNE? First, an MNE will expect to be treated no less well than a host country firm. Ideally, the costs, procedures, and requirements for establishment and operations will be the same for all firms regardless of the location of their headquarters. MNE costs will be lower if the laws and regulations of establishment and operations are easily accessible, even to foreigners, and if the administration of the laws and regulations is clearly understood, non-discriminatory, and consistent over time. An MNE will find an effective and efficient dispute-settlement apparatus advantageous from a cost perspective when inevitable disputes arise with host government agencies. Host country compliance with international standards of conduct regarding expropriation and trade related investment measures (domestic content or export requirements) will benefit an MNE by stabilizing expectations. For a discussion of these international standards, see Graham [1994, 19-22].

The conditions that would maximize the welfare of a MNE may impinge on the welfare aspirations of the host country. This is especially so because an MNE may have such a dominant place in the host country market that excess profits can be extracted to the detriment of the citizenry. In addition, since a multinational firm has little control over international prices, and therefore over overall MNE profits, its managers think they must minimize cost to produce a desired profit. Efforts to minimize costs could unfavorably affect the welfare of citizens of the host country. The problem becomes one of optimizing global welfare by working out arrangements that promote the most efficient allocation of resources among MNE interests, citizens of the host country, and citizens of the rest of the world.

To some degree, market forces can be used to accomplish the goal. As I have argued elsewhere:

> Invariably the host country market is less competitive before the arrival of an international entrepreneur [an entrepreneurial MNE or a EMNE] than it is immediately afterwards. The entrepreneurial activity associated with MNE expansion can be expected to yield increased profits for the firm involved . . . [as a result] of a cost advantage possessed by the EMNE. [In the host country] . . . relatively competitive equilibrium will be attained if producers in the host country can reduce costs sufficiently to be competitive with the EMNE. If host country "competitors" are unable to compete with the EMNE and exit the industry, EMNE returns are likely to remain extraordinary and be transformed from entrepreneurial profit into economic rents. The continuation of the EMNE's extraordinary returns might be stopped,

> however, if "copycat" MNEs enter the host country's market, essentially an international version of the process postulated by [Joseph] Schumpeter [Scaperlanda 1994, 345-46].

If either domestic producers or copycat MNEs compete with the EMNE, then the EMNE will be constrained by market forces and consumers will benefit through lower prices. Other things being equal, consumers will lose only if the EMNE can sustain a sufficiently dominant market position so that economic rents (in contrast to entrepreneurial profits) can be reaped and repatriated to MNE headquarters.

Changes in the host country's factor markets will influence that nation's net welfare. Those factors important to the output of the EMNE and its competitors will unquestionably gain; however, to compete, domestic producers must cut costs, thereby precipitating downward pressure on wages of those persons supplying labor services for which demand does not increase and on the prices of domestically-produced primary and intermediate products. On balance, these welfare effects will be negative in the short run if the downward pressure on factor income is dramatic enough to make the suppliers of some factor services noticeably worse off. This could occur either because output prices decline less than factor prices or because the depression of factor income is concentrated, thereby excessively affecting a particular segment of the population. Short-run negative welfare effects can be overcome in the longer run by MNE-stimulated growth of the host country's economy.

AN OMNE AND THE GENERAL WELFARE

If MNE expansion, being technologically driven, is inevitable and if positive welfare effects can, and probably will, result from this expansion, what institutional arrangement will minimize the costs both to MNEs and to citizens of host countries while simultaneously optimizing the global distribution of the gains associated with MNE expansion? One obtains a comprehensive understanding of the scope that an institution or organization for multinational enterprises will need if the proposals of Paul Goldberg and Charles Kindleberger [1970], Fred Bergsten and Edward Graham [1992], the NAFTA FDI provisions [Graham and Wilkie 1994], and Graham [1994] are combined. Another possible model for a GATT-type OMNE is being developed by the European Union (EU). The EU has been active in establishing a comprehensive approach to "controlling" MNEs operating within its jurisdiction [Scaperlanda, 1992; Groenewegen and Beije, 1992]. Bergsten and Graham [1992, 29-41] identify the variety of disputes that may arise for which settlement procedures should be developed. They suggest a different dispute settlement processes for each category of potential dispute.

Existing proposals for and precursors of an OMNE can be labelled "instrumentalist or institutionalist" because each pragmatically addresses a prevailing problem. The overall NAFTA negotiations, for example, led to the identification of a need for investment provisions to which negotiators reacted positively. The Asia Pacific Economic Cooperation (APEC) Eminent Persons Group [1993, quoted in Graham 1994, 1] also thought that the proposed Asia Pacific Investment Code (APIC) was needed "to reduce the uncertainties and transactions costs of trade and investment in the region." Graham reports that "[i]n mid-November 1994, the APEC ministers endorsed a set of non-binding investment principles" but that they "did not meet the standards recommended by" him [Graham 1994, 25].

Although these proposals divide, in approach, between global and subglobal, they have a common aim of creating an environment favorable to the growth of multinational enterprises.[4] Graham's analysis of the proposed Asia-Pacific Investment Code (APIC), follows the ratification of the NAFTA, and is therefore the most advanced of contemporary proposals for some sort of OMNE. Graham says that "[a]n effective investment code would contain five central elements, of which three are statements of basic obligations of [host] countries to investors, one is an institutional arrangement, and one is a set of additional obligations of countries and of investors" [1994, 9]. An investment code should commit the host country to insuring (1) the transparency of, or intellectual accessibility to, national laws and regulations (and the procedures by which they are administered) that are relevant to an MNEs establishment and operations, (2) the right of an MNE to establish itself in the host country subject to the same laws and regulations as domestic investors, and (3) the right of the MNE to be treated in post-establishment operations just like domestic investors [Graham 1994, 9-15]. In the view of Graham and others, the institutional element that is required, an effective dispute-settlement mechanism, is "at the heart of any investment code. It is also the investment issue on which [host] countries are the most reluctant to act, given its implications for [infringing on] national sovereignty" [Graham 1994, 15].[5] A fifth, catch-all element in an investment code would commit the host country to at least (1) following internationally accepted standards and guidelines if expropriation of MNE assets is deemed necessary, and (2) designing and using tax laws and policies, investment incentives, and MNE performance requirements in ways that do not distort international investment patterns [Graham 1994, 19-23].

Graham [1994, 25] envisions the likelihood that investment codes used within the context of Asia Pacific Economic Cooperation, the APIC, by NAFTA, and by the OECD will eventually lead to a global investment code that is an extension of the responsibilities of the World Trade Organization. One drawback to at least some aspects of contemporary regional plans and to the process by which WTO investment-code responsibilities would be extended is that negotiations often lead to minimal solutions rather than optimal ones. For a variety of reasons it is unlikely that a consensual approach to negotiations will lead to such high standards that the political hassles and threats often encountered in MNE expansion will become negligible. Rather, it is more likely that investment code standards will be set close to the preferences of the weakest or the most inward-looking host country. In practice, one process of reaching consensus has yielded only a voluntary code of conduct, drafted by the OECD in 1976, a result that Gordon has said "can scarcely accomplish very much" [1980, 269].

An alternative approach to the development of an OMNE was proposed by Wendell Gordon over 35 years ago. The principles underpinning his proposal at that time were:

> . . . a whole lot could be done toward improving the "investment climate" if investors would appreciate that they must operate under labor, social security, and health laws that give reasonable protection to the workers, and under a general pattern of local laws . . . which are a matter for local determination . . .
>
> As a corollary, local governments should . . . pass laws that are really intended to raise the level of living and increase the freedom of action of their people, but which are in general nondiscriminatory against foreigners and foreign investors, and then insist on the observance of the laws [Gordon 1958, 498-99].

In addition to these principles to guide MNE-host country relations, Gordon recognized the multinational, potentially resource-distorting dimension of MNE operations and expansion when he said that "Centralized responsibility for the behavior of a business organization which is itself centrally controlled is desirable [1958, 496]. In 1980, Gordon extended this idea when he wrote: "There is probably no satisfactory way to deal with the . . . power of the multinational corporation . . . short of international incorporation of multinational firms and taxation by the United Nations of corporations which operate internationally" [1980, 269].

In his 1994 book, *The United Nations at the Crossroads of Reform*, Gordon advocates the U.N. as the institution best suited to incorporate MNEs. If the U.N. organization were modified as Gordon suggests, the office that issued corporate charters might be developed out of the U.N.'s Transnational Corporations and Management Division, which has been working since 1975 with the U.N.'s Commission on Transnational Corporations to develop codes of conduct for host countries and MNEs to follow, the better to insure that all parties connected with the MNE receive equitable and fair treatment [United Nations 1993, 652-53]. A U.N. Charter amended to permit the legal incorporation of private enterprises could delineate, in the documents of incorporation, the rights and responsibilities of host countries and of MNEs along the lines identified by Bergsten and Graham [1992] and Graham [1994]. To accomplish the crucial dispute-settlement function, Gordon forwards the idea of amending the statute of the International Court of Justice so that MNEs could appeal decisions of national supreme courts to that court. The right of appeal would be available if, and only if, the U.N. were the venue of legal incorporation for the MNE that wished to make the appeal [Gordon 1994, 112-13].

If the U.N. Charter is modified to allow for the legal incorporation of private enterprises, and if MNEs found it advantageous to incorporate under U.N. auspices, an international corporate income tax could be established. If established, it would provide a source of U.N. revenue that is not attached to the political whims or the budgetary limits of national governments. National governments would benefit if the United Nations levied a corporate income tax because MNE tax evasion practices would be muted. With taxes "more equitably levied" from the host country's point of view, the climate for cooperation between MNE and host country should be enhanced. Gordon recognizes that MNEs will not be anxious to be internationally chartered unless the right to appeal national judicial decisions exists [1994, 112]. In addition, he thinks that MNEs would be more interested in being U.N. chartered if national corporate income taxes could be deducted from taxes due to the United Nations, say up to 50 percent [1994, 113].

U.N. chartering of MNEs accompanied by an effective corporate income tax that is uniform across nations should result in tax neutrality that, in turn, results in lower firm costs because of a more efficient location of facilities around the world. This benefit probably would be supplemented by greater transparency and predictability of regulations in general. That change, in turn, should further reduce social and pecuniary costs. If both the host country and the MNE are more certain of being treated "fairly" as a result of the presence of the International Court of Justice in the system, it will be politically easier for host country controls on MNEs to be permissive, thereby minimizing interferences with the expansion of MNEs.

A possible scenario of the dynamics involved begins by noting that increased international competition, fostered by MNE expansion, seems to have advantaged owners and top managers to the disadvantage of many workers who are downsized out of a job. Since national governments are currently the only source of protection for workers, there is a chance that restrictions will be placed on MNEs in an attempt to protect workers and local producers. If protection is extended, chances are that it will be excessive. Alternatively, a U.N. agency for chartering enterprises might protect workers and simultaneously reduce the worldwide disruption of the allocation of resources by requiring that competition-prompted downward adjustment of the work force be spread over time and over space. Spreading the adjustment cost over several countries will prevent one country or one group of people from taking the full hit. A U.N.-based cost-spreading policy will also help to eliminate even the perception that an MNE's downsizing is punishment to the host country's leaders and citizens for the being uncooperative in the treatment of the guest MNE.

A new U.N. agency to charter MNEs would have its actual authority (in contrast to theoretical authority) worked out over time as attempts are made to accomplish its mission.[6] For one thing, national statutes under which enterprises currently operate would have to be adapted to allow for U.N. incorporation. Once the United Nations developed the legal capacity to charter MNEs, it would become a focal point, albeit initially a relatively weak one, whenever a new enterprise considered the benefits and costs of being chartered in the range of jurisdictions available. Global standardizing of norms for host countries and for MNEs is likely to make U.N. enterprise-incorporation effective more quickly than the alternative route of institution building by which nations join together voluntarily to develop a similar agreement. If a U.N. agency were established, important to its successful evolution is that all parties (home and host countries and the MNEs) come to understand the benefits and costs to be derived from the international incorporation of an MNE. If the U.N. conditions for incorporation were favorable and if they were known, U.N. incorporation can be expected to be the jurisdiction of choice.

CONCLUSIONS

If MNEs expansion stands to promote pervasive improvements in the standard of living of the earth's population and if they must organize and use resources efficiently to survive, it is important to minimize resistance to MNE expansion. A transnational organization for multinational enterprises (an OMNE) would remove impediments to MNE expansion because it would provide assurance that the citizens of the countries in which an MNE is located share in the rents generated by the MNE's expansion. Since an OMNE is potentially beneficial to many, attention should be turned to the strategy of developing such an organization.

Placing a chapter dealing with FDI (MNE expansion) in the North American Free Trade Agreement, incorporating such matters into the ongoing work of the European Union, and developing an Asia Pacific

Investment Code are piecemeal, albeit well drawn, approaches to developing an OMNE. The Trade Related Investment Measures that are part of the Final Act of the Uruguay Round of the GATT (WTO) negotiations are piecemeal, as well.[7] Gordon's idea of global incorporation of MNEs would complement the existing reactive, restrictive oversight of MNEs. If the United Nations were given the authority to incorporate enterprises, MNEs would have an additional choice in their strategic planning. National governments would be freed from concerns about transfer pricing and similar actions that reduce the rents due their citizens, while MNEs would stand to make substantial gains as well.

From an enterprise perspective, all nations agreeing to a multinational business incorporation mechanism would be required to implement a common set of investment laws, regulations, and policies. They would, in effect, be required to harmonize their treatment of MNEs. Such harmonization should be attractive to MNEs because of the cost reductions that would result from dealing with simpler requirements. If an MNE found the benefits sufficient, it could opt for U.N. incorporation. This voluntary process could be considered experimental: after a decade or two the U.N. alternative could be dropped if an insufficient number of MNEs availed themselves of U.N. incorporation. The ideas of Goldberg and Kindleberger [1970], Bergsten and Graham [1992], Graham and Wilkie [1994], and Graham [1994] can and should be incorporated into the charter and by-laws of any U.N. agency that provides enterprise incorporation and oversight. Their ideas are compatible and complementary with those of institutionalists.

During the nearly four decades through which a theory of multinational enterprise expansion (foreign direct investment) has been evolving, institutional economists, especially Wendell Gordon, have made major contributions to the literature. In addition, scholars like John Dunning, although not calling themselves institutionalists, have worked in much the same tradition by proceeding with an eclectic approach that focused on what was actually happening in connection with MNE expansion. Institutional economics, that is, offers a platform from which all scholars working with the contemporary theory of multinational enterprise expansion and related policy issues can construct ever more meaningful contributions.

ENDNOTES

1. In *International Trade* [1958], Wendell Gordon offered empirical evidence that over periods as short as 35 years foreign investors withdrew from the host country interest and dividends equal or nearly equal to the total value of the investment made. Gordon concludes in his monograph, *Foreign Investments* [1962], that for the United States "The foreign investment process . . . may have occurred in a manner that results in debt service being as

large as new investment virtually from the beginning of the process" [1962, 27]. One implication of his analysis is that developing countries could finance their own development if they have exportable products, can secure markets for them, and can channel foreign exchange earnings to finance the import of the capital equipment and technical expertise that an MNE often supplies. Gordon summarizes the empirical relationship between FDI and economic development in this way: "no country in the last two hundred years has grown substantially after experiencing over a period of years a foreign-investment financed import balance on goods and services (debt service excluded)" [1984, 305-6]. Bill Wilkins found support for this hypothesis in his case study of Venezuela [Wilkins 1963].

2. The product life cycle process represents one avenue by which a potential MNE can evaluate the domestic market conditions in a potential host country.

3. Because Wendell Gordon's earliest concerns regarding FDI were centered on the contribution made by foreign investment to the general welfare, especially in developing countries, it is not surprising that his work includes an extensive review of the attitudes toward FDI in both home (creditor) and host (debtor) countries [Gordon 1958, ch. 27; 1962, 62-65].

4. Graham [1994, 11-12] also notes that the Organization for Economic Cooperation and Development (OECD) member countries have subscribed to two codes that are related to these proposals and that in principle are binding for all OECD members. The Code of Liberalization of Capital Movements and the Code of Liberalization of Current Invisible Operations commit each member country, subject to declared, existing long- and short-run exceptions, to remove barriers to inward and outward foreign direct investment and to flows of financial capital related to the FDI.

5. The two global organizations that might settle disputes between host countries and MNEs, the World Bank's International Centre for Settlement of Investment Disputes and the U.N. Commission on International Trade Law are both inadequate for at least three reasons. First, neither has jurisdiction unless both the country and the MNE agree to use it to settle the dispute. Second, even if a settlement is reached, neither institution has any ability or leverage to enforce it. Third, both are perceived as being biased against MNEs (in favor of host countries) and of being excessively legalistic [Graham 1994, 15].

6. The impetus and direction of MNE policy formation that has arisen from the "creative tension" between the members' national governments and the European Union's (EU) Commission is one aspect of the EU experience that might be instructive in formulating a global approach to overseeing MNEs. The Commission's "theoretical" mission was set forth in general terms in 1958 while its "actual" mission is ever evolving. An important part of the evolution is the continuous struggle for sovereignty between the member nation states and the Commission. References to aspects of the EU process are found in Scaperlanda [1992]. In a related vein, Graham [1994, 25] thinks that a global OMNE will eventually benefit if "policy competition" among subglobal OMNEs like the OECD, the APEC, and the NAFTA occurs.

7. These measures exclusively emphasize the prohibition of performance standards such as domestic content requirements or export goals that can be imposed on an MNE and that distort trade. See GATT, *Draft Final Act of the Uruguay Round*, Section N.

REFERENCES

Bergsten, C. Fred, and Edward M. Graham. "Needed: New International Rules for Foreign Direct Investment." *The International Trade Journal* 7 (Fall 1992): 15-44.

Bhagwati, Jagdish N., et al. "Quid Pro Quo Foreign Investment and Welfare--A Political-Economy-Theoretic Model." *Journal of Development Economics* 27 (1987): 127-38.

Chandler, Alfred D. "Organizational Capabilities and the Economic History of the Industrial Enterprise." *Journal of Economic Perspectives* 6 (Summer 1992): 79-100.

Dunning, John H. "Governments, Markets, and Multinational Enterprises: Some Emerging Issues." *The International Trade Journal* 7 (Fall 1992): 1-14.

The Economist. "An India That Still Says No." (August 12-18, 1995): 12.

Ethier, Wilfred J. "The Multinational Firm." *The Quarterly Journal of Economics* 101 (November 1986): 805-33.

General Agreement on Tariffs and Trade. "Trade-Related Aspects of Investment Measures." Section N of the *Draft Final Act of the Uruguay Round.* Geneva, Switzerland: GATT Information Division, September 28, 1993.

Goldberg, Paul M., and Charles P. Kindleberger. "Toward a GATT for Investment: A Proposal for Supervision of the International Corporation." *Law and Policy in International Business* 2 (Summer 1970): 295-325.

Gordon, Wendell C. *Foreign Investments.* University of Houston, *The Business Review* 9 (Fall 1962).

———. *Institutional Economics.* Austin: The University of Texas Press, 1980.

———. *International Trade.* New York: Alfred A. Knopf, 1958.

———. *The United Nations at the Crossroads of Reform.* Armonk, New York: M. E. Sharpe, 1994.

Graham, Edward M. "Towards an Asia-Pacific Investment Code." *Transnational Corporations* 3 (August 1994): 1-27.

Graham, Edward M. and Christopher Wilkie. "Multinationals and the Investment Provisions of the NAFTA." *The International Trade Journal* 8 (Spring 1994): 9-38.

Groenewegen, J. and P. R. Beije. "The European Answer to the Dilemmas of Competition, Cooperation, and Mergers." *Journal of Economic Issues* 26 (June 1992): 493-511.

Helmberger, Peter and Andrew Schmitz. "Factor Mobility and International Trade: The Case of Complementarity." *The American Economic Review* 60 (September 1970): 761-67.

Hymer, Stephen H. *The International Operations of National Firms: A Study of Direct Investment.* Cambridge, MA: MIT Doctoral Dissertation, 1960.

Kelly, Jim. "Leading Companies Face Tougher Tax Line Over Transfer Pricing." *Financial Times* (July 17, 1995): 1 & 14.

Krugman, Paul. *Geography and Trade.* Cambridge, MA: The MIT Press, 1991.

MacDougall, C. D. A. "The Benefits and Costs of Private Investment from Abroad: A Theoretical Approach." *Bulletin of the Oxford University Institute of Statistics* 22 (1960): 189-211. Reproduced as chapter 10 in Richard E. Caves and Harry G. Johnson, eds., *Readings in International Economics.* Homewood, Illinois: Richard D. Irwin, Inc., 1968.

McClintock, Brent. "Recent Theories of Direct Foreign Investment: An Institutionalist Perspective." *Journal of Economic Issues* 22 (June 1988): 477-84.

———. "Direct Foreign Investment: A Reply." *Journal of Economic Issues* 23 (September 1989): 885-88.

Mundell, Robert A. "International Trade and Factor Mobility." *The American Economic Review* 47 (June 1957): 321-35.
Robinson, Richard D. *National Control of Foreign Business Entry: A Survey of Fifteen Countries*. New York: Praeger Publishers, 1976.
Rugman, Alan M. "Internalization as a General Theory of Foreign Direct Investment: A Re-appraisal of the Literature." *Weltwirtshaftliches Archiv* 116 (1980): 366-79.
———. "Internalization is Still a General Theory of Foreign Direct Investment." *Weltwirtshaftliches Archiv* 121 (1985): 570-75.
Rutter, John. "Recent Trends in International Direct Investment." Washington, DC: U.S. Department of Commerce, International Trade Administration, Trade Development, August 1992. (Analytic Document).
Safarian, A. Edward. *Multinational Enterprise and Public Policy: A Study of the Industrial Countries*. Brookfield, VT: Edward Elgar, 1993.
Scaperlanda, Anthony. "Multinational Enterprises and the Global Market." *Journal of Economic Issues* 27 (June 1993): 605-16.
———. "Schumpeterian Entrepreneurship and Multinational Enterprises: Implications for Social Economics." *Review of Social Economy* 52 (Winter 1994): 338-52.
———. "The European Community and Multinational Enterprises: Lessons in the Social Control of Industry." *Journal of Economic Issues* 26 (June 1992): 421-32.
Scaperlanda, Anthony, and Robert Balough. "Determinants of U.S. Direct Investment in the E.E.C.: Revisited." *European Economic Review* 21 (1983): 381-90.
United Nations. *Yearbook of the United Nations, 1992*. Boston, Massachusetts: Martinus Nijhoff Publishers, 1993.
Vernon, Raymond. "International Investment and International Trade in the Product Cycle." *Quarterly Journal of Economics* 80 (1966): 190-207.
Wilkins, B. Hughel. "Foreign Investment and Internally Generated Funds: A Venezuelan Case." *Inter-American Economic Affairs* 16 (Spring 1963): 3-10.
Williamson, Oliver E. "Strategizing, Economizing, and Economic Organization." *Strategic Management Journal* 12 (Winter 1991): 75-94.

III. LABOR, RESOURCES, AND TECHNOLOGY IN THE INTERNATIONAL ECONOMY

CHAPTER 7

TECHNOLOGY TRANSFER, ECONOMIC DEVELOPMENT, AND THE PERPETUATION OF POVERTY: RESOURCE CREATION VERSUS FRUGALITY

Thomas R. DeGregori
University of Houston

Distrust of new technologies is deeply rooted in Western culture. Some forms of resistance to new technology are endemic to the societal process of innovating technology. Technology, as ideas, as skills, and as behavior, involves a complex of institutional beliefs and practices, sentiments, and symbols, to which people acquire an emotional attachment that makes them resistant to change. Though much of the criticism of modern technology emerges out of the Western cultural tradition, the movements seeking alternate technologies have found resonance and respectability among thinkers of vastly diverse cultural, institutional, and educational backgrounds. Though many of the movements' leaders have advanced degrees, most of their members fundamentally do not understand modern technology and science.

The anti-science, anti-technology dogma reaches a level of virtual certainty on questions concerning the research and implementation in agriculture in what has popularly become known as the Green Revolution and on questions involving resource-creating technologies and sustainability. These are technologies that have helped to feed hundreds of millions of people, yet they are condemned in torrents of misinformation by otherwise well-informed, well-intentioned people. The anti-technology bias is not only elitist, but it is destructive of the well-being of the poorest and most powerless of the world's inhabitants.

RESOURCE CREATION: AN INSTITUTIONAL THEORY

The very use of the term "natural resources" is not only incorrect but is misleading and has policy implications that are potentially deleterious to the human endeavor of reducing or eliminating poverty. Institutional economic theorists such as C. E. Ayres and Erich Zimmermann developed the theory of resources as a logical extension of the institutional theory of technology and in response to the conceptualization of resource scarcity that was, and to some extent remains, central to mainstream economics. Qualifying the centrality of resource scarcity with the phrase "to some extent" is deliberate. Though basic economics texts still define the discipline as the allocation of scarce resources among alternative uses, mainstream economists have been in the lead in arguing against limits-to-growth theories of likely resource exhaustion. In fact, during the two centuries since the Industrial Revolution the utilization of raw materials has vastly increased, while their scarcity has steadily decreased as measured by real prices, as a percent of output, or as the worker time necessary to obtain them. For roughly the last 100 years, the real price of other raw materials and basic foodstuffs have likewise steadily fallen even as population and demand have steadily and rapidly increased. Unfortunately, the economic theory of resources is inadequate to explain this long-term trend, although it can contribute to the understanding of short-run effects. Clearly, no one using economic theory would have guessed the trend of decreasing resource scarcity prior to the massive accumulation of evidence.

In advance of the modern statistical studies, the institutional theory that technology creates resources refuted the thesis of increasing resource scarcity. It provides a solid theory explaining the trends as well as predicting them. It also provides a firm foundation for using this understanding of resource creation to frame policies on some of the most critical issues of our time.

The framework for the institutional theory of resources is that the raw stuff of the universe, material and immaterial, matter and energy, are not resources but only potentially so. Stuff becomes resources only when human ingenuity allows us to use it for a human purpose. Being a resource then is not an inherent property of the raw stuff but involves a relationship between this stuff and human beings. The dynamic creative force in the process is the human intelligence that generates the means which we call technology. Institutionalism has, therefore, an anthropocentric theory of resources and their creation. This is understandable since the institutional theory is predicated on an anthropocentric theory of value. Human beings are the primary actors, in many ways the only actors, in institutional theory and nowhere is this perspective more important than in the theory of resources. Institutional theory not only covers raw materials as "natural" resources but also foodstuffs, the land upon which crops are grown, access to water and its potability, energy, the shelters that we create, and the air within them that we breathe.

Biologically, we originated as tropical primates that could survive only in a limited range of habitats. The fact that we have spread over the globe without speciation means that we have used our technology to transform the environment to make it habitable. All the elements of human survival outside the original ecological niche are resources as a result of our technological capability to access them. The "resources" of these diverse environments that technology made habitable would no more logically be considered resources without human technology than would the minerals on the moon be *currently* considered as part of the inventory of human resources. Both are only potential resources until the technology of utilization in all aspects, including access, is adequately developed.

Popular conceptions of technology still stress its hardware or material aspect, but even the simplest tool is the embodiment of an idea. One does not have to be a follower of Plato to understand the centrality of ideas in technology and therefore in resource creation. The ideational process that creates technology simultaneously creates resources. When the emerging humans had an idea and a skill to make stone tools, then this technological action endowed certain types of stones with the property of being resources. "Resources are not, they become," and their becoming is the consequence of technological change. Zimmermann adds that resources "are not static but expand and contract in response to human wants and human actions" [1951, 15]. Zimmermann's analysis is called a "functional" appraisal of resources.

Technology is first and foremost ideas. We have evolved into homo sapiens as tool users and become dependent on technology and resource creation even in our original ecological niche. In other words, we were tool users and therefore resource creators even before we were fully human. In the words of the anthropologist, Clifford Geertz: "Tools, hunting, family organization, and later, art, religion, and a primitive form of 'science,' molded man somatically; they are therefore necessary not merely to his survival but to his existential realization" [1973, 83; 1977, 30-31]. Geertz adds, the "slogan 'man makes himself' now comes to have a more literal meaning than originally supposed" [1977, 27]. The phrase "man makes himself" is from the title of a book by V. Gordon Childe [1951]. Geertz counters that "rather than culture acting only to supplement, develop, and extend organically-based capacities genetically prior to it, it would seem to be an ingredient to those capacities themselves" [1977, 28]. Geertz goes on to indicate how meaningless it is to conceive of a "cultureless human." Included in the analysis is the homo sapiens' brain which, "having arisen within the framework of human culture, would not be viable outside it" [Geertz 1973, 68; Geertz 1977, 28]. It would be equally meaningless to conceive of human culture without technology and resource creation.

For those of us privileged to have had a seminar from C. E. Ayres, one of his phrases on resource scarcity stands out; namely, that defining economics in terms of the allocation of scarce resources is pointless since the way that we allocate them will determine their scarcity. In other words, if we allocate resources in a manner that furthers the technological process, then we will be creating resources as we are using them. If our actions and policies hinder the further development of the technological process, then we will truly be using up resources.

Any policy based on resources being fixed, finite, and exhaustible will become self-fulfilling. In terms of any existing complement of science and technology, there will be a finite set of resources that will vary only in terms of price. No matter how frugal we are in using and recycling them, as long as recycling is less than 100 percent, then we are certain to experience a sustained increase in price as our utilization eventually leads to resource exhaustion. Perversely, then, each theory if correctly implemented can lead to its own predicted outcome. Obviously, if true, we should prefer to operate in terms of the most optimistic theory.

In some small respects, mainstream economics seems at least superficially to have accepted the notion that technology and science create resources and that therefore we need not exhaust them as long as we create them faster than we use them; however, other groups have arisen with romantic conceptions of human beings, our place in the "natural" world, and a conceptualization of resources being fixed and finite and likely to be exhausted.

Romantic notions about resources, the environment, and technology are harmful. With these ideas, when policies and actions are put in action, they will lower levels of living and worsen the problems that they are supposed to solve. In the 1970s, theories on treating natural resources and their exhaustion led to decisions in developing countries that perpetuated poverty. In recent years, as environmental and conservation groups have become more influential, they are beginning to have a significant and potentially adverse impact upon development in poor countries particularly in the areas of agriculture, food supply, and human health. In general, the impact of wrong ideas is greater, even devastating, in developing countries. Even if these romantic ideas about the environment and resource sustainability were correct, the costs of saving the planet would still fall on those least able to bear the burden. Unfortunately, environmentalist ideas about sustainability and resource exhaustion are often the exact opposite of the truth and have contributed to worsening the already bad situation of poor people.

The anti-science and anti-technology perspectives of these groups is the source of the difficulties that they create. E. F. Schumacher, one of the modern heroes of the back-to-nature enthusiasts and a promoter of "small-is-beautiful" and "intermediate" technology categorically stated that knowledge of science is not necessary in order to be educated and to understand the world. Intermediate technology was about using resources "gently" and not about creating them. "What do I miss as a human being if I never heard of the Second Law of Thermodynamics? The answer is nothing" [Schumacher 1973, 80].

OWNERSHIP OR AUTHORSHIP?: COMPETING CLAIMS

Most foreign investors in raw material resources become crypto-institutionalists when justifying their pecuniary gains from resource extraction in another country. They claim that the stuff was worthless until they brought the technology to extract and utilize it. Although it might superficially appear that institutional theory supports this claim, in fact the institutional theory of technology, in distinguishing between authorship and ownership of technology, denies any specific group exclusive claim to a technology and its usufruct. Wendell Gordon's theory of investment argues that technology can only move from where it is to where it is not [1962, 14-15]. Gordon speaks of a "technological commitment" to a certain type of production and a body of "technological knowledge" necessary to carry it out [1962, 14-15]. This technological knowledge and commitment is what determines the resource character of raw materials and not their happenstance existence within particular political, cultural, or corporate boundaries.

If technology is truly the heritage of all humankind, then so are resources. It is interesting that the discourse on resources in the Law of the Sea Treaty uses the phrase "heritage of mankind." In other words, those who currently have command of a particular body of technology knowledge may have a legitimate ownership claim through research and discovery to its latest iteration but they cannot lay claim to the larger historical resource-creating process without which their advancement would not have been possible. This provides a broad framework within which competing claims can be understood in terms of the location of resources, the historical process of their creation, and recent contributions to resource creation.

TECHNOLOGY AND RESOURCE SCARCITY

The intermediate or appropriate technology movement had a considerable following in the 1970s and was heralded as the answer to problems allegedly created by large, sophisticated "inappropriate" technologies. Yet it is hard to find among today's economic success stories any countries that followed the prescriptions of this movement. Many countries, such as Tanzania, that to a significant degree were influenced by the movement later recanted and were forced to make a major policy adjustment. Both the original policy and the later policy adoptions cost the people of Tanzania and elsewhere dearly in terms of sustaining poverty.

It is not hard to see why, for the basic analysis on resources was fundamentally wrong. As I have argued, technology creates resources. The raw stuff of the universe takes on the characteristic of being a resource when humans acquire the ability to transform and use it. It is through technology and science that we endow the stuff of the universe with the characteristic of being a resource. Over the last two centuries, through science and technology, we have been creating resources faster than we have been using them and their real prices have been steadily declining. This has been very much true in the two decades since we were offered the thesis of "soon-to-be-exhausted" natural resources. By every measure that we have of resource availability--price, reserves, etc.--resources have become less scarce and not more scarce [DeGregori 1987, 4].

RENEWABLE VERSUS NONRENEWABLE RESOURCES

In the 1970s, the limits-to-growth theorists and the appropriate technology movement argued that we should make a transition to renewable resources from dependence on nonrenewable resources that were rapidly being exhausted. Contrary to their prophesies, nonrenewable resources have become less scarce while the resources that are currently most threatened are renewable, biological resources. Further, countries which followed these strategies have paid a high price in perpetuation of poverty both from the policies themselves and the actions that have been taken to correct them. Technology and resource creation are not about living within limits but of the human endeavor to transform them. An understanding of the institutional theory of technology and resources could have saved a lot of people from falling deeper into poverty and a lot of academics from writing nonsense.

The great irony of the advocacy in the 1960s and 1970s of the shift to renewable resources is that many of these same groups are concerned about loss of tropical rainforests, habitat, biological diversity, and agricultural lands and soils. In other words, nonrenewable resources (as well as some renewable commodities such as cocoa) are cheap and abundant while it is the above-mentioned renewable resources that are deemed threatened. In addition, renewable energy sources such as wood and charcoal are highly polluting and deleterious to human health.

The use of some renewable resources is not only inefficient and polluting, but harmful to human health. Open fires, such as cookstoves, produce particulate matter and toxic chemicals, including benzo-b-pyrene that some consider one of the most carcinogenic substances produced by industry or by everyday activities. Globally, it is estimated conservatively that "acute respiratory infections caused by indoor air pollution from biomass burning contributes to some four million deaths annually among infants and children" [Hansen 1992, 121]. Other estimates run to seven million or more deaths.

Traditional indoor fuels have been advocated as appropriate technologies without regard to their harmful impact on human health. Unfortunately, designing stoves to increase the efficiency of burning wood increases some pollutants while reducing others. "The more efficient the stove, the more pollutants it releases. Indeed, in extreme cases the stove that is clamped down to make it barely stay alight . . . may behave like a wood gassifier or pyroliser, heating the wood in the absence of air to produce great amounts of organic matter for discharge into the air" [Allaby and Lovelock 1980, 422]. Among these pollutants are carbon monoxide, and formaldehyde.

R. Terry Rambo examines the conventional wisdom that "primitive people live in harmony with nature whereas civilized societies wantonly degrade their environments" [1985, 1]. In *Primitive Polluters*, he investigates the impact on the environment of the Semang peoples of the Malaysian tropical rain forest. Because they are few in number, he finds that their aggregate impact upon the environment is low even though their practices of burning trash and swidden agriculture are locally polluting. Semang pollution in relation to the group's numbers and level of living is actually quite high. Modern technology is polluting but it is almost always less polluting per unit of output than less advanced technologies.

Rambo wisely includes the air the Semang actually breathe as a critical part of the environment [1985, 48-51]. From Belize to Borneo, houses are built on stilts of various kinds so that items, such as coconut shells, can be burned underneath the house, thus filling the residence with carcinogenic smoke that kills insects, including malaria-bearing mosquitos. Even where it is not deliberate, cooking and heating in colder climates fill dwellings with smoke. This is as true for the ancestors of the contemporary affluent people of the developed countries as it is for today's poor.

> Indoor particulate concentrations, probably the best single indicator of toxic (noncarcinogenic) effects, are twenty times higher in villages of developing countries than in households where two packs of cigarettes are smoked per day. Several studies in developing countries have suggested that an increased incidence of pneumonia is associated with exposure to organic fuel emissions, although several studies have had problems with controlling variables such as socioeconomic crowding [Stansfield and Shepard 1993, 69-70].

Rambo found it "surprising" that "at the local scale," the Semang impact on the environment was "not invariably quantitatively less significant than ours, despite the immense differences in technological power between primitive and modern societies" [1985, 78-79]. He further argues:

> Although the Semang do not cause significant air pollution at the regional or global level, they achieve quite respectable pollution levels in terms of the immediate life space of the individual and the household. Burning of domestic fires and heavy smoking of cigarettes results in atmospheric contamination with noxious gases and particulate matter equalling or surpassing the norm in modern cities. If citizens of Malaysia's capital city of Kuala Lumpur were confronted with air pollution of the intensity normal in Semang households, they would rise up in outrage over the terrible state of the city's environment, and they would blame it on modernization and capitalism [1985, 79].

Historically, the indoor air that humans have had to breathe was as bad as that described above. In the densely packed houses

> the occupants breathed and rebreathed each other's air, increasing the risk of respiratory diseases. Animal exhalations, animal dander, and dried animal excreta were . . . added to the indoor air, which could become heavy with methane and the decomposition products of urea. Living in close proximity with animals gave our Old World ancestors tuberculosis, influenza, measles, and smallpox among other diseases that followed Columbus into the New World [Garn 1994, 94].

Conversely, we can examine some of the resources that are essential to our survival and the role that technologies play in their availability. Today, we see industrially produced chemicals as pollutants of water. Given our phobias about chemicals, it should be recognized that humankind did not regularly drink hygienically clean water until purification processes, which included adding chemicals, were introduced in this century. The eighteenth-century developments in basic science of Joseph Priestley and Antoine Lavoisier allowed later researchers to gain a better understanding of respiration. Further, Lavoisier's work led to the "secularization and demystification of water by analyzing it and showing that it could be broken down into hydrogen and oxygen" [Goubert 1989, 2]. In the middle of the nineteenth century, there were the observations of the physician, John Snow, who identified the water from one well as the source for an outbreak of cholera. This was followed by Louis Pasteur's recognition of the microbial origin of water-borne diseases.

Previously water could be visually clean or ritually clean but now with this new knowledge and chemical intervention people could have hygienically clean water. In short, water became an industrial product [Goubert 1989, ch. 7; Hamlin 1990, 301]. Despite the fact that "millions of lives have been saved by the use of chlorine for disinfection of water," there are some who would ban its further use even though the evidence for its dangers is meager [Abelson 1994, 183]. Gordon Gibble, in fact, clearly describes the benefits of chlorine [1995].

Cultures are unique and distinctive in the way in which they assemble their complexes of resource traits and technologies. Although many seek technology transfer for their countries, there is for others a stigma attached to borrowing Western technologies. Considerable effort is being expended to develop indigenous technologies. To some, technology, and scientific and technological ways of thinking, are unique attributes of Western culture. Nothing could be farther from the truth. Most major cultural areas have experienced periods of technological dominance. Northern Europe, in many respects a latecomer, came to technological dominance by borrowing from Asia and the Near East. In the process of colonialization, Europeans instilled the notion of their singular capability for science and technology. This belief was unfortunately internalized by some of those colonized and in reaction, being non-technological was often proclaimed a virtue.

AN INSTITUTIONAL THEORY OF RESOURCES: REINTERPRETING CURRENT ISSUES AND CONCERNS

For issues such as the environment, seabed resources, and genetic resources the institutional theory of resources leads to solutions that are equitable and facilitate continued resource creation and utilization. Our evolution as human beings depended on the creation and utilization of non-renewable resources. The human dispersal across the globe was predicated on technological transformation of the environment. We can neither reverse the biological evolution that made us resource-creating nor can we bottle up the multiplying 5.7 billion people on this planet in the tropical environment of our early ancestors. Environmental issues must therefore be framed in the context that humans survive by disrupting the environment with technology. Our task is to identify the technological processes by which our environmental transformations are sustainable. For this we will need more technology and not less.

To oppose technology is not only meaningless, but is simply counterproductive to environmental preservation. Humans will eventually disrupt and destroy the environment unless we create the means for intensive and sustainable utilization of those portions devoted to economic management. Unless we do so, there will not be any areas available for wilderness or other conservation purposes.

Romantic notions about the superior lifeways of earlier peoples are simply delusions that stand in the way of intelligent discourse and problem-solving. It is an irony of more recent romantics that they have accepted this civilizational hierarchy of the colonial mentality and its alleged empirical foundations and have turned it upside down. Highest honors are awarded to those with the simpler ways who live "lightly" on the land and are in "harmony with nature." Their life is one of stasis and sustainability. Many of these perceptions come from the environmental and organic agricultural movements. Not only is "natural" not necessarily better, the transformation of foodstuffs by processing has historically been a vital part of human livelihood.

Even those who argue the superiority of hunting and gathering over the civilizations that followed recognize that diseases can be caught from wild animals. One could catch rabies; or, tularemia, a disease related to bubonic plague, "may have been a significant cause of sickness and death among American Indians who regularly handled game and fur-bearing animals." Cohen adds: "Handling wild animals or their remains can also result in infection with such other diseases as toxoplasmosis, hemorrhagic fevers, leptospirosis, brucellosis, anthrax, salmonellosis, and a long list of lesser-known infections. In addition, people can encounter a variety of highly lethal anaerobic bacteria, including the agents of gangrene, botulism, and tetanus, if they expose themselves to the intestinal contents of animals while butchering a kill" [Cohen 1989, 33]. Add in trichina worms that cause trichinosis, and an occasional staphylcoccal infection, and it is clear that food harvested in the wild is not necessarily clean, wholesome, and natural. Drinking water in the wild can cause "beaver belly" or be a source of "microorganisms derived from moose, ducks, and geese as well" [Garn 1994, 92]. If you think that we eat contaminated food today, as is often claimed, and that we ate clean food in earlier times in human history, think again.

As Rene Dubos has said, "Like it or not, from the moment we learned to transform things according to functions we developed a hundred thousand years ago, we drove the natural out" [Dubos and Escande 1980, 99]. Dubos characterizes the nature-knows-best school of thought as a twentieth century version of Dr. Pangloss, who thought we lived in the best of all possible worlds. This is ironic, because critics of modern technology frequently refer to its supporters as being Panglossian.

A NOTE ON BIOLOGICAL RESOURCES

The biological resources of the rainforest or of evolutionary diversity are resources because we have the science and technology to utilize them. Similarly, when emphasis is placed on ethnobotany and local knowledge or on farmer's rights, these are simply different forms of cumulated technological knowledge. From an institutional perspective, all are part of the unity of knowledge and the resource-creating process, so that it is not a question of favoring one or the other process.

The importance of ethnobotany and local knowledge demonstrates the diverse nature of technological knowledge for resource creation. The dichotomies between "high tech" and "low tech" or between appropriate and modern technology are artificial creations of ideologues and not the result of serious thought. The knowledge of the indigenous denizens of the rainforest is vital when forest products may become pharmaceutical resources. So are the modern science and technologies of biological assay. The skills of the anthropologists and ethnobotanists are essential in making local knowledge available and usable by the global scientific research community. In other words, the rainforest is in fact a source of potential resources whose character is realizable as a result of a combination of useful knowledge and technologies. The science and technology that many romantics condemn is precisely the resource-creating endeavor that can provide impetus and economic incentives for rainforest preservation.

Many who would have us live "in harmony with nature" fail to realize that this is inherently impossible. In evolving with our technology, we have survived outside our original natural environment by transforming it to make it suitable for our habitation and to accomodate increasing densities of population. Agriculture is a disruption of the environment and involves defending the crop from animals, insects, or micro-organisms. Innumerable substances have been used to protect crops. A major impetus for the riseof the modern consumer movement in the United States in the 1920s and 1930s was concern over the use of lead arsenate as a pesticide [Paehlke 1989, 24]. Other poisons used for crop and livestock protection before modern chemical pesticides include the alkaloid nicotine, copper acetoarsenite, potassium 4,6-dinitro-o-cresylate, lime sulfur spray, hydrogen cyanide, sodium arsenite, and potassium antimonyl tartate [Metcalf 1980, 220; Metcalf 1986, 253, 259]. Modern chemical pesticides are more benign to the worker and consumer than most other substances used throughout human history.

Organic material must be broken down by bacteria into its inorganic components before it can be absorbed and used by plants. Its components, manure and artificial fertilizers, are indistinguishable to the plant, but there are two important differences. Artificial fertilizers can be composed of the right combination of nutrients for the soil in order for the crop to be grown. The contents of manures vary and do not always provide nutrients in correct proportions to meet agricultural needs. Manure is better for the soil structure, though it can have toxic chemicals or a high salt content and may harbor harmful bacteria, insects, worms, and other pests [Hall 1974, 137; *Consumer Reports* 1980, 413].

Manure is no longer available in sufficient quantities to provide the soil nutrients needed to raise enough crops to feed the world's population. In the late 1980s, "about 4.4 billion tons of composted organic animal manure (1.5 percent nitrogen on a dry-weight basis) [would have been required] to produce the equivalent of the 65 million tons of chemical nitrogen" used at that time. As the use of chemical nitrogen increases, so does the volume of manure needed to replace it. "To produce it would require a three- to four-fold increase in world animal production, necessitating in turn, huge increases in the output of feed grains and pasturage. Furthermore, the transportation costs associated with distributing these fertilizers would be prohibitive" [Borlaug and Dowswell 1988, 14]. Currently, global production of chemical nitrogen is between 80 and 90 million tons, supplying better than twice as much of the world's nitrogen needs for agriculture as does manure, which provides about 35 million tons of nitrogen, and about 40 to 50 percent of all the nitrogen needs of the world's crops [Smil 1991, 573, 575, 577, 580; Smil 1993, 69-70]. "By the late 1980s, this also meant that these [synthetic] fertilizers provided an identical share [40-50%] of all nutrients incorporated in the annual global crop harvest" [Smil 1991, 577]. Given that "about three-quarters of all nitrogen in proteins comes from arable land, and if synthetic fertilizers provide about half of all nitrogen in harvested crops then at least every third person and more likely two out of every five, get the protein in the currently prevailing diets thanks to synthetic fertilizers [Smil 1991, 582]. In terms of the institutional economics framework, artificial fertilizer and plant breeding are technologies of resource-creation, namely of the "land" resources to feed people.

Many who would have us return to organic agriculture would have us cut back, if not eliminate, the consumption of meat. Simply stated, they wish us to use more manure while simultaneously having us produce less of it. Every environmental and health sin imaginable is attributed to the raising of cattle and the consumption of meat, particularly beef. For samples of the "cattle battle," see Wuerther [1993], Avery [1993], and Savory [1993]. The environmental costs of bringing more land into cultivation for grain crops, converting more land to pasture, and hauling several billion tons of manure, would undoubtedly be far greater than those environmental costs that result from the manufacture and transportation of chemical fertilizers.

The problems of sufficient energy, feeding the world's growing population, and preserving the environment continue, but our ability to deal with them is hampered by political polarization and disputes over symbols rather than over meaningful, substantive ways of solving problems. There are poverty problems that can be meliorated by known technologies. Strange combinations of interest and ideological groups often combine to make access to these technologies difficult. Since the mid-1970s, environmental groups have not only successfully prevented the export of certain categories of pesticides but have succeeded in restricting their use in many developing countries. Recently, protectionists have joined with environmentalists in seeking to limit imports of products that were manufactured or grown under conditions that violate United States environmental laws. For the domestic growers, this means less competition and therefore higher prices for their produce. For the developing-country producer it means lower sales and income. For the American consumer, including the domestic poor, it would mean higher prices for food. From the perspective of developing countries, this is another instance of shifting the burden of environmental protection to those least responsible for creating the problem and those least able to afford the remedies. In many instances, it is questionable whether the proffered legislation is dealing with scientifically verifiable health and environmental concerns or the phobias of an affluent anti-technology elite. Whether well-intentioned or motivated by crass vested interests, most of these efforts are fundamentally misguided. Even if some of the alleged carcinogenic effects of these pesticides are valid, there may be anti-poverty trade-offs in developing countries that are different from those chosen in developed countries.

POLICY IMPLICATIONS

Resource creation is at the core of any economic development policy. Resources are fixed and finite and become progressively less available unless technology and science are creating them. In the long term, in the absence of technological advances, population growth and resource utilization will inevitably engender economic decline [DeGregori and Rodgers 1994, part III]. The institutional theory of resource creation reflects the historical process by which human development has taken place. There is considerable virtue and benefit in making this process of resource creation more explicit so that those in a position to do so can frame policies that take maximum advantage of it. This understanding becomes an absolute imperative when we are confronted with limits-to-growth theories that would perpetuate poverty in the name of resource conservation. There are any number of economic issues, from alternative technologies to care for the environment, in which the question of resource creation must be addressed if reasonable, equitable, and sustainable solutions are to be found, widely understood, and appropriately acted upon.

REFERENCES

Abelson, Philip H. "Chemicals: Perceptions versus Facts." *Science* 264 (April 8, 1994): 183.

Allaby, Michael and Jim Lovelock. "Wood Stoves: The Trendy Pollutant." *New Scientists* 88 (November 13, 1980): 420-422.

Avery, Dennis. "Cattle are the Green Revolution." *Earthwatch* 12 (July/August 1993): 26-28.

Brady, N. C. "Poverty and the Green Revolution." In T. R. DeGregori and H. R. Rodgers eds., *Poverty Policy in Developing Nations*. Greenwich, CN: JAI Press, 1994, pp. 215-230.

Childe, V. Gordon. *Man Makes Himself*. New York: Mentor Books, 1951 [1936].

Cohen, Mark Nathan. *Health and the Rise of Civilization*. New Haven, CT: Yale University Press, 1989, p. 285.

Consumer Reports. "It's Natural: It's Organic, or Is It?" *Consumer Reports* 45 (July, 1980).

DeGregori, Thomas R. "Resources Are Not; They Become--An Institutional Theory." *Journal of Economic Issues* 21 (September 1987): 1241-1263.

DeGregori, Thomas R. and Harrell R. Rodgers, eds. *Poverty Policy in Developing Countries*. Vol. 1 of *Policy Studies in Developing Nations*. Greenwich, CN: JAI Press, 1994.

Dubos, Rene and Jean Paul Escande. *Quest: Reflections on Medicine, Science, and Humanity* (translated by Patricia Ramum). New York: Harcourt, Brace, Jovanovich, 1980.

The Economist. "Black Marks for Greens." *The Economist* 321 (October 21, 1991): 39-40.

The Economist. "Power to the People: A Survey of Energy." *The Economist* 331 (June 18, 1994): 1-18.

Garn, Stanley M. "Uses of the Past." *American Journal of Human Biology* 6 (1994): 89-96.

Geertz, Clifford. *The Interpretation of Culture: Selected Essays*. New York: Basic Books, 1973.

———. "The Transition to Humanity." *Tax and Freeman* (1977): 21-32.

Glickman, Theodore S. and Michael Gough, eds. "Resources for the Future." *Readings in Risk*. Washington, DC: 1990.

Gordon, Wendell C. *Foreign Investment*. Special issue of the *Business Review of the University of Houston*, Vol. 9, (Fall 1962).

Goubert, Jean-Pierre. *The Conquest of Water: The Advent of Health in the Industrial Age*. Translated by Andrew Wilson. Introduction by Emmanuel LeRoy Ladurie. Princeton, NJ: Princeton University Press, 1989.

Gribble, Gordon W. *Chlorine and Health*. New York: American Council on Science and Health, 1995.

Hall, Ross Hume. *Food for Nought: The Decline in Nutrition*. Baltimore: Harper and Row, 1974.

Hamlin, Christopher. *A Science of Impurity: Water Analysis in Nineteenth Century Britain*. Berkeley and Los Angeles: University of California Press, 1990.

Hansen, Stein. "Population and the Environment." *African Development Review: A Journal of the African Development Bank for the Study and Analysis of Development Issues in Africa, Special Issue on Population Growth and Sustainable Development in Africa* 4 (December 1992): 118-164.

Henderson, D. A. "Health Issues." In T. R. DeGregori and H. R. Rodgers eds., *Poverty Policy in Developing Nations*. Greenwich, CN: JAI Press, 1994, pp. 231-244.

Jamison, Dean T., W. Henry Mosley, Anthony R. Meacham, and Jose Luis Babadilla eds., *Disease Control Priorities in Developing Countries*. New York: Oxford University Press for the World Bank, 1993.

Johnson, Pamela R. and Ann Van Dusen. "Poverty Policies: The Role of Research, Lessons from the Health Sector." In T. R. DeGregori and H. R. Rodgers eds., *Poverty Policy in Developing Nations*. Greenwich, CN: JAI Press, 1994, pp. 197-214.

Kogan, Marcos, ed. *Ecological Theory and Integrated Pest Management Practice*. New York: John Wiley, 1986.

Lehr, Jay H., ed. *Rational Readings on Environmental Concerns*. New York: Van Nostrand Reinhold, 1992.

Mazur, Laurie Ann, ed. *Beyond the Numbers: A Reader on Population, Consumption, and the Environment*. Washington, DC: Island Press, 1994.

Metcalf, R. L. "Changing Role of Insecticides in Crop Production." *Annual Review of Entomology* 25 [1980]: 219-256.

———. "The Ecology of Insecticides and the Chemical Control of Insects." In M. Kogan, ed., *Ecological Theory and Integrated Pest Management Practice*. New York: John Wiley, 1986.

Olson, Paul A., ed., *The Struggle for Land: Indigenous Insight and Industrial Empire in the Semiarid World*. Lincoln: University of Nebraska Press, 1990.

Paehlke, Robert C. *Environmentalism and the Future of Progressive Politics*. New Haven, CT: Yale University Press, 1989.

Rambo, A. Terry. *Primitive Polluters: Semang Impact on the Malaysian Tropical Rainforest Ecosystem*. University of Michigan Museum of Anthropology, *Anthropological Paper No. 76*. Ann Arbor, Michigan, 1985.

Recheigl, Miloslav Jr., ed. *Man, Food, and Nutrition: Strategies and Technological Measures for Alleviating the World Food Problem.* Cleveland, OH: CRC Press, 1973.

Rossiter, Bryant W. "Opportunities in energy-photovoltaics." In T. R. DeGregori and H. R. Rodgers eds., *Poverty Policy in Developing Nations.* Greenwich, CN: JAI Press, 1994.

Sanford, Richard F. "Environmentalism and the Assault on Reason." In J. H. Lehr, *Rational Readings on Environmental Concerns.* New York: Van Nostrand Reinhold, 1992.

Savory, Allan. "The Necessary Evil." *Earthwatch* 12 (July/August 1993): pp. 28-29.

Schumacher, E. F. *Small is Beautiful: Economics as if People Mattered.* New York: Harper and Row, 1973.

Smil, Vaclav. "The Critical Link Between Population Growth and Nitrogen." *Population and Development Review* 17 (December 1991): pp. 569-601.

Stansfield, Sally and Donald S. Shepard. "Acute Respiratory Infection." In D. T. Jamison, et al., eds., *Disease Control Priorities in Developing Countries.* New York: Oxford University Press for the World Bank, 1993, pp. 67-90.

Tax, Sol and Leslie G. Freeman, eds. *Horizons of Anthropology,* (2nd edition). Chicago: Aldine Publishing Co., 1977.

Tulchin, Joseph S., ed. with Andrew I. Rudman. *Economic Development & Environmental Protection in Latin America.* Boulder, CO: Lynne Rienner Publishers for the Woodrow Wilson Center, Current Studies on Latin America, 1991.

Wirth, Timothy E. "Foreword." In L. A. Mazur, *Beyond the Numbers: A Reader on Population, Consumption, and the Environment.* Washington, DC: Island Press, 1994, pp. 13-16.

World Bank. *World Development Report 1993: Investing in Health.* New York: Oxford University Press, 1993.

Wuerther, George. "The Real Cost of Hamburger." *Earthwatch* 12 (July/August 1993): 24-26.

Zimmermann, Erich W. *World Resources and Industries: A Functional Appraisal of Availability of Agricultural and Industrial Materials.* New York: Harper & Brothers, 1951.

CHAPTER 8

TECHNOLOGY AND THIRD-WORLD DEVELOPMENT: A TWENTY- TO THIRTY-YEAR RETROSPECTIVE

Dilmus D. James
University of Texas, El Paso

Hardly an important economic variable is unaffected by technological change and, in the longer term, technological transformation has a bearing on cultural values, social relationships, and configurations of political power. Little wonder, then, that the dynamics of technological advance continue to attract increasing attention among scholars and decision-makers, a concern that now extends to problems of, and promises for, the social and economic development of the Third World.

For institutional economists, technology has always been viewed as a core element in economic development, but alas, they have not been sufficiently influential in the field of development economics beyond their own circle. Although there are notable exceptions like Wendell Gordon, James Street, and Thomas DeGregori, there has never been a significant core of institutionalists who concentrated their energies on the role of science and technology in developing countries. Both the structuralist and the dependency schools recognized the importance of technology, but with few exceptions did little beyond making general pronouncements as to the desirability of achieving technological progress by means of industrialization [Street and James 1982; Sunkel 1989]. Then, during the late 1960s and early 1970s some development economists, called "developmentalists" here for convenience, began to sense that the very levels of abstraction and restrictiveness of assumptions that had lent elegance and broad applicability to orthodox economics, rendered the approach too limited when assessing the origins and consequences of technological change. During the period 1965 to 1975, economists such as Ajit Bhalla, Charles Cooper, Amilcar Herrera, Francisco Sercovich, Francisco Sagasti, Frances Stewart, Constantine Vaitsos, and Miguel Wionczek began treating technology transfer and technological innovation within a political economy context and as endogenous analytical variables that are major elements in determining economic growth and social development.[1]

The emergence of developmentalist thought is sufficient reason for singling out the period 1965 to 1975, but it was also a time when many large developing countries initiated regulations governing technology imports. Many also established, or significantly strengthened, national science and technology councils. It is obvious then that there was a growing dissatisfaction with the manner in which technology was being handled analytically, as well as with existing institutional mechanisms through which developing countries acquired technology. Thus, the period can serve as a convenient base for identifying major differences in past and present treatment of technological change relating directly or indirectly to the development of the Third World.

Indeed, the primary purpose of this chapter is to provide a perspective on the manner in which heterodox development economists currently view technology and Third-World development vis-à-vis the period roughly between 1965 and 1975. In short, an attempt is made to present a 20 to 30 year retrospective, selective to be sure, on what we thought we knew about science, technology, and development during the earlier period and what we fancy that we now know. The chapter continues with a skeletal presentation of the traditional, neoclassical treatment of technology; reviews the positions of heterodox development economists on the role of technology and development around 1965-1975; concentrates on various events since the mid-1970s that were particularly instrumental in reshaping or augmenting heterodox, developmentalist insights into technology and development; and presents the current configuration of the developmentalist position. The essay closes by alleging that most developing countries are underutilizing the new insights and that the principal technology-related problems center around inadequate institutional arrangements.

THE NEOCLASSICAL POSITION

Although technology was prominent in the works of influential writers with widely divergent ideological convictions such as Karl Marx, Joseph Schumpeter, and Thorstein Veblen, their insights were not absorbed into the main corpus of orthodox economics. It is fair to say that until quite recently neoclassical economics took technological progress for granted. In their microeconomic analysis the production function is the locus of the firm's technological knowledge. Inventions and discoveries are generally considered as exogenous factors which create a supply of readily available technology from which firms can choose. Typically, in the neoclassical analysis, the acquisition of knowledge from the existing stock is costless, or at most, incurs only a modest one-off expense in mastering the new technique. The element of time is ordinarily deemphasized by positing instantaneous acquisition of technology, the employment of which is divorced from the firm's past learning experiences. In brief, history does not count.

When the analysis does focus on generating technology de novo, the analogy with an ordinary investment decision is very close. The firm compares the cost with prospective returns, both properly discounted, after weighing the probabilities of success or failure. Very often the analysis assumes perfect competition, which means, among other things, that the entrepreneur is omniscient about the market for inputs, including technology. Relative product and factor prices constitute the core data dominating technical, and all other, decisions by the firm. By and large, the most fundamental line of causation is from prices to technological change, not the reverse. Ex post results of technological change are of considerable interest, but the neoclassical world regards alterations in relative prices as the primary engine of economic growth and structural change while technological change is seen as a passive response to purely market-driven forces.

In the late 1950s, mainstream economics did become more appreciative of the role of technological change in the process of economic growth, when it was found that the accumulation of productive factors (capital and labor) could explain only a fraction of actual growth. Among other elements in the unexplained "residual," technological dynamics was regarded as extremely important. In addition, traditional economics recognized imperfections and externalities in the market for technology, such as information asymmetries between buyer and seller [Arrow 1962], problems with appropriating the benefits of R&D [Nelson 1959; Arrow 1962], real-world institutional arrangements dealing with intellectual property protection, and so forth. For the most part, however, the origin, pace, and direction of technological change continues to be largely ignored by neoclassical economists. When orthodox economists do focus on technology, their examination proceeds in a highly reductionist and abstract framework, with the brunt of their attention centered on the consequences of introducing new technologies, not on how they originate, are selected, and are mastered.

This sketch of the neoclassical position is, of course, so brief that it borders on a caricature. As orthodoxy fans out into new territory and delves into more diverse aspects of science and technology, the line of demarcation between traditional and heterodox economics has become anything but air tight. Yet, I think it is fair to say that the characterization presented above remains a legitimate one for today's starker textbook renditions.

DEVELOPMENTALISTS: 1965-1975

This section establishes a benchmark for comparison by examining selected aspects of heterodox thinking during 1965-1975 on the role of science and technology in furthering the economic development of the Third World.

The International Technology Market

Between 1965 and 1975, emphasis was not exclusively, but very heavily, on the transfer of technology rather than its generation within developing countries [Fransman, 1984]. Although developmentalists saw some room for expanding domestic innovational activities, the discussion revolved primarily around acquiring technology from abroad because there was little recognition of existing endogenous technological capability in the South.[2] This perception, combined with the Ricardian doctrine of comparative advantage, seemed to dictate against significant domestic R&D efforts.

There was a tendency to treat technologies as if they were discreet entities or commodities and to stress imperfections in the international market for technology. In addition, a prevalent belief was that technology developed in mature industrial countries fit poorly with factor endowments, market sizes, and production geared to the satisfaction of basic needs. Powerful multinational enterprises were viewed as the chief means for transferring technology under market conditions allegedly rigged against buyers of technology [Vaitsos 1970, 1974]. Multinationals were accused, among other criticisms, of charging high prices for technology when the marginal cost to them for supplying already existing technology was zero or very close to it [Vaitsos, 1970; Stewart, 1977]. Accordingly, one strand of the literature concentrated on monopolistic elements in the market and was instrumental in convincing policymakers to establish regulations governing technology imports with the intent of ameliorating some of the most undesirable outcomes for technology importers. The thrust of the literature and policy prescriptions were definitely directed at defensive measures to remedy defects in the international market for technology rather than positive actions fostering indigenous technological capability-building.

Transfer and Absorption of Technology

Between 1965 and 1975, most literature discussed technological conditions in Third-World regions or nations; very little attention was focused on technology or technical learning at the enterprise level. This might seem odd since received microeconomics had routinely concentrated on analyzing the behavior of the firm; however, by assuming perfect knowledge about the market and the ability to adopt technology at trivial cost, and instantaneously in an ahistorical setting, there was not much interesting to explore. Although heterodox economists began questioning these sterilizing stipulations, it took some time before the importance of the firm as an instrument for technological advance became apparent. Furthermore, when considering suitable examples for transferring to developing countries, the concept of technology transfer usually fit comfortably with the "linear" thesis of science, in which technology and development were almost exclusively focused on technology coming out of the applied end of the R&D pipeline.

Alternative Technologies and Choice of Techniques

Between 1965 and 1975, complaints that imported technologies were ill-suited to developing country needs led to much weight being placed on choosing more suitable production techniques [Stewart and James, 1982; Fransman, 1984]. One strand of this literature drew heavily on neoclassical foundations properly adapted for developing country conditions, which focused on differences in factor costs as the fundamental criterion for choosing techniques. Another group spawned the intermediate technology movement which, as the word "movement" implies, went beyond purely economic criteria in advocating the adoption of technologies positioned somewhere between traditional-indigenous and modern-conventional technologies. The notion of intermediate technology is inextricably bound with its champion, E. F. Schumacher, who founded the Intermediate Technology Development Group in 1965, an organization that remains extremely active in promoting technological progress in the Third World.

His emotive, influential work, *Small is Beautiful: Economics as if People Mattered* [1973], attracted an enormous following.

INTERVENING EVENTS

Much water has flowed under the bridge over the past two decades and, with no attempt at being exhaustive, I turn to a few of the major transitions and developments that were particularly influential in altering our view of science, technology, and development.

Technology and Trade Theory

Today's global economy is far more market-driven than was the case during the period between 1965 and 1975, a condition that has heightened interest in technology as a primary ingredient in attaining and maintaining international competitiveness. Furthermore, the inroads by technology-related analyses begun by Posner [1961] and Vernon [1966] on the product-cycle have continued, as witnessed by the technology-gap literature [Krugman 1986, 1990; Grossman and Helpman 1990]. Dosi et al. [1990], in an important and pioneering work, also in the technology-gap mode, suggest that much of today's international commercial flows are based on absolute advantages in technology rather than on Ricardian dictates.[3] Technology-related advances in the field continue to attract scholarly attention and further undermine the faith in the older Ricardian and Heckscher-Ohlin underpinnings of trade theory.

Recognition of Technology Capacity in the South

Several events and trends led to a greater interest in learning more about the origins and disposition of technology in developing countries and were responsible for a growing realization that countries of the South were not devoid of internal technological capacity. As evidence that many Third-World firms did innovate, one can cite (1) the emergence of the East Asian superexporters, (2) studies on innovational activities in mature developed countries[4] which greatly advanced the understanding of how technological change comes about, and (3) research in the Third World, partly inspired by studies in advanced countries. A few firms were able to undergo major technological transformations; and several developing countries were exporting some goods and services with high technology content.

Measuring Scientific and Technological Activity

Until the late 1970s it was not unusual to see inflows of foreign direct investment, capital-labor ratios, or rates of industrialization used as proxies for gauging technological progress. Considerable progress has been made, however, in devising science and technology indicators that facilitate international comparisons of scientific-technological-innovational resources, activities, and outputs. Dosi et al. [1990] identify three main sources: (1) the Organization for Economic Development and Cooperation on R&D activities, the data for which can be compared internationally; (2) the National Science Board in the United States which inspired a "science indicators" movement; and (3) academics and commercial organizations that pioneered the gathering of data on scientific publications, citations, and innovations.

New Emerging Technologies

In the earlier period, mention of the impact that newly emerging technologies might have on developing countries was rare and understandably speculative, while at present the literature is replete with studies dealing with the actual consequences of these technologies, especially microelectronic innovations and biotechnology.[5] The possibilities include "technology blending" which has come to mean the constructive integration of new emerging technologies with traditional modes of production in developing countries [Bhalla and James 1991].

THE CURRENT HETERODOX POSITION

By no means does this review exhaust the catalog of momentous transitions during the past 20 to 30 years. I have selected those that had a clearly identifiable and palpable effect on the field of technological change and development in the Third World. Precisely how have these events altered our thinking on the technological dimension of development economics? Observations will be grouped under (1) the international market for technology, (2) a new emphasis on learning linkages and innovation systems, (3) a diminution of concern with alternative technologies, and (4) the fact that previous actions by nations and enterprises matter a great deal.

The International Technology Market

The concern of technology-oriented development economists has shifted from a preoccupation with technology transfer to developing countries to the goal of internal technological capacity-building. There is little doubt that imported technology is an extremely important element of capacity-building, but rather than being an end unto itself, today it is subordinated to fostering local technological mastery.[6]

In obtaining technology from abroad, large multinational enterprises headquartered in mature industrial economies remain extremely important as providers of technology to developing countries, but alternative sources have proliferated. Today small and medium-sized enterprises from developed countries transmit technology to countries of the South [Herbolzheimer and Ouane 1985]. Smaller multinationals are also active [Bell and Scott-Kemmis 1985; TCMD 1992]. Centrally-planned Eastern European nations have become sources of technology [Monkiewicz 1989] and are now even more aggressive in marketing technology during the current period of transition. Technology is available from developing countries [Tolentino 1993].

There is ample evidence that effective transfer of technology often means that sellers, far from incurring zero or trivial expenses, face substantial costs. Originally documented in the work of Teece [1977], corroborating evidence is plentiful. After surveying 93 technology transfer agreements between British providing and Indian receiving firms, Bell and Scott-Kemmis observed "few of the supplier firms incurred trivial or zero costs--for most firms they were clearly of considerable significance [1985, 1978]."

The proliferating sources from which technology can be secured, the better bargaining skills of purchasing entities, a recognition that sellers frequently must absorb substantial costs, and the marked trend toward global trade liberalization have caused concerns with monopolistic imperfections in the international technology market and regulations on technology imports to be far less prominent on the agenda. Early leaders in controlling incoming technology, including Brazil, India, and Mexico, have markedly reduced restrictions on acquiring technology from abroad.

Technology is bought and sold in the international technology market, so there is a some justification for viewing it as a commodity, yet such a view is seriously incomplete for at least two reasons. First, some types of technical knowledge partially or completely defy codification. First mentioned by Polanyi [1965], and later popularized by Nelson and Winter [1982], this attribute of "tacitness" means that for mastery, some in-house learning is mandatory and cannot be bought like a commodity. The idea that some technology will have varying degrees of "firm specificity" has been accepted by many working in the field of the economics of innovation. Compare purchasing a bicycle complete with instructions with then learning to ride (Polanyi's example), or purchasing a tennis racket with then playing the game, an analogy favored by Nelson [1990]. Furthermore, many fruitful linkages through which enterprises acquire technological competence are not purely commercial.

Learning Linkages and Innovation Systems

The long neglect of the individual enterprise as an important generator and repository of technology has ended; indeed, enterprise-level analysis has moved to the center of current concern with technology capacity-building. According to John Enos [1991]: "The evidence for a few rapidly industrializing countries is overwhelming: the producing firm is the most important creator of technological capacity. If technical competence resides anywhere, it is within the producing firm" [85]. Cemoli and Dosi [1990] concur: "at a micro level, 'technologies' are to a fair extent incorporated in institutions, the firms, whose characteristics, decision rules, capabilities, and behaviors are fundamental in shaping the rates and directions of technological change" [52].

The enterprise sits at the nexus of an elaborate and rich network of linkages through which various agents transmit and receive technical information. These learning linkages include interfirm circulation of workers and key personnel, subcontracting arrangements, spin-offs from parent firms, user-producer interactions, equipment suppliers, membership in professional associations, and contacts with friends, family, and old school chums who are in the same or similar occupations.[7] Some of these learning linkages have varying combinations of commercial and social content, another reason that the purely "commodity" conception of technology is incomplete. Research on industrial districts and other geographic agglomerations, on strategic alliances among firms, and on national innovation systems indicates the heightened recognition of the importance of interactive learning linkages.

This systemic view of technological advance is at considerable odds with a linear thesis. Rather than a typical "lock-step" from basic research, through directed basic research, experimental design, applied development, to pilot project and full-scale production, each stage often influences the others in a multidirectional fashion, and what is more, according to the literature on the "continuous improvement firm," innovation can emerge in a relatively costless and serendipitous fashion at all stages of production [Cole and Mogab 1995].

Alternative Technology

Although the topic remains obligatory for a major section or a chapter in standard texts on economic development, the choice of the most appropriate production technique or technology is far less conspicuous in recent literature on economic development. The Intermediate Technology Development Group and many other specialized agencies remain active, but in the more prominent economic journals the emphasis has shifted from the initial selection of technology to that of achieving continuous improvement in utilizing the technology once it is secured.[8]

History Counts

The experiences of Japan, South Korea, and Taiwan provide considerable evidence that the nations best positioned to select and receive technology from abroad are those that establish an economic atmosphere conducive to innovation; integrate science and technology policy with employment, industrial, financial, and trade policies in a coherent fashion; provide scientific and technological institutions and infrastructure; and stress education and training. Equally important, they master imported technology and use it to complement domestically generated technologies. Thus, history does count and it favors nations that are proactive in their efforts to build technological capacity.

The historical dimension is stressed by the neo-Schumpeterian school which has, inter alia, examined the cumulative, evolutionary, and irreversible nature of technological advance and the concept of technological trajectories. They make it abundantly clear that, in terms of technology capacity-building, past practices matter at the enterprise level. The neo-Schumpeterians are marshalling the most telling challenge to economic orthodoxy on matters pertaining to the processes by which enterprises and nations accumulate technological capabilities, although the bulk of their energies have been directed to technological change in mature industrial countries.[9]

THE PROPER EMPHASIS: TECHNOLOGY PUSH OR INSTITUTIONAL PREPARATION?

The preceding discussion shows that we know a great deal more now about the nature of technology and development than we did 20 to 30 years ago. The historical example of Japan and the contemporary experiences of South Korea and Taiwan indicate that those nations placing a very high priority on technology capacity-building, with adequate coordination with overall development efforts, will make remarkable strides. In addition, it is wise to stress the complementary aspects between the acquisition of technology from abroad and local scientific, technological, and innovative undertakings. Rather than being unduly preoccupied with acquiring technologies as they are squeezed out of the end of the toothpaste tube, as the linear thesis would have it, the proper focus is on an entire system of learning linkages that ultimately affect the technological capabilities of individual enterprises. Finally, there is the realization that, although the initial selection of technology should not be approached cavalierly, innovative activity can be enormously rewarding once hard technology is in place. In this concluding section I want to elaborate two assertions. (1) The Third-World science and technology policy in practice fails to exploit these insights to a large extent. (2) Most of the shortcomings responsible for this failure are institutional in nature rather that purely technological.

Technology and the Ultra-Poor

There is general agreement that extremely low income populations have not shared proportionally in the benefits flowing from technological progress. Having noted this, however, the fundamental barrier to improving the lot of extremely poor populations is not a dearth of techniques. Indeed, while not complete, the "shelf" is well-stocked. The task, a daunting one, is to create conditions under which the poor can access, select, adapt, deploy, and improve technologies. A United Nations study on technology for basic needs[10] identified six "pillars," none of which deals directly with the generation of technology: (1) education, particularly basic education, (2) access to information, (3) participatory action, (4) health, (5) basic infrastructure, and (6) small-scale economic activities. It is attention to physical, organizational, and attitudinal preconditions paving the way for fruitful absorption of technology that is fundamental to any technology-related strategy for poverty alleviation.

To emphasize the point, since the overwhelming preponderance of what the United Nations classifies as least developed countries are located in Africa, it may be instructive to consider the enormous amount of World Bank lending for information technology in Africa during the 1980s and early 1990s. Evaluations of the provision of information technology by Moussa and Schware [1992] and Gahan [1992] lead one to conclude that the efforts were concentrated largely on providing technology rather than on physical, organizational, and attitudinal preconditions. I do not doubt that there were successful applications of information technology in Africa, but the impression from the two studies cited is that, on the whole, results have been disappointing, a situation raising serious questions about the sequencing of, and relative emphasis on, pushing technology vis-à-vis establishing a reasonably receptive environment. All of these problems raise many issues regarding the lack of understanding of the long-term cumulative process necessary to master technology, and an underappreciation of the role of complementary capacities, not the least of which is the ability of managerial systems to learn and reconfigure themselves rapidly.

Problems with Innovation Systems in the South.[11]

Although it is possible to identify world-class scientific and technological undertakings in the Third World, in general, they display a host of shortcomings, of which the selection of research projects is but one. The portfolios of R&D projects in developing countries are too heavily skewed toward the pure or basic end of the R&D spectrum, as opposed to the more applied segment. They are inordinately influenced by what is in vogue in the international scientific community rather that addressing bona fide, locally pressing development problems. Many agendas are laden with projects that, while intrinsically promising, are not backed by a critical minimum threshold of resources, human and otherwise, to have much of a chance for succeeding. The project selection process contributes to the serious disarticulation between R&D activities that are being carried out and the R&D results sought by producing enterprises.

In addition, R&D in developing countries very often suffers from a variety of inefficiencies within research institutes:

- overly hierarchical managerial structures,
- equipment chosen by administrators rather than the users,
- severe neglect or obstacles to equipment maintenance,
- a low ratio of supporting technicians to scientists,
- a paltry incidence of sharing expensive equipment,
- almost no inter-institutional sharing of expensive equipment, and
- a biased incentive structure leading scientists to abandon research in favor of careers in administration--the list could go on.

As to finance, there is the obstacle presented by volatile fluctuations in government financing for public R&D, a practice especially pernicious for scientific and technological endeavors which, by their nature, require lengthy gestation periods. There are the further frustrations due to premature withdrawal of external financial aid to R&D institutes of the South by funding sources that are overly myopic in their assessment of the time it takes to launch an R&D project or institute.

There is a more fundamental obstacle. It is impossible to read reviews of science, technology, and innovation systems of, as examples, Argentina, Brazil, India, and Mexico without coming away with the impression that science and technology policy is nowhere near the center of economic policy. Manufacturing firms in Argentina confine innovation primarily to adaptive engineering activities [Katz and Bercovich, 470]. During the 1970s, Brazil's undergraduate university enrollment tripled while full-time faculty declined [Dahlman and Frisctak 1993]! An OECD [1994] study on Mexico concluded that science and technology policy instruments are outdated and fragmented, considerations suggesting "that profound structural change is required for the Mexican science and technology system" [53].[12] Citing government sources, Bhalla and Reddy [1994] point out that in India, at most, only 14 percent of R&D expenditures have a rural orientation. One would expect that science and technology policy is likely to fare even less well in very low income nations. Speaking of African science and technology policy bodies, Paul Vitta [1992] observes: "In practice, the formality does not stop heads of state from consigning them to the big scrap heap of other institutions" [33].[13]

CONCLUSION

The main two points of the preceding discussion are (1) that the insights regarding science, technology, and development gained over the past several decades are not being satisfactorily exploited; and (2) that the primary locus of the problem is in inadequate institutions that are severely inhibiting the process of technology transfer, local technology generation, and post-acquisition dissemination and innovation--in short, the whole route to technology capacity-building. The catalog of deficiencies is perpetuated by political myopia, inadequate incentive structures, and misguided attitudes about the role of science and technology in development. These, rather than the inadequacies in the international market for technology, are the institutional arrangements that need remedial attention.

This is not the proper place to offer detailed policy prescriptions, but if the heterodox view offers any insight, it is that technical change lies at the heart of the process of development. Nations continuing to treat science and technology efforts as a marginal adjunct to other policy considerations are very unlikely to achieve sustained long-term economic progress.

ENDNOTES

1. Bhalla played a major role by editing *Technology and Employment in Industry* [1975], a volume that has seen three revised editions; see his concluding chapter [1975]. For representative works see Cooper [1974] and Cooper and Sercovich [1971]; Herrera [1969 and 1971]; Sagasti [1975] and Sagasti and Guerrero [1974]; Sercovich [1974 and 1975]; Vaitsos [1970 and 1974]; Wionczek [1968 and 1971]. Although slightly later than the period under discussion, see Stewart [1977] which reflects much of her thinking on technology and development that had incubated during 1965-1975. Works written by, or heavily influenced by, members of the Science Policy Research Unit of the University of Sussex are: Oldham et al. [1967], Sussex Group [1970], and Cooper [1973].

It should be stressed that all of these developmentalists continued to develop and refine their views on science, technology, and innovation in the Third World and most continue to make contributions to current policy considerations in this area.

2. Herbert-Copley [1990: 14] points out that even as late as the mid-1970s, after a survey of literature on technology in developing countries, Crane remarked on "the relative absence of technological innovation in the developing countries" [Crane, 1977: 378].

3. For a review of technology-gap literature, see Goglio [1991].

4. For a review of some of these studies, along with a case that they have relevance to the South, see Cooper [1994].

5. For thorough reviews of the literature on microelectronics and biotechnology in developing countries see, respectively, James [1994] and Fransman 1994].

6. In a review essay [James 1993] encompassing seven volumes on technology in developing countries I observed: "The reviewed volumes illustrate how, over the past ten or fifteen years, the preoccupation with technology transfer as an end in itself has waned. Not one of the volumes emphasizes technology transfer. In different ways, they all focus on the importance of accumulating internal technological capability" [100].

7. Examples and citations for each category of learning linkages can be found in UNCTAD [forthcoming].

8. I first became aware of the waning interest in alternative technologies in the literature after completing the review essay mentioned in endnote 6. The collection of books contained only one bare mention of appropriate technology [James 1993]. A stint while working with the Division for Science and Technology of UNCTAD on a review and analysis of the literature on technology capacity-building during 1992-1993 reinforced this impression.

9. The best single source of neo-Schumpeterian writing is Dosi et al. [1988].

10. United Nations, Economic and Social Council, Commission on Science and Technology for Development. *Science and Technology for Basic Needs: A Bridge*. Report of the Panel on Technology for Small-Scale Economic Activities to Address the Basic Needs of Low-Income Populations. New York: United Nations, 1995.

11. Substantiating examples, details and citations can be found in James [1990] and UNCTAD [forthcoming].

12. For an even more pessimistic assessment of Mexico's science and technology policy, see Wionczek and Marquez [1993].

13. James [1995] reviews some of the literature on the crisis of science and technology in lower income African countries.

REFERENCES

Arrow, Kenneth. "Economic Welfare and the Allocation of Resources for Invention." In *The Rate and Direction of Inventive Activity*, National Bureau of Economic Research. Princeton: Princeton University Press, 1962, pp. 609-25.

Bhalla, Ajit S. "Lessons from the Case Studies." In Bhalla 1975, pp. 309-324.

———, ed. *Technology and Employment in Industry*. Geneva: International Labour Office, 1975.

Bhalla, Ajit S., and Dilmus D. James. "Integrating New Technologies with Traditional Economic Activities in Developing Countries: An Evaluative Look at Technology Blending." *Journal of Developing Areas* 25 (July 1991): 477-496.

Bhalla, Ajit S. and Amulya K. N. Reddy, eds. *The Technological Transformation of Rural India*. London: Intermediate Technology Publications, 1994.

Bell, Martin and Don Scott-Kemmis. "Technology Import Policy: Have the Problems Changed?" *Economic and Political Weekly* 20 (November 1985): 1975-1990.

Cemoli, Mario, and Giovanni Dosi. "The Characteristics of the Development Process: Some Introductory Notes." In Manas Chatterji, ed., *Technology Transfer in the Developing Countries*. London: Macmillan, 1990.

Cole, William E., and John W. Mogab. *The Economics of Quality Management: Clashing Paradigms in a Global Market*. Cambridge, MA: Blackwell, 1995.

Cooper, Charles. "Science Policy and Technological Change in Underdeveloped Economies." *World Development* 2 (March 1974): 55-64.

———. "Relevance of Innovation Studies to Developing Countries." In Cooper 1994, pp. 1-40.

———, ed. *Science, Technology and Development*. London: Frank Cass, 1973.

———, ed. *Technology and Innovation in the International Economy*. Tokyo: United Nations University Press, 1994.

Cooper, Charles and Francisco Sercovich. *The Channels and Mechanisms for the Transfer of Technology from Developed to Developing Countries*. Geneva: UNCTAD, 1971.

Crane, Diana. "Technological Innovation in Developing Countries: A Review of the Literature." *Research Policy*, 6 (October 1977): 374-395.

Dahlman, Carl J., and Claudio R. Frischtak. "National Systems Supporting Technical Advance in Industry: The Brazilian Experience." In Nelson 1993: 414-450.

Dosi, Giovanni, Christopher Freeman, Richard Nelson, Gerald Silverberg, and Luc Soete, eds. *Technical Change and Economic Theory*. London: Pinter, 1988.

Dosi, Giovanni, Keith Pavitt, and Luc Soete. *The Economics of Technical Change and International Trade*. New York: New York University Press, 1990.

Enos, John L. *The Creation of Technological Capacity in Developing Countries*. London: Pinter, 1991.

Fransman, Martin. "Technological Capability in the Third World: An Overview and Introduction to Some of the Issues Raised in This Book." In Martin Fransman and Kenneth King, eds., *Technological Capability in the Third World*. London: Macmillan, 1984, pp. 3-30.

———. "Biotechnology: Generation, Diffusion, and Policy." In Cooper 1994, pp. 41-147.

Gahan, Eoin. "Computers for Industrial Management in Africa: An Overview of Issues." *Industry and Development* 31 (1992): 1-65.

Goglio, Alessandro. *"Technology Gap" Theory of International Trade: A Survey*. Geneva: UNCTAD, 1991 .

Grossman, Gene, and Elhanan Helpman. "Trade, Innovation and Growth." *American Economic Review* 80 (May 1990): 86-91.

Herbert-Copley, Brent. "Technical Change in Latin American Manufacturing Firms: Review and Synthesis." *World Development* 18 (November 1990): 1457-1469.

Herbolzheimer, Emil, and Habib Ouane. "The Transfer of Technology to Developing Countries by Small and Medium-Sized Enterprises of Developed Countries." *Trade and Development* 6 (1985): 131-148.

Herrera, Amilcar O. "La Ciencia en el Desarrollo de America Latina." *Comercio Exterior* 19 (Septiembre 1969): 704-712.

———. *Ciencia y Politica en America Latina.* Mexico, D.F.: Siglo Veintiuno, 1971.

James, Dilmus D. "Science, Technology and Development." In James L. Dietz and Dilmus D. James, eds., *Progress Toward Development in Latin America: From Prebisch to Technology Autonomy* (1990), pp. 159-176.

———. "Technology Policy and Technological Change: A Latin American Emphasis" *Latin American Research Review* 28 (1993): 89-101.

———. "Technology-Related Development Models for Africa: Review and Synthesis of Recent Literature." Paper, Southwestern Economic Association (March 22-25 1995) Dallas.

James, Jeffrey. "Microelectronics in the Third World." In Cooper 1994, pp. 149-230.

Katz, Jorge M. and Nestor A. Bercovich. "National Systems of Innovation Supporting Technical Advance in Industry: The Case of Argentina." In Nelson 1993, pp. 451-475.

Krugman, Paul, ed. "Increasing Returns and the Theory of International Trade," In *Rethinking International Trade.* Cambridge, MA: MIT Press, 1990.

———, ed. *Strategic Trade Policy and the New International Economics.* Cambridge, Mass.: MIT Press, 1986.

Monkiewicz, Jan. *International Technology Flows and the Technology Gap: CMEA Experience in International Perspective.* Boulder, CO: Westview, 1989.

Moussa, A. and R. Schwartz. "Informatics in Africa: Lessons from World Bank Experience." *World Development* 20 (December 1992): 1737-1752.

Nelson, Richard R. "The Simple Economics of Basic Scientific Research." *Journal of Political Economy* 67 (June, 1959): 297-306.

———. "Acquiring Technology." In H. Soesastro and M. Pangestu, eds., *Technological Change in the Asian Pacific Economy.* Sidney: Allen & Unwin, 1990.

———, ed. *National Innovation Systems: A Comparative Analysis.* New York: Oxford University Press, 1993.

Nelson, Richard R., and Sidney Winter. *An Evolutionary Theory of Economic Change.* Cambridge, MA: Belknap Press of Harvard University Press, 1982.

Oldham, Geoffrey, Christopher Freeman, and Freeman E. Turkcan. *Transfer of Technology to Developing Countries with Special Reference to Licensing and 'Know-how' Agreements.* Geneva: UNCTAD, 1967.

Organization for Economic Co-operation and Development. *Reviews of National Science and Technology Policy: Mexico.* Paris: OECD, 1994.

Polanyi, M. *The Tacit Dimension.* London: Routledge and Kegan Paul, 1965.

Posner, M. V. "International Trade and Technical Change." *Oxford Economic Papers* (October 1961): 323-341.

Sagasti, Francisco R. "Integracion Economica y Politica Technologica: El Caso del Pacto Andino." *Comercio Exterior* 25 (Enero 1975): 46-49.

Sagasti, Francisco R. and Mauricio Guerrero C. *El Desarrollo Cientifico y Tecnologico de America Latina*. Buenos Aires: Banco Interamericano de Desarrollo and Instituto para la Integracion de America Latina, 1974.

Schumacher, E. F. *Small Is Beautiful: Economics As If People Mattered*. London: Blond and Briggs, Ltd., 1973.

Sercovich, Francisco C. "Dependencia Technologica en la Industria Argentina." *Desarrollo Economico* 14 (April-June 1974): 33-67.

———. *Tecnologia y Control Extranjeros de la Industria Argentina*. Mexico: D.F.: Siglo Veintiuno, 1975.

Stewart, Frances. *Technology and Underdevelopment*. London: Macmillan, 1977.

Stewart, Frances, and Jeffrey James. 1982. "Introduction." In Frances Stewart and Jeffrey James, eds., *The Economics of New Technology in Developing Countries*. London: Pinter, 1982, pp. 1-16.

Street, James H., and Dilmus D. James. "Institutionalism, Structuralism and Dependency in Latin America." *Journal of Economic Issues* 26 (September 1982): 673-689.

Sunkel, Osvaldo. "Structuralism, Dependency, and Institutionalism: An Exploration of Common Ground and Disparities." *Journal of Economic Issues* 22 (June 1989): 519-533.

Sussex Group. "Draft Introductory Statement for the World Plan of Action for the Application of Science and Technology to Development." Annex II of *Science and Technology for Development: Proposals for the Second Development Decade*. New York: United Nations, 1970.

Teece, D. J. "Technology Transfer by Multinational Firms: The Resource Cost of Transferring Technological Know-how." *Economic Journal* 87 (June 1977): 242-261.

Tolentino, Paz E. *Technological Innovation and Third World Multinationals*. London and New York: Routledge, 1993.

Transnational Corporations and Management Division (UN). "Small Transnationals: No Less Than Larger Ones." *Transnationals* 4 (December 1992): 1, 6.

United Nations Conference on Trade and Development. *Fostering Technological Dynamism: Technology Capacity Building and Competitiveness*. Geneva: UNCTAD, forthcoming.

Vaitsos, Constantine. "Bargaining and the Distribution of Returns in the Purchase of Technology by Developing Countries." *Bulletin of the Institute of Development Studies* 3 (1970): 16-23.

———. *Intercountry Income Distribution and Transnational Enterprises*. Oxford: Clarendon Press, 1974.

Vernon, Raymond. "International Investment and International Trade in the Product Cycle." *Quarterly Journal of Economics* 80 (May 1966): 190-207.

Vitta, Paul B. "Management of Technology Policy in Sub-Saharan Africa: The Policy Researcher's Burden." *Journal of Asian and African Studies* 17 (January/April 1982): 32-40.

Wionczek, Miguel S. "La Transmision de la Tecnologia a los Paises en Desarrollo: Proyecto de un Estudio sobre Mexico." *Comercio Exterior* 18 (Mayo 1968): 404-413.

———. *Inversion y Tecnologia Extranjera en America Latina*. Mexico, D.F.: Joaquin Mortiz, 1971.

Wionczek, Miguel and Miguel H. Marquez. "Mexico." In Surendra J. Patel, ed., *Technology Transformation in the Third World: Latin America* (Vol. IV). Aldershot: Avebury (1992), pp. 1-100.

CHAPTER 9

LABOR MIGRATION AND URBAN EMPLOYMENT IN DEVELOPING COUNTRIES: THE IMPACT OF POPULATION GROWTH AND PROPERTY INSTITUTIONS[1]

William E. Cole
University of Tennessee

In this chapter I will argue that the standard analyses of rural-urban migration and urbanization have limited explanatory power because they fail to take certain important variables into account. Specifically, the standard models have focused too narrowly on wage differentials to the neglect of population growth and institutional arrangements. By refracting migration data through models that are exclusively demand-pull in nature for cases where supply-push factors are obviously operating, analysts have come out with policy prescriptions that are palpably suspect.

Urbanization and rural-urban migration are two, often remarked upon, phenomena of Third World economic development. Because the standard economic transformation involves the proportional decline of agriculture, both in output and labor utilization, and because industry, being subject to external economies, prefers urban locations, one could anticipate both of these phenomena. Over the past couple of decades, however, economic development analysts have argued that the labor force aspect of the transformation has proceeded at an unduly fast pace. "Urban bias" and "over-urbanization" are terms often encountered in the ongoing discussions.[2]

Misplaced policies that distort the demand side of the market are blamed for this apparently outsized growth of the urban services sector, especially its informal component, and open urban unemployment. Sometimes stated, other times implied, a redirection of resource flows so that agriculture gets more attention and industry less is taken to be a prerequisite to slowing the pace of urbanization. The discussion that follows demonstrates how population growth operates as a push factor that helps explain both migration and urbanization. Moreover, situations in Latin America and India will be contrasted to demonstrate how key institutions play important roles in the process, in some cases amplifying the push of population growth, and in others, ameliorating it. Neither analysis nor policy can safely neglect these factors.

STRUCTURAL TRANSFORMATION: REALITY OR MIRAGE?

The underlying mechanics of the structural transformation are put succinctly by Poulson: "High rates of growth of per capita product and productivity are closely associated with, and indeed require, changes in economic structure; the latter are connected with, and indeed require, shifts in population structure [1994, 341]." Following the work of Kuznets, this transformation is often associated with the changing structure of demand that is reflected in Engel's Law [Poulson 1994, 347]. As per capita income grows, the structure of demand changes to reflect disproportionate growth, first for manufactured goods and then for services. This transformation, documented by Kuznets for the developed countries, has proceeded at varying rates for many LDCs. The experience of developed and developing economies is shown in table 9.1.

If the structural transformation is viewed as a two-stage affair in which an industrial emphasis occurs first and is followed by a shift toward services, most developing countries have completed the first phase. If the least developed are singled out, they remain in the first phase, with the preponderance of GDP originating more or less equally in services and agriculture. If the focus is on the Latin American countries presented in table 9.1, it appears that they have largely proceeded through both phases. It is obvious, nevertheless, that none of the countries listed is considered developed in a way analogous to the United States, Western Europe, or Japan. For one thing, the per capita income gulf is wide between those two groups. In explaining the apparent anomaly between achievement of structural transformation and relatively low per capita income, some observers argue that services employment data mask a dual phenomenon.

For many, informal sector services employment, often self-employment, represents a residual category of last-resort employment.

Table 9.1

SECTORAL ORIGIN OF GDP (1992) (percent of total)			
	Agriculture	Industry	Services
Industrial Countries	4	37	59
All Developing Countries	17	36	47
Least Developed Countries	37	20	43
Mexico	9	30	61
Brazil	10	39	51
Peru	7	37	57
Venezuela	5	47	48

Totals may not add to 100 because of rounding.

Source: UNDP, *Human Development Report 1994.* New York: Oxford University Press, 1994.

THE ECONOMICS OF LABOR TRANSFER

In the tradition of economics, the intersectoral or geographic movement of labor is explained by wage differentials.[3] Supposedly, therefore, it is always a matter of the relative pull of the various employment choices available across the economy. In the well-known genre of dualism models pioneered by Lewis, it was necessary to posit a modern urban wage higher than that in the traditional rural sector in order to explain the movement of surplus labor into the modern sector."[4] Apparently, then, even perceived conditions of surplus labor in the rural environs have not deserved a push designation. Poulson tells us that "[t]here is no evidence that migrants are pushed out of the rural sector by unfavorable conditions [1994, 228]."

Such complete denial of push factors is implicit in the migration model of Todaro [1969]. He considers the potential rural emigrant's probability of rural employment at the existing wage unity.[5] Given the apparent certainty of a rural income, the potential migrant is enticed to move when the present value of expected urban earnings, adjusted for the probability of obtaining the requisite urban employment, exceeds the seemingly guaranteed expected rural earnings. This is what amounts to the standard explanation of labor migration in current economic development theory.[6] It is within this context that misplaced policies and institutional wages are said to swell the migrant stream artificially, with the size of the employment probability acting to equilibrate prospective earnings between sectors [Todaro 1969]. Any policy action that increases the urban wage or the probability of employment, assertedly, will spur migration and thereby exacerbate the degree of over-urbanization. This is demonstrated by Sabot's [1977] analysis, which models an urban residual sector that catches all labor force aspirants who cannot find employment in the urban modern sector.

The analysis that follows will swim against the current and argue that population growth has been a major factor in Third-World urbanization, affecting the urban-rural mix directly through natural increase and indirectly through intersectoral and spatial migration. Furthermore, it will be argued that population growth is a push factor that can be considered independently from wage differentials. This is not to say that such differentials are of no importance, but that they are only one aspect, and one that diminishes in relevance when the other factors are considered. When the push factor is combined with the natural rate of urbanization, we then have two new causes in addition to wage differentials to explain urbanization. It is from this new platform that a look at policy implications is informative.

ON THE ARITHMETIC OF NATURAL URBANIZATION

Two popular measures of urbanization are the percent of the population that is urban and the percent of the population living in cities of one million or more. The former is thought to reflect the expected decline in the importance of agriculture and the latter is used by some to suggest the presence of over-urbanization. Table 9.2 displays data based on these measures.

Table 9.2 indicates that the pace of urbanization has been much more rapid in Latin America than in the developing countries on the average. Indeed, the profile for the selected Latin American countries more or less matches that for the industrial countries. If we are to find examples of hyper-urbanization, these Latin American countries should provide fertile ground.

Natural increase always constitutes a component of a city's overall increase in population size. That it also contributes to relative urbanization may be less obvious. If the age composition and crude birth and death rates were uniform across a nation's territory, and if there were no migration from place to place, there would still be a significant change in the rural-urban division of the population, especially if the natural rate of increase is large.

Table 9.2

URBAN POPULATION AS PERCENT OF TOTAL				
	1960	1992	2000 (est.)	Pop. in cities of more than 1 million
Industrial Countries	61	74	78	33
All Developing Countries	22	35	49	14
Least Developed	9	21	28	8
Mexico	51	74	77	31
Brazil	45	77	81	39
Chile	68	85	89	37
Peru	46	71	75	30
Venezuela	67	91	94	31

Source: UNDP, *Human Development Report 1994*. New York: Oxford University Press, 1994.

This is shown in table 9.3, where country X has a population of 20 million persons in year t = 0. That population is distributed among various sizes of population centers as shown by rows A through H. Here we define rural as all population in centers of less than 15,625,[7] leaving 44 percent of the population defined as rural, and 8 percent residing in cities of one million or more.

Next, we make the critical stipulation that population is increasing at a uniform rate of 3.5 percent per annum. Given that growth rate, population size would double in 20 years. With the assumption of no geographic migration, each population center would double in size. We therefore find the new distribution shown in the column for year t = 20. Because each of the represented population centers has doubled in size, each urban unit represented in rows B through H moves to the next higher classification. The larger population under I now constitutes the whole population of H and I. Only 22 percent of the 40 million current residents of X now reside in areas designated as rural, down from 44 percent earlier.

Furthermore, the proportion of the population in the top category (one million and up) has doubled, to 16 percent.

What appears to be occurring in table 9.3 has all of the markings of urbanization that is fueled by rural-urban migration. The importance of the rural population has been reduced by half and the largest centers have doubled in importance. The big jump in the importance of the smaller cities represented by row G mimics a standard description of the migration process in which rural persons are said to make their first move to smaller, nearby cities. That move is said to allow them to develop some urban skills and to gather more complete information on employment opportunities before making an ultimate move to a metropolis.[8] To the extent that the exercise in table 9.3 illustrates small-city growth as a stepping stone movement of population, it is a mirage.

Table 9.3

Urbanization Without Migration: An Exercise				
Urban Size	Total Population in t=0 (millions)	Percent of Total	Total Population in t=20 (millions)	Percent of Total
A. 1 million and up	1.6	8	6.4	16
B. 500,000 - 999,999	1.6	8	3.2	8
C. 250,000 - 499,999	1.6	8	3.2	8
D. 125,000 - 249,999	1.6	8	3.2	8
E. 62,500 - 124,999	1.6	8	3.2	8
F. 31,250 - 62,499	1.6	8	3.2	8
G. 15,625 - 31,249	1.6	8	8.8	22
H. 7,813 - 15,624	4.4	22	8.8	22
I. Below 7,813	4.4	22		
Total Population (Millions)	20.0	100	40.0	100

The underlying logic inherent in this example is at work in the real world situations of the Third World. Population growth alone will account for some of the apparent urbanization. Increasing urbanization would occur even if there were no structural transformation and if there were no policies that could be construed as having an urban bias. It would be there with or without wage differentials. This is not to say that those other factors are not in fact present, but to show that they can be perceived as add-ons to the demographic trend. The fact that population growth rates have been higher than average in Latin America surely suggests that the phenomenon of an underlying natural urbanization has proceeded more rapidly there than elsewhere. Moreover, as the ensuing sections will show, the impact of population growth on urbanization goes far beyond this particular arithmetical phenomenon.

RELEVANCE OF THE INSTITUTIONAL CONTEXT

Those who study rural-urban migration as an aspect of economic development usually equate it with a net movement of labor from the agriculture sector to the industrial and services sectors. Furthermore, the full focus of analysis has been on urban activities, thereby limiting interest to the demand side, or pull effects. In focusing on the supply side, I recognize that the impacts of population and labor force increments are more usefully analyzed within a disaggregated context that reflects key institutional factors. Indeed the important role of the push metaphor associated with population growth emerges only when we consider specific aspects of the institutional settings in which migration decisions are made. Likewise, the standard analysis and associated policy prescriptions that are based on conceptualizing labor and land as aggregates diminish in explanatory power when the context is a specific but still typical household in a specific but still typical village of a particular country. In order to stress the role of institutional specificity in the analysis, my focus will be on Latin America and, more often than not, on Mexico in particular. From time to time the argument that has been developed will be refracted through the prism of institutional factors of other regions. As is the case with any useful analysis, the range of validity of any generality is circumscribed by the relevance of the specific institutions under study.

Analysis usually takes a macroeconomic approach to population growth, viewing it as an increase in the labor force at some nebulous margin. Population-cum-labor is modeled as a global variable that is combined with the stocks of capital and land, so that the marginal product of labor declines whenever population (labor) grows at a faster rate than capital and land.[9]

Population growth, whatever its rate, originates largely within families, each increment to the population becoming a member of a family.[10] An analysis of migratory decisions must take into account specific parameters of the broader institutional setting. For present purposes, therefore, it is assumed that the family unit is located in an *ejido* village in Mexico. The *ejido* is an institution patterned after the Aztec *calpulli* [Gordon 1950, 38] and constitutes an agricultural village in which the land is owned by the community as a persona. In theory, *ejidos* may be cultivated collectively or by households. In practice, relatively few present-day *ejido* villages are organized collectively. In most cases, individual households work the land on the basis of a usufruct provided to the head. Such would be a typical agricultural unit, representing more or less half of Mexico's agricultural labor force.

The village should be seen as one of thousands that are located in the densely populated central plateau of Mexico. There, most villages abut other villages because the area has represented an agricultural heartland since ancient times. For most of these *ejido* villages, therefore, there is no idle land to be brought into cultivation by the resident families. This accurately reflects the situation of most of the several million *ejido* families in Mexico.[11] Land is available only in frontier settings, which, in most cases, would require considerable effort to clear or drain and a sizable public commitment of infrastructure before its exploitation would be economically feasible. In other words, incremental additions to agricultural land are not part of the decision matrix of a potential migrant, or even of a few operating together.

For analytical simplicity, assume that the prototypical village contains families in which an average size of six is uniformly represented by two parents, M and F, two sons, S_1 and S_2, and two daughters, D_1 and D_2. The law governing *ejidos* provides that the family continue to enjoy the usufruct of the family plot so long as the land is cultivated,[12] and that it may be passed on in inheritance to a family member, who according to Mexican tradition is likely to be the oldest surviving male.[13] Important to this discussion is the fact that the parcel of land will pass intact to one survivor. There is a provision in the law that the inheritor must permit surviving children under the age of 15 and any incapacitated siblings or parents to remain on the subject land.

The intent is that the integrity of the plot should remain intact and serve as the source of sustenance of the nuclear family of the inheritor. Therefore, by depicting each family as having an identical composition, each S_1 is likely to inherit the family plot. In fact, this passing of the usufruct often happens prior to the death of the father. In such cases, the aged parents, or parent, typically remain in the household, working at a diminished pace for as long as possible. This scenario is faithful to the available data that show that the average size of nuclear families in typical *ejido* regions to be 6.3 persons [Barbosa-Ramirez 1979, 225]. Nuclear families and extended families that include grandparents make up 76 percent of the *ejido* families [Barbosa-Ramirez 1979, 228].

For ease of illustration, assume that each S_1 finds a marriage partner among the females of the village from the pool of D_1s. This couple then constitutes a nuclear family that takes over the household and plot inherited by S_1. This context establishes important parameters for the not unusual case of a teen-aged female, D_2, living in a village household with male siblings in a society that traditionally accepts primogeniture as a guide for inheritance. If she has not been asked for in marriage by a landowner or potential landowner, she will have to seek wage employment. Whether or not agricultural wage employment is available locally depends on a number of factors, often including the sex of the aspirant. In the Latin America context, she will probably find no significant employment opportunities in the agricultural village. This is manifest in data showing that less than five percent of Mexico's agricultural labor force consists of females [IV Direccion General de Estadistica 1965, table 12]. By considering the concrete situation within which the migration decision is being made, we see that, in this case, the aspirant's probability of finding employment at the rural point of decision making is essentially zero.

The second son, S_2, faces a somewhat different set of alternatives, and normally one of those is not to stay on the family plot. In the Mexican tradition, a male is more likely than a female to obtain wage labor in agriculture. Although some wage opportunities are available in the small-scale *ejido* sector, they are seasonal in nature and not likely to sustain an individual, let alone a family. In most cases, S_2 would find it necessary to change place of residence, whether employment is found in agriculture, industry, or services.[14]

The reasonableness of the portraits of the prototype migrants is supported by the facts that more females than males migrate from rural to urban environs and that migrants, male and female, are young [Munos et al. 1977, 42-45].[15] The facts call into question the standard assumption that the potential migrant is fully employed in the rural economy at the time of decision. Indeed, in many cases migration will lead to the individual's initial entry into the labor market, previous work having been in the form of contributions to housework and chores on the farm. According to Gregory, 76 percent of female migrants have no work experience, in comparison to 43 percent of male migrants [1986, 163].

In the depicted scenario, the probability of employment at the point of decision making is zero rather than unity. That certainly approximates the case of females like D_2. Demand factors, therefore, will determine where she goes, but not if she goes. The if is determined by her untenable situation at home, and the where is determined by the location of job opportunities that are largely urban. Even in the case of S_2s, the probability of remaining as an adult in the family household is nearly zero. Spatial movement, rural-urban or rural-rural, is forced upon them by the nature of the institutional arrangements. Only S_1 and D_1 would find themselves with a unit probability of rural employment at the existing wage, the situation depicted as typical by standard migration theory. Of the four siblings, only they would be comparing their current conditions in agriculture as reflected by earnings associated with their landholding, to the opportunities in urban industry and services. While emigration of S_2 and D_2 might be seen as triggered by a differential between wageless rural and wage-paying urban situations, it is more reasonable to see their move as triggered by the peculiar domestic situation. The key variable is family size and the key institutional factor is primogeniture.

Increasing population will be directly reflected in average family size, whether the underlying cause is declining mortality or increasing birth rates. For most developing countries, the population growth rate increased significantly during the mid-twentieth century because death rates declined. That was certainly the case in Mexico where the natural rate of population growth jumped from an annual rate of 1.3 percent in 1930 to 3.5 percent in 1960, exclusively because of a declining mortality rate [*Nacional Financiera*, 1965]. This phenomenon was followed by the increased movement of persons from rural to urban environs to such an extent that half of the migrant population of Mexico City in 1970 had arrived since 1960.[16]

A comprehensive study of migrants to Mexico City gives additional evidence corroborating the broad outlines of the scenario. Some 55 percent of the migrant population of Mexico City is female [Munos et al. 1977, 133]. Furthermore, 38 percent of the city's women and 33 percent of the males are migrants. As time passes, the migrant profile more and more reflects rural origins and declining average educational attainment. Both of these factors suggest that migrants are pushed. For the period 1935-1944, 40 percent of arriving migrants came from population centers of less than 5,000 persons, whereas that fraction rose to more than 53 percent for the period 1965-1970. Furthermore, educational attainment fell for migrants. The age cohort 21-30 years that arrived in Mexico City in the interval 1935-1944 featured an average of 7.3 years of education. The average had dropped to 5.0 years for the same cohort arriving during the period 1965-1977 [Munos et al. 1977, 103].

Given the described rural conditions, agricultural employment opportunities must be viewed as limited by all landless labor force members, new entrants or otherwise. That is especially the case for females. In contrast, given that the economy is undergoing a standard economic transformation, demand for labor should be relatively robust in industry and services. Moreover, as argued by Cole and Sanders [1985], the subsistence sector of large, growing cities offers opportunities for self-employment to practically anyone who will take them.[17] Consequently, there are likely to be many aspirants whose probability of rural employment approaches zero, while the probability of urban employment in a subsistence setting approaches unity. Consideration of such concrete cases may help explain the several situations in which analysts have found urban-bound migration occurring in the context of an urban informal wage lower than its rural counterpart.[18] Sabot [1977] explains this phenomenon as a result of persons being enticed to queue in the informal sector while awaiting employment in the relatively attractive modern urban sector, but a significant number of migrants having been pushed into marginal urban employment is at least as likely.

Because primogeniture is the traditional inheritance standard in much of Latin America, similar pressures to quit the land are present even where small-scale private farms dominate or where the more tenuous situation of sharecroppers' rights are involved. In other words, the intent of the *ejido* system to protect the integrity of the holding is nothing unusual in Latin America; the codification of custom by Mexican law merely places in relief a tradition found throughout Latin America.

AN ASIAN COUNTERPOINT

To emphasize the role of institutional arrangements, let us momentarily step out of the Latin America setting and look to India. There, neither the structural transformation nor urbanization has proceeded at a pace comparable to that of Latin America. In 1990, only 27 percent of India's population was urban and only 9 percent lived in cities of more than one million persons [UNDP 1990, table 22]. In terms of the transformation of the labor force, 62 percent of workers were employed in agriculture in 1991, while only 11 percent were associated with industry and 27 percent with services.[19] Let us assume a family in village India whose composition is similar to that of our hypothetical Mexican *ejido* family: father, mother, two sons, and two daughters.

The natural rate of population increase has been lower in India than in Mexico. For the period 1965-80, the reported rates were 3.1 percent per annum in Mexico and 2.3 percent for India [World Bank 1987, table 26]. Although the rate was lower for India, population growth nevertheless pressed on the carrying capacity of the cultivable land. The average farm size declined from 6.25 acres to 3.84 acres between 1953 to 1972 [Dantwala, 60, table 1]. The crucial questions concern how this pressure has been transmitted to individuals and, more specifically, how it has affected decisions to migrate. There are crucial differences in Mexican and Indian institutional factors, notably inheritance. According to Myrdal [241], Hindu and Muslim traditions provide for the division of a property inheritance among all siblings. In the context of standard migration models, each of the siblings is in the same boat. Because each sibling inherits land, the odds are enhanced for each finding a marriage partner in the home village or nearby. Where the Mexican system accelerates migration, faster than would occur in the standard structural transformation, inheritance institutions in India slow the process. This is the case because, for the most part, each child or sibling of a landholder can expect to enjoy a probability of unity to have some agricultural employment.

Although the Indian inheritance systems slow emigration, they simultaneously promote a preeminent problem of Indian agriculture. Indeed, Myrdal [1972, 241-2] singled out this factor as a major cause of the widely noted fragmentation of rural holdings in India.[20] Because of fragmentation, the expected earnings from each one of the siblings' holdings will likely be smaller than those of the parents. In India, over the period 1953-1972, the number of households with agricultural holdings of less than one acre grew by 132 percent, 15,360,000 to 35,640,000 [Dantwala 1986, table 1]. In 1971-2, this category of households accounted for 44.0 percent of all agricultural households, up from 31.5 percent in 1953-4. Moreover, the average size of these small holdings declined by about 50 percent. Because fragmentation pressures the rural wage to fall over time, it promotes rural-urban migration. If the focus is on population growth, the higher the rate of natural increase, the larger will be average family size, In turn, the greater the size of the family, the smaller will be each inherited plot. It follows that, with urban conditions given, the higher the rate of population growth, the larger will be the flow of migrants from rural environs.[21]

When we juxtapose the hypothetical Indian family with its Mexican counterpart, the Hindu and Muslim inheritance systems slow the transformation of the labor force. Indeed, when we compare the respective situations within the context of the standard migration model, the difference is starkly apparent. For some Mexican siblings, the expected rural earnings calculation yields a value of zero, making a spatial migratory move a certainty. For Indian siblings, a landholding may offer only a modicum of income in many instances, but there are associated advantages. It provides a place for constructing a residence which, in any case, is a major component in a poor family's economic struggle. Moreover, an humble rural residence serves as a base for operating in other economic sectors. Such options as craft manufacture and petty trade become possibilities whenever there are enough villages and small urban centers within a reasonably short radius to constitute a viable market. For the noninheriting Mexican siblings, the *ejido* village usually affords no opportunity to construct even a very modest dwelling.[22] They are pushed to make a spatial move if they are to enjoy the economic necessity of a dwelling.

In determining where to move, larger urban environs will be attractive to many young rural Mexicans. In a megalopolis such as the Mexican Federal District, there are hundreds of thousands of households that hire servants, the demand for which rises as the size and income of the modern sector grows. There are other menial wage employment opportunities that require little or no human capital, such as those associated with the hotel and restaurant trades. The urban economy offers economies of scale for many low-income self-employment categories as well as external economies [Cole and Sanders, 1985]. This is the case with the ubiquitous repair shops for automobiles and appliances as well as petty vending, shoe-shining, supervision of street parking, and impromptu services such as auto washing. Even begging requires some critical minimum of population to provide a precarious existence. At these lowest levels of urban self-employment, there are few barriers to entry.[23] The situation is at the opposite end of the spectrum from that encountered in the agricultural village where the probability of finding some form of employment is zero for many.

POPULATION GROWTH: GIVING THE DEVIL HIS DUE

The early dualism models treated population growth as a source of surplus labor and its pace determined the time required to complete the take off stage.[24] Because these were simple two-sector models, there was no anticipation of the development of large urban subsistence populations. There were only sketchy data on the incipient trends in fertility and mortality rates, so the modellers may be excused for slighting so important a factor. Its significance stands in relief only in hindsight. Indeed, when Lewis published his now classic article, few censuses had been taken after World War II and fewer still had been published. It was well into the 1960s before we began to get widespread confirmation that death rates had plummeted in many countries because of the introduction of Western medical technology, sanitation techniques, and pesticides (DDT) in the years immediately following World War II. By that time, apparently, the course of development theory was pretty much set. The theory was conceived in light of modest population growth. Not only did observers assume that the underlying rates were modest, they were even more naive about possibilities. Hagen placed the maximum biological growth rate at three percent per year and assumed that few, if any countries would ever approach it.[25] Against that backdrop, Todaro [1969] devised a migration theory that put all the explanatory eggs into the pull basket.

By now it should be manifest that population growth is intimately intertwined with several phenomena that characterize Latin America in the post-World War II decades: industrialization, urbanization, and extreme inequality. With Raul Prebisch and the Economic Commission for Latin America providing the intellectual cover, many Latin American countries embarked upon industrialization strategies that relied on import substitution. Several, including Mexico, were sufficiently successful to gain the status of a newly industrializing country or NIC. In those cases, the industrial mix became varied and deep enough to include capital goods production. Even analysts who decried protection and its price distortions conceded that industry was the engine of growth over that period. It is interesting, therefore, that it is the services sector that has shown the greatest growth, to 61 percent of GDP in 1992 (see table 1). Equally interesting is the fact that although services accounted for the lion's share of employment, 48 percent, that sector's share of output was much greater.

On the basis of simple averages, the service sector appears to represent the prosperous portion of the labor force. That, however, would be only a half truth. The likelihood is that the services sector is a source of the income inequality that has marked, or one might say, marred, Mexico's development efforts. Indeed, it is surely another example of dualism, featuring the extremely high incomes of financiers and professional persons, on the one hand, and the poverty-level incomes of urban subsistence laborers on the other. According to Munos et al., 73.5 percent of Mexico City's labor force of 1970 was in services [1977, 144]. Of that group, domestic, laundry, restaurant and hotel, and miscellaneous personal services accounted for about 25 percent and featured extremely low wages. Furthermore, of the women employed in all of the services sectors, 72 percent were unskilled [Munos et al. 1977, 83].

The comparison of the Mexican situation with that of India shows that not only did the economic transformation proceed further in Mexico, but so did urbanization and inequality. In 1990, 31 percent of India's GDP came from agriculture as compared to 9 percent of Mexico's. As earlier noted, only 26 percent of India's population was urban in 1992, compared to 74 percent for Mexico. India's income distribution demonstrates considerably more equality. When household income is distributed by quintiles, the upper fifth of households receives 5 times the amount of the lowest fifth. In Mexico, the top quintile receives 14 times the income going to the bottom quintile.

The analysis presented in this chapter shows that part of the explanation of these differences lies in the fact that the population growth rate has been significantly higher in Mexico. For the period 1960-70, India's rate of population increase averaged 2.3 percent while Mexico's average rate was 3.4 percent. In proportional terms, the economy of Mexico had to accommodate increasing numbers faster than did India's. It follows that the rate of natural urbanization was larger in Mexico. Moreover, the institutions of inheritance provide that fewer rural-born Mexicans than Indians were able to remain on the land. The analysis speaks clearly to the efficacy of using a rural incomes policy to stem rural-urban population flows. The provision of subsidies to agricultural producers would do little to raise the expected rural income for those whose probability of land ownership is zero or very low. Such policies would be efficacious in India, but not in Mexico. An edifice of effective policies requires a foundation of realistic analysis, which, itself, requires the consideration of the key institutional factors of the country or region under study.

ENDNOTES

1. Walter C. Neale's helpful comments are gratefully acknowledged. The usual caveats apply.

2. Michael Lipton [1988] and Michael Todaro [1969] are prime examples of this trend.

3. That is the case whether the movement is geographic, such as from one city to another or from the countryside to a primate city, or merely conceptual, as between economic sectors. Of course, one migratory event may involve the simultaneous change of economic sector and a geographic move. Whichever the case, the move is sparked by the existence of a higher wage at the end point of the move than at the origin. All of this is implicit in the general equilibrium model that demonstrates under restrictive assumptions that returns on investments will be equalized across firms and sectors in the long run. The movement of labor is part of that equilibrating mechanism, albeit a passive part. The development of the argument with specific relation to labor migration is found at least as early as Ravenstein [1885].

4. While Lewis [1954] did not equate traditional with rural, that became more or less a habit in the literature that followed. Especially noteworthy in that regard is the work of Ranis and Fei [1961]. Lewis [410-11] says "[E]arnings in the subsistence sector set a floor to wages in the [modern] sector, but in practice wages have to be higher than this, and there is usually a gap of 30 percent or more between [modern sector] wages and subsistence earnings." Cost-of-living differences, psychological factors, and conventions are said to account for the differential.

5. This assumption is implicit in Todaro's [1969] equation for expected rural income wherein no employment probability coefficient is used to discount the existing rural wage.

6. This approach first appeared in Todaro [1969]. Cole and Sanders [1985] argued that the rural-urban migration movement is better understood when a distinction is made between the spatial movement of the educated and the relatively uneducated. They granted, nevertheless, that even the uneducated were attracted by the wage differential between what they called the rural subsistence and the urban subsistence sectors.

7. The United Nations endeavors to have member countries use 20,000 inhabitants as the watershed marker between rural and urban. Obviously, I have chosen a figure that is reasonably close to that marker, but which allows us ease in calculation. In practice, not many countries comply with United Nations wishes on this matter. In some cases, the break occurs with a population as low as 2,500.

8. Drakakis-Smith [33] says that a stereotypical pattern has assumed that most migrants "sought work in a series of step-like moves up the urban hierarchy at increasing distance from their point of origin. In other words, they would first migrate to a nearby small town."

9. When there is spatial movement of labor, it is rationalized as labor increments at the margin moving to match up with complementary resources in a way that maximizes the return to labor. In that context, it makes sense to say that the unit of labor was pulled or attracted to its sectoral or spatial destinations.

10. In theory, the increase in the population growth rate might occur because life expectancy has increased for any and every age cohort. In the Mexican case, as in others, the decrease in the death rate has affected all ages, but the impact has been greatest among infants and children. This is clear when one compares population pyramids (bar graphs of population displayed by age cohorts) for successive censuses in Mexico [*Mexico Demografico*, 17-21].

11. In 1960, at a time when the pressure of urban-bound migration was accelerating, 54 percent of all agriculturalists in Mexico were found on small farms (5 hectares or less). Furthermore, the *ejido* farms accounted for 85 percent of farmland cultivated by the small farmer group. These data are taken from the *IV Censos Agricola, Ganadero, y Ejidal, 1960*, tables 2 and 12.

12. The usufruct, or use right, is forfeited if the land remains uncultivated for two consecutive years.

13. Articles 81 and 82 of the *Ley Federal de Reforma Agraria* treat inheritance of the usufruct. It provides that the *ejitario* (head of household) has the right to designate the successor to the usufruct. This is accomplished by presenting a succession list, in order of preference, to the *ejido* assembly. The list may include any children and the spouse. In theory, any one of them may head the list. The operative point is that only one person can inherit the plot.

14. Some males, therefore, are engaged in rural-rural migration. Furthermore, they move with the harvests: the work itself is migratory in nature.

15. For example, 56.3 percent of the migrant population of Mexico City and environs was female (43.7 percent was male) in 1970 [Munos, 45].

16. This is shown in Mexican census data reported in Munos [43].

17. Using economic terminology, barriers to entry are very low for self-employment as street vendors, shoe-shiners, and operators of charcoal-fired taco stands.

18. Sabot [1977] discusses this phenomenon and refers to studies that have reported observing it.

19. *Human Development Report 1993*, table 17, and the dates refer specifically to the years 1989-91.

20. Fragmentation should be understood separately from the declining size of average holding. A holding is often composed of several plots that are not contiguous. This occurs largely because of the inheritance system that calls for equal division among all siblings. When two village members marry, each may bring to the union a holding consisting of several scattered plots. Obviously the degree of fragmentation will increase over time.

21. Put in terms of Todaro's model, smaller plot size would translate to a lower level of expected rural income.

23. This discussion of barriers to entry and probability of employment in the urban subsistence sector is taken from Cole and Fayissa [783-4].

24. Specifically, Ranis and Fei argued that the faster population grew, the more prolonged would be the take-off period.

25. Quoted in Higgins [318].

REFERENCES

Barbosa-Ramirez, Rene. *Empleo, Desempleo, y Subempleo en el Sector* Agropecuerio. Mexico City: Centro de Investigaciones Agrarias, 1979.

Cole, William and Bichaka Fayissa. "The Urban Subsistence Labor Force: Toward a Policy-Oriented and Empirically Accessible Taxonomy." *World Development* 19 (July 1991): 779-89.

Cole, William and Richard Sanders. "Internal Migration and Urban Employment in the Third World." *American Economic Review* 75 (June 1985): 481-94.

Consejo Nacional de Poblacion. *Mexico Demografico*. Mexico City, 1982.

Dantwala, M. L. *Indian Agricultural Development since Independence*. New Delhi: Oxford and IBH Publishing Co., 1986.

Direccion General de Estadistica. *IV Censos Agricola, Ganadero, y Ejidal*. Mexico City, 1965.

Drakakis-Smith, David. *The Third World City*. New York: Methuen, 1987.

Gordon, Wendell. *The Economy of Latin America*. New York: Columbia University Press, 1950.

Gregory, Peter. *The Myth of Market Failure*. Baltimore: The Johns Hopkins University Press, 1986.

Higgins, Benjamin. *Economic Development*. New York: W. W. Norton, 1959.

Lewis, W. Arthur. "Economic Development with Unlimited Supplies of Labour." *The Manchester School* 22 (May 1954): 139-91.

Lipton, Michael. "Why Poor People Stay Poor: Urban Bias in World Development." In Josef Gugler, ed., *The Urbanization of the Third World*. New York: Oxford University Press, 1988.

Munos, Humberto, et al. *Migracion y Desigualidad Social en la Ciudad de Mexico*. Mexico City: Instituto de Investigaciones Sociales (UNAM) and Colegio de Mexico, 1977.

Myrdal, Gunnar. *Asian Drama* (abridged). New York: Vintage Books, 1972.

Nacional Financiera. *La Economia Mexicana en Cifras*. Mexico City, 1965.

Poulson, Barry. *Economic Development: Private and Public Choice*. St. Paul: West Publishing Co., 1994.

Ranis, Gustav and J. C. H. Fei. "A Theory of Economic Development." *American Economic Review*. (September 1961): 333-58.

Ravenstein, E. G. "The Laws of Migration." *Journal of the Royal Statistical Society* 48 (June 1885): 167-227, and 52 (June 1889): 241-89.

Rincon Serrano, Romeo. *El Ejido Mexicano*. Mexico City: Centro Nacional de Investigaciones Agrarias, 1980.

Sabot, R. H. "The Meaning and Measurement of Urban Surplus Labour," *Oxford Economic Papers* 29 (November 1977): 389-411.

Todaro, Michael. "A Model of Labor Migration and Urban Unemployment in Less Developed Countries." *American Economic Review* 59 (March 1969): 138-48.

United Nations Development Program. *Human Development Report*. New York: Oxford University Press, 1990.

World Bank, *World Development Report*. New York: Oxford University Press, various years.

IV. INSTITUTIONAL CHANGE IN THE INTERNATIONAL ECONOMY

CHAPTER 10

INSTITUTIONAL ADJUSTMENT AND ECONOMIC DEVELOPMENT: INSIGHTS FROM THE ETIOLOGY OF PRIVATIZATION

William P. Glade
University of Texas

POLICY TRAILBLAZING ALONG TWO PATHS

The year 1917 was pivotal in the emergence of economic development policy, for in that year two countries embarked on radically new paths of growth in which social and political reconstruction was linked with state-management of economic relationships. Although, as Alexander Gerschenkron and others have noted, late industrializers on the Continent and in Japan had already resorted to state intervention and/or development banking to accelerate and redirect change into patterns different from what the market, unaided, would have supported,[1] the Soviet Union and Mexico, as precursors of mid-century developments, went much beyond the earlier cases. Differing from each other in the route chosen, as a policy pioneer, each was caught up in years of path-dependent experimentation and adaptation. Neither country had precedents to emulate, neither could draw on technical assistance from multilateral agencies or aid from leading countries, and each had to chart its new course before development studies had provided empirical and theoretical guidelines.

The Soviet Union, notwithstanding (or, *après* Crane Brinton, because of) a growth spurt in late Czarist years, launched the policy trajectory of the Great October Socialist Revolution by massive seizures of property. There soon followed the modern era's first privatization program when War Communism gave way to the New Economic Policy in an effort to restore some measure of organizational discipline and to rescue production. In time, the NEP was itself displaced by a radical reorganization of land tenure and by centralized economic planning, changes that consolidated a regime in which power and decisional authority of all sorts were as concentrated and hierarchical as the planning mechanism itself. In this regime the development of heavy industry became the centerpiece of policy. The civil strife of this era laid waste a vast amount of territory, physical capital, and cultural resources, not to mention an appalling loss of life. Of greater relevance to this analysis, however, is the nature of the institutional system that composed the new structure of central planning, which obliterated most pre-revolutionary organizational forms and the behavioral instructions encoded therein, save for the instruments of autocratic control and terror.

The second pioneering country, Mexico, had just come out of several years of revolutionary turbulence, with considerable sacrifice of life and property, when in 1917 it enacted a new constitution.[2] This was to serve as a general blueprint for the social and economic architecture it then proceeded to build as a replacement for the several decades of export-led growth that had preceded the Revolution. The vehicle chosen for the new pattern of development was a mixed economy under the tutelage of the state and its bureaucracy, for which the point of departure was likewise a sweeping change in land tenure.[3] In time, industrial development was promoted by both market circumstances and policy, and by the late 1940s this was expressed formally in a policy model christened import substituting industrialization (I-S-I). In Mexico (and in Turkey) public authorities did not attempt to repeal all, or even most, prerevolutionary institutions, including the market, although the social organization of the economy was certainly modified in ways that selectively muted the force of the market. Other institutions--in governance, religion, cultural expression, and so on--were in varying degrees reconfigured as well. Thus, the Banco Nacional de Mexico, established in the early 1880s, continues to operate to this day, while the famous Fundidora of Monterrey, the first integrated iron and steel works in Latin America, lasted from its establishment just before the turn of the century until it closed in the 1980s.

Whereas the policy regime put together by Soviet authorities was in due course imposed on the country's western neighbors and exported east to China, North Korea, and eventually Southeast Asia as well, the policy designs that were devised in the 1940s and 1950s in a great many other countries of the so-called Third World came to look very much like the Mexican (and Turkish) template. Thus, the two development strategies that originated in the events of 1917 are invested with an analytical interest that considerably transcends a comparative study of policy systems of the two countries alone. The growth paths initiated by the USSR on the one hand and Mexico and Turkey on the other differed, however, quite substantially from each other, not least in the process of institution building they implied. This chapter explores the institution-building process fundamental to these two historic growth paths.

Developments that came to a head in both the Soviet Union and Mexico in the 1970s and '80s motivated each country to undertake comprehensive economic reform, which has embraced two conceptually distinct but complementary sets of policies: those that stabilize and restructure the macro-level environment and those that alter micro-level behavior. The evacuation by the state of significant portions of the economic territory it once dominated through direct and indirect intervention has reshaped macroeconomic dynamics at the same time that it has compelled firms to deal with types and degrees of competition from which they were long sheltered. Moreover, the policy process itself has changed in ways that were scarcely anticipated only a few years ago when Communist rule seemed permanently ensconced throughout the Soviet Bloc and the I-S-I model of industrialization looked to be no less durable.[4] That structural adjustment is so pervasive nowadays, in less developed and newly industrialized countries (LDCs and NICs) as well as in former centrally planned economies (ex-CPEs), indicates that in late twentieth-century policy discourse, markets have become more contestable than they have been for decades.

In advanced industrial economies, no less than in developing economies and economies in transition, market-based growth has come to be seen by many as preferable to the modernist tradition in which the invisible hand of supply and demand was, in varying measure, overshadowed by the very visible hand of activist public policy. The long-reigning interventionism that began with Otto von Bismarck and grew almost steadily thereafter, with the evolution of the regulatory state, got a special impetus with the arrival of the Keynesian revolution in macroeconomic management, and the hubris of the brief era of "fine tuning." Lately, however, this interventionist policy framework has been challenged increasingly by policy options that seem, at least on the surface, to be notably less statist. Under the Margaret Thatcher government in England and a series of administrations in the United States, beginning with that of President Jimmy Carter, the downsizing of the public sector has, accompanied by deregulation, become almost a leitmotif of policy [Swann 1988]. In Germany, France, Spain, Italy, and even Sweden and Austria, the change in policy direction has been no less notable.[5]

As time went on, the rich theoretical and analytical literature on market failure, which was for a long time used to interpret, if not justify, so much intervention, was overtaken by a no less compelling literature on public-sector failure and rent-seeking.[6] In advanced industrial economies, concerns with crowding-out, faltering productivity, and stagflation were added to the mix, while in developing and newly industrialized countries the denouement of the debt crisis seemed to signal the exhaustion of the policy model first concocted in Mexico (and Turkey) and then taken aboard, with variations, on such a widespread basis elsewhere.[7] For these, the fiscal crisis of the state, under prevailing circumstances, left few policy options open.[8] Meanwhile, in a process still not fully understood, the CPEs reached the end of the line and one after another abandoned the policy itinerary that had been envisioned, at least partly, some 70 years before in St. Petersburg. The contrasting experiences with structural reform are unusually instructive for the light they shed on the nature of development and the exigencies of transition. And although privatization is only a part of this complex enterprise, it nevertheless affords a particularly revealing glimpse into the social processes that undergird economic growth.

THE CONTEXTUAL ANALYSIS OF ECONOMIC RESTRUCTURING

Structural adjustment, as policy reform is usually styled, has sometimes been called marketization, a somewhat inelegant term for the ensemble of policies that broaden the decisional domain determined by market forces. Thus, liberalization of foreign trade and exchange markets, the abolition of price controls and subsidies in product and factor markets, the ending of financial repression and the reduction or abolition of qualitative or selective credit controls, and the removal of restrictions on foreign and domestic investment all aim to introduce more market signals and relationships into allocative decisions. For its part, macroeconomic stabilization, through a combination of fiscal and monetary reforms, provides the foundation on which this canonical World Bank and International Monetary Fund (IMF) policy package depends for its efficacy; absent stabilization, the difficulty of implementing the other policies is compounded.[9]

The micro-level policy of privatization and macroeconomic stabilization are, with deregulation, subsumed under marketization and economic restructuring. But privatization, though only part of the prescription, can be taken as emblematic of the broader reform program and considered separately to trace the connection of all these processes with relationships not fully captured in most discussion of the macro policies of structural adjustment or micro strategies of privatization. Macroeconomic stabilization and "getting prices right" through deregulation are, for example, of undeniable importance in promoting economic recovery; without them other adjustments in policy, including privatization, are rendered much more difficult if not impossible. Yet, macroeconomic stabilization and the other conventional props of structural adjustment, like privatization itself, elide a number of more fundamental changes that need to be taken into account when either LDC or ex-CPE reform strategies are examined. The conventional approach usually takes the efficiency conditions of privatization as sufficient to indicate why we can take privatization alone as our focus in this inquiry.[10]

Privatization policies in their several variants conform managerial behavior in enterprises to market guidelines, above all in the substitution of a hard budget constraint for a soft budget constraint.[11] A shift in asset ownership may or may not be involved; the key is the kind of managerial decision-making that results from the policy structure in a given environment. Hence, though privatization deals with firms' behavior while marketization refers to the context within which firms operate, the structural features of the economy that are relevant for designing and assessing reform measures, macro- as well as micro-level, necessarily include factors of the institutional environment that fall into the aforementioned elision. For example, marketization, in practice, must involve not only privatization of decision-making at the firm level but also deprivatization at the macro-level: i.e., extinguishing the opportunities for rent-seeking that have proliferated over the years in the public policy framework. While deregulation is the essence of today's reforms, the process may also involve initiating regulation to deal with information problems that might otherwise impair market performance and ensure that enterprises that confront neither domestic nor foreign competition, even with economic opening, behave as if they were operating in a competitive environment. A fair number of countries on the privatization path have discovered needs for regulation in public utility fields, safeguards for the integrity and stability of banking and insurance institutions, and for the proper working of security exchanges.[12]

All this, in turn, implies looking into the social matrix of market-based and power-based behavior to examine the extent to which the private management of non-market relationships, especially the levers of public policy, are habitually used to manipulate a system's economic opportunity structure and access thereto. Hence, though privatization and the larger program of restructuring center on market signalled behaviors, modified where necessary by regulations, the whole project of policy therapy with which they are associated requires, for successful design and implementation, the kind of understanding of systemic structure that generally comes from the analytical territory covered by political economy.[13]

By the same token, the social efficiency of managerial decisions taken in a marketized context of macroeconomic stability, deregulation, and so on will depend on the degree to which the decisional process is vulnerable to market failure in one guise or another. Absent a carefully calibrated intervention to rectify conditions that produce market failure, the hoped-for gains from marketization and privatization will likely prove illusory. Successful privatization, therefore, requires not only a reasonably reliable overarching market framework, it also presupposes, as an integral feature of that framework, broad development of the institutional capacity needed to support productivity-enhancing privatized decision making at the managerial level. And institution building, historically a time-consuming and complicated process that involves, essentially, the production of public goods, has perforce entailed at least some degree of state initiative and sanction.[14] Laying down the "legal foundations of capitalism," to invoke a familiar phrase, is, along with much else that sails under the banner of institution building, primarily a state-based process, even when the actual elaboration and management of economic organizations falls on the shoulders of the private sector.[15]

The context in which privatization operates will vary from place to place, and along with it the variables that need to be taken into account. In Nigeria and Malaysia questions of ethnicity intrude because in each, one ethnic group has tended to dominate the market-guided domain while another has held the advantage in the political arena. Ethnonationalism also played a role in the separation of the Czech and Slovak republics during their reform process, just as it has, in a more sanguinary way, in the states that once composed Yugoslavia. In other instances, it may be necessary to disentangle, both analytically and in policy, the organization of state-owned enterprises from the party apparatus that once sat, or still sits, in control of government and that customarily used, or still uses, the armamentarium of interventionist measures to fashion whatever degree of political equilibrium has been achieved. India and Mexico come to mind in this respect, so far as concerns still-ruling parties, while the situation that bedevils Russia and other ex-CPEs demonstrates how a self-aggrandizing and tenacious nomenklatura has proved adept in perpetuating its privileged position.[16] Even in economies in which civil society has waxed strong, as in the United States, any alteration in public expenditure runs up against the reality that preparation of the fiscal budget occurs amid a vast encampment of interest-groups, each mobilized to defend and, if possible, expand the piece of the rent-producing expenditure-tax territory it has come to view as an entitlement.

A review of different conditions that have given birth to privatization programs clarifies the factors that are relevant to both the design of policy and the prospects for successful implementation, to say nothing of understanding the social processes that envelop and shape economic reform programs in general. To construct an etiology of privatization, we take most of our observations from the recent experience of Russia and other ex-CPEs, on the one hand, and Mexico and other Latin American cases on the other. Although privatization is usually associated with failure, this juxtaposition of cases shows that it is important to distinguish the level at which failure occurs and to differentiate the cases of failure from instances in which privatization is actually indicative of a more positive set of circumstances.

PRIVATIZATION TO REMEDY SYSTEMIC FAILURE

It is certainly the case that in Latin American economies, as in other LDCs, the shortcomings of the parastatal sector often originated beyond the organizational boundaries of the enterprises themselves and in this sense may be chalked up not so much to poor management as to policy failure or public-sector failure: e.g., the use of regulated prices on parastatal output, or parastatal purchases to subsidize favored firms and populations, the required employment of redundant or ill-qualified workers for political patronage, and the location of parastatal operations in inhospitable backward regions to jumpstart their development. Poor management, itself, generally is found nested in a larger failure: i.e., in faulty administrative and/or legislative oversight (the principal-agent problem). Problems of enterprise accountability abounded from the start. When the size of the parastatal sector grew relative to GDP, and its complexity increased as well, the accountability problem was compounded. As time went on, the public treasury was burdened with mounting bills, and frequently foreign debts, for covering the deficits of the parastatal companies whose performance was so weakly monitored.

Throughout Latin America a variety of deficiencies in the organization of the public sector chronically hindered the ability of state-owned firms to meet economic performance standards consistent with sustained growth. Besides the problems already noted, decisional rigidity, bureaucratic suboptimization through goal displacement and substitution, corruption, and so on grew worse as the parastatal sector expanded, generally unchecked by market discipline. In due course, the fiscal congestion to which this gave rise not only led to crowding out and macroeconomic instability (with the monetization of swelling deficits) but also to undermining the capacity of the state to invest in welfare, education, and health.[17] What is more, the decisions taken by parastatal management often proved no more likely than those of private firms to internalize externalities for social benefit. Though less immediately threatening than Chernobyl, the damage inflicted on both the natural and cultural environment by Petroleos Mexicanos, a government-owned oil and petrochemical company, has easily matched the notorious environmental contamination produced by state industry in the ex-CPEs. All over the continent, public policy failures have accelerated environmental degradation in a multitude of forms: e.g., massive deforestation, erosion, destruction of coastal ecology, rising salinity in irrigated land. Government failure has done as much as market failure to sap the chances for sustained development.

Directly and indirectly, weaknesses of the parastatal sector contributed to overborrowing by almost all the Latin American countries, save Colombia, during the 1970s and early '80s, so that when the end of debt-led development came in 1982, privatization was but one of several measures instituted to restore some capacity for growth to countries which had no possibility for continuing to pursue their customary policy preferences.[18] Although the ensuing years have often been labeled a "lost decade of development," Pedro Aspe has rightly noted that the real "lost decades" consisted of the excesses and policy failures of the run-up to 1982, when policy rectification could have made far better use of the external resources then available.

Troublesome as were the problems of the NICs, they pale by comparison with those of the ex-CPEs. By far the most dramatic instance of systemic failure took place in the Soviet Bloc economies where, following a protracted period of poor economic performance, planning regimes imploded in a process still not altogether clear.[19] Here, as in Chile, or even the early NEP, the resuscitation of production has been the primary motive for privatization, though in most of the ex-CPEs the efficacy of such programs has been problematic as the agenda of reform entails a reconstitution of virtually the whole economic structure. To be sure, in Hungary, Poland, the Czech and Slovak Republics, Slovenia, and Croatia, the prospects for success seem reasonably bright, thanks to the greater historical proximity of experience with a market-organized economy, the earlier introduction of partial reforms in the post-war period (except in Czechoslovakia), and to greater interaction with the West prior to 1989.[20] In Poland and Hungary, even before the demise of Communism, some Western price ratios were imported, albeit on a quite limited basis, in an incipient cross-border trade that expanded rapidly after the end of central planning and the opening of the economy. In Hungary, the retail and service sector, as well as some manufacturing plants, had experienced a series of reforms dating back to the late 1960s when the New Economic Mechanism shifted the locus of more decision making to enterprise managers.[21] The Yugoslav economy, meanwhile, had become even more marketized, and for a longer period of time. In these economies, the changes of 1989 did not launch them entirely into a total institutional void, and a modest amount of multilateral help and foreign direct investment since 1989 must be reckoned additional advantages.[22]

For the cases that stretch from the Baltic states through Croatia and Slovenia, its proved possible, for reasons of proximity and outsider interest, to import substantial blocs of organizational structure and practice. Large sections of the Western price structure moved with traded goods, at least as reference prices for anchoring the eventual adjustment. Commercial and banking practices were revised through emulation or, as in Poland, through restructuring the old banking system as regional banking networks and relying on management contracts to prepare institutions for privatization. In some cases, firms were converted into joint ventures with foreign banking concerns. Also imported by CEF countries were business school and social science curricula, securities exchanges with an appropriate regulatory framework, commercial and property law in general, managerial and cost accounting practices, marketing and distribution systems, and industry standards as the targets for eventual attainment.

The former German Democratic Republic is a special case, having been taken, tout ensemble, into the protective custody of the strongest of the Western European economies.[23] Even there, the incompatibility of the pre-reform system with the operating requirements of modern industrial economy posed obstacles that have made absorption of the *funf neuer Länder* an unexpectedly expensive and thorny process. As one recent work puts it, in alluding to the reunification of Germany, "A description of the East German economic system prior to 1990 (supposedly the best case of the Soviet bloc) reads like an economist's nightmare" [Giersch et al. 1993, 257]. This much conceded, wholesale institutional importation, managed by the Treuhandanstalt, has been an option unavailable to any of the others, along with massive subsidy through the currency conversion, the setting of wage scales in post-unified eastern firms, and the conferring on the new population of all the benefits of the social market economy, undiluted.

In the successor states to the former Soviet Union, however, the challenge of systemic reconstruction has been particularly formidable, owing to the longevity and rigor of the central planning experience, the greater isolation of firms from contact with the market economy of the West,[24] and the resultant greater degradation of whatever market-friendly institutional "software" had been incorporated into Russian economic organization prior to wholesale nationalization and the institution of central planning in the Soviet period.[25] A multitude of studies have over the years revealed how shot through with organizational weaknesses was the institutional style of central planning, starting with the lack of transparency in allocational decision processes and the unavailability of market prices to provide reliable information on preferences and relative scarcity and, hence to signal alternative values. The outright suppression of markets in capital and land complicated allocative processes and contributed further to the informational asphyxiation that plagued the economy, growing worse as the industrial structure increased in complexity [Banerjee and Spagat 1991, 646-660]. Alongside the deleterious impacts of the soft-budget constraint and the lack of competition on enterprise efficiency, the risk-averse incentive structure discouraged innovation and led to pervasive technological backwardness outside such priority fields as weaponry,[26] for which condition the barriers to interaction between Soviet firms and the rest of the world posed an addition complication. Withal, the forfeiting of enterprise flexibility and the built-in combination of hoarding and scarcity decried by Janos Kornai created persisting difficulties at the microeconomic level. Of special relevance to performance potential in a market context was the tendency of ministry-led combines to go overboard on vertical integration and minimize transactional dependence on other decisional nodes at the cost of building greater connectivity among firms scattered across industries and sectors. Considering the distorted nature of information flows[27] and the very limited play afforded feedback mechanisms, it was a system that was afflicted by a radical learning disability.

Against this background, it is not merely the strained political situation that has produced so much expectational and policy uncertainty in the economies in transition.[28] Policy credibility and predictability have been undermined by the existence of so many lacunae in the institutional fabric of the ex-CPEs, such that the linkage between policy inputs and policy outcomes is subject to much greater uncertainty than it is in the West, where, even in more certain circumstances, lags of various sorts render imprecise the application of corrective or compensatory fiscal and monetary policies.[29] In the new Russian economy, in particular, the market-compatible, behavioral programming contained in the organizational DNA, as it were, of the firm is conspicuously scarce.[30] Thus, market-based reforms have been difficult to implement, with any confidence in the reliability of assumptions about the firm behavior that results, so long as the institutions that constitute the market are still in embryonic form, at best. Understandably, the fragile new governments of the region have not exactly jumped with alacrity into the shock therapy that some have counselled, however compelling the case for catching potential resistance off guard and shifting resources quickly into more productive uses. That the outcome of shock therapy programs has been salutary at all can probably be attributable not to successive approximations of market optimality in any refined sense but to the distance to which economies were operating behind their production possibility frontiers and to the fact that waste composed such a large portion of output that almost any redirection of productive factors would likely result in a net gain.

PRIVATIZATION, MICRO-LEVEL FAILURE, AND SYSTEMIC GROWTH

Most anecdotal discussions of privatization in LDCs emphasize really egregious cases of micro-level mismanagement where the evidence of failure tends to be unmistakable and the arguments for remedial privatization the most persuasive. For example, managerial deficiencies in the state-owned petroleum company of Argentina, the YPF, were notorious and could hardly be concealed when contrasted with the well-run Venezuelan nationalized oil enterprise, or the reasonably efficient Brazilian version, because international industry performance standards are so readily available. So, too, with the Argentine government's telephone company, its gas company, and its flagship airline. The examples abound: e.g., Petroleos Mexicanos or Pemex, Aeromexico, the bulk of the Peruvian parastatal sector, and a host of other cases exhibiting very nearly every business shortcoming that one could imagine. Labor redundancy, the favoritism shown privileged suppliers and privileged customers of parastatals, patronage sinecures in management (the Brazilian "maharajahs," the Argentine military officers managing Fabricaciones Militares), the benefits reaped by private investors in joint ventures with the state--the list of problems is almost endless.

Nonetheless, although privatization is often enough a child of failure, another reading of the record yields the conclusion that it can sometimes, perhaps more often than one might expect, be construed a child of success. In most privatizations in Western Europe, for example, this is abundantly plain. In the first place, one force driving the process was the success of regional integration, which had limited the ability of governments to operate their firms in ways much different from private management and thus inadvertently facilitated their later absorption by the private sector. More fundamentally, no doubt, it was the high quality of managerial, technical, and skilled labor resources generally available in the European labor market that combined with strong standards of professionalism and the prestige of positions in parastatal service to reinforce the organizational capacity of the state-owned firms, and their efficiency.[31] While it might seem odd to interpret many Latin American privatizations as likewise a product of success, such a case can certainly be made.

Even before the reforms of recent times, the growing business resiliency of the region was foreshadowed in the growth of manufacturing exports from Brazil, Mexico,[32] and elsewhere from the 1960s onward, including, as a particularly challenging case, sales of aircraft into highly competitive international markets by Embraer, a Brazilian government-owned corporation [Lord 1992]. The technical and business solidity of Petrobras, Brazil's nationalized oil company, of Braspetro, its affiliate for international operations, and of the state-owned Companhia Vale do Rio Doce, an immense mining conglomerate now being privatized, were also widely recognized.[33] So, too, with the internationally respected Petroleos de Venezuela, which even embarked on a profitable program of vertical integration by downstream acquisitions in the European and U.S. markets. These are only some of the most newsworthy instances, barometers of the build up of a much more widespread economic capacity. One has only to compare, for example, the yellow pages in a current telephone directory of any Latin American capital city or other major metropolitan area with the same section of, say, 30 years ago. The variety of business, professional, and engineering services that support investment and operating efficiency in the industrial sector has grown enormously, and so have the number and quality of institutions of higher education and research, to say nothing of the diversity of the industrial sector itself, wherein a great amount of organizational learning, no small part of it under challenging circumstances, has taken place.[34]

The survival capacity of Chilean manufacturing stands as a particular case in point. Nurtured during decades of secular inflation by the standard package of government inducements and protections, the long-coddled sector was in short order subjected to two successive wrenching reorientations of public policy in the 1970s: first the impulsive but comprehensive nationalizations undertaken by President Salvador Allende, which produced an extensive breakdown of management and in time a dramatic fall in output, and then the no less far-reaching and abrupt reversal of policy by General Augusto Pinochet. On top of these dislocations, the Pinochet reprivatizations took place amid a rapid lowering of tariff barriers and non-tariff forms of protection, accompanied by a deliberately overvalued exchange rate that, in effect, subsidized imports. To be sure, manufacturing output fell initially, though this was partly attributable to recession, and to the privileged price of imports, but the industrial sector proved able to endure these troubles and in time resumed its expansion, with reorganized product lines and improved products and production methods, in the context of an open economy. Further, notwithstanding the havoc that shook Chilean banking in the early 1980s, when the system collapsed, the striking aspect of the restructuring that Chile undertook is how quickly economic authorities moved along the learning curve. They introduced mid-course policy corrections, and carried out a privatization project that was highly complementary to the other policies of the day.[35] In a very few cases was there any difficulty in divesting enterprises from the state's portfolio of holdings, and, indeed, innovative privatization of the social security system was a major step forward in augmenting the investible resources available through the capital market.

No less striking has been the rapidity with which Argentina and Mexico have been able to implement large-scale privatization programs and Brazil's success in privatizing such major industries as iron-and-steel, petrochemicals, and fertilizers despite the indecisive policies of the presidency prior to Fernando Henrique Cardoso. The capacity of these economies to handle massive rebalancing of the public and private sectors while regenerating themselves attests to their success over the years in building up the institutional accoutrements of a market economy and well-qualified, experienced enterprise management. Such was, for instance, demonstrated in the exceptionally quick turnaround of the Argentine YPF oil company, which moved from deficits and demoralized management to profitability and the beginning of an aggressive overseas expansion through the acquisition of a U.S. oil company with far-flung international holdings. In fact, the new vigor of Latin American capital markets and their ability to recover from the Mexican peso shock, the renewal of portfolio investments and general foreign investor interest in the emerging markets of the region, and the return of Latin American borrowers to Euromoney and New York markets all point to a new maturity of institutional capacity that is the product of decades of evolution--not the quick switch in policy of the last decade.

Perhaps no evidence is more telling than the unprecedented growth of foreign direct investment by Latin American firms in each other's markets through the acquisition of privatized assets and FDI, and even in Europe and the United States. Increasingly, Latin American firms also participate in strategic business alliances. These changes mark the coming of age, as it were, of the region's enterprise sector. The Mexican cement company that has operating subsidiaries in Spain, Venezuela, and the United States; the Mexican-Venezuelan joint venture in setting up a hemispheric-wide television production and broadcasting enterprise (which also enjoys a significant share of the Hispanic market in the United States); the export of television programming to Europe from Mexico and Brazil; and the acquisition by Mexican firms of a major seed company, of glass-making operations, and of plants and companies in still other branches of production in the United States all point to the maturation of a business system that has been able to move well beyond the sheltered markets of yesteryear.

Indeed, no marker of this institutional maturation, and the increasing density of organizational structure, is more convincing than the fact that Mexico has felt able to enter into a free trade agreement with Canada and the United States and that in the same period it qualified for admission into the OECD. The former, especially, was a giant step forward. Never before had economies so disparate in the levels of development been able to negotiate such an arrangement with the reasonable expectation that it would eventually come to full fruition.

CONCLUSIONS

So viewed, the strategy of state-led growth and change that was announced in Mexico in 1917, began on a regional basis in the 1930s and ended with a national debt crisis in the 1980s, can be seen as a period of rather more positive accomplishment than emerges from the conventional neoclassical reading. Behind the moving frontier of industrial policy and other forms of intervention, in commercial policy and financial markets particularly, there was a great deal of institutional infilling, an impressive accumulation of human and organizational capital that enabled the economies of the region to carry off effective economic restructuring with much more ease than was possible in the countries that followed the Soviet route.[36] In retrospect, while in Mexico the market was accorded a hegemonic position rather than nullified, as in the Bolshevik experiment, it was by no means left untouched. In fact, the market in Mexico was reshaped and subordinated continuously and extensively to the ends of public policy. The results were historically quite respectable increases in real factor productivity, sustained through several decades [Maddison et al. 1992].

Thanks to the institution-building carried out over decades as the very cornerstone of the national development project, a process explicitly envisaged in the 1917 Mexican Constitution, the economic landscape of Mexico, and of the region that followed in train, has been transformed. Countries that only ten years ago looked to be mired in a so-called "lost decade of development" have rebounded to display a resiliency and versatility that augurs well for the future. The structural undergirding of social or organizational capital provided by policy, and no little investment of resources, has paid off as a type of public good generating a wide range of externalities useful in reconfiguring the Mexican economy.[37] Clearly, institutions matter, and they matter so much that getting prices right is essentially epiphenominal compared with getting institutions right. This, together with the growing evidence from East Asia on successful strategies of governmental guidance and market management, suggests that economies in transition could profitably study both sets of Latin American and Asian experiences to find alternatives to the strategies for systemic rehabilitation that have been proposed with such fanfare from the West.

In point of fact, advocated macro-level treatments often have been modified in actual practice by provision of a considerable amount of technical assistance that has to do with building a more productive institutional framework for economic transactions. Nowhere is this plainer than in the case of the restructuring programs enunciated by the World Bank, in which a subtext of micro-level organizational reformation had, in fact, been a recurrent leitmotif. For that matter, the inter-governmental programs initiated by the United States, modest as they have been, and by the European Commission and some of its constituent governments, have centered on this understanding even more explicitly than have the multilateral programs of the World Bank and the IMF.[38]

For both diagnostic or analytical purposes and therapeutic or normative purposes, therefore, it is essential to unpack the related but different social processes that are so often conflated in discussions of restructuring, which, at most, get into questions of sequencing but not implementing components--except insofar as this latter is implied, but seldom much developed, by those who favor gradualism over the "big bang" strategies. The larger vision of transformation portrayed by grand strategy is, of course, necessary to map the general direction of change, to help reduce uncertainties to calculable risks, and, perhaps, to inspire. But ultimately it is what goes on at the ground-level, where organizational or social capital is accumulated and human resources developed, that will ultimately decide which grand strategy is ultimately successful and therefore instrumentally valid, the point that has consistently been the position of institutional and structuralist schools of development. Once again we are reminded that, as the contrasting historical experiences of Mexico and the Soviet Union ironically attest, God (or the Devil) is in the details.

ENDNOTES

1. Gerschenkron [1962] and Lockwood [1954], among others, including Veblen in his essays on Japan and Germany, observed that the late developing capitalist industrializers relied heavily on public policy to promote structural transformation.

2. The policy strategy that took shape in Mexico during the long ordeal of revolution and social transformation bears a remarkable similarity to what evolved, quite independently, during the same era in Turkey, where social engineering likewise moved in tandem with political reorganization and economic reconstruction. It was in 1917 that the fate of the Ottoman Empire was sealed by the collapse of the Czarist regime, the entry of the United States into the Great War, and the new military operations mounted by the Allies in the Balkans and the Middle East. Owing to these, the actual demise of the regime came close

on the heels of the end of the Great War. The Turkish case is set in a wider context of late nineteenth century industrialization in Aitken [1959], and related to other contemporary policy experiences in Ranis [1971].

3. In both countries, which were overwhelmingly agrarian, land tenure changes were the means of rupturing and refashioning relations of production that involved a great majority of the population, thereby inducting them into the new system. This measure was, interestingly, not so important in the third of the earliest cases of modernizing development, Turkey, although there the large majority of the labor force also worked in agriculture.

4. The growing public-sector involvement in Western industrial economies is analyzed in an abundant literature, while the scholarship on centrally planned economies is no less prolific. The latter, however, gave little hint--apart from the work of Lange, Sik, Kornai, and a few others--that profound changes were in the offing. Third-World economies, meanwhile, were widely assumed to have settled into a pattern of state-managed development that, save for such weaknesses as those described in the analysis of macroeconomic populism, seemed more-or-less durable. It was rarely recognized that the formation of regional integration schemes, which in Latin America seemed to be a way to prolong I-S-I, might chip away at the policy autonomy of the state and the monopoly power (and soft budget constraints) of parastatal enterprises while eroding the privileges of protected private firms, a point made by Glade [1977].

5. See Jessop, Kastendiek, Nielsen, and Pedersen [1991], and Maclean [1995, 273-91], the latter for recent developments in the country that created the terms dirigisme and étatisme. On a broader canvass, these national cases call to mind the playing out of forces explored by Schumpeter [1950] and by Olson [1982].

6. The huge volume of writing on public choice, rent seeking, bureaucratic politics and other bureaucratic problems, the myriad problems of regulation, the various lags in the policy process, and so on have sharpened our understanding of policy failure on many fronts. For two recent outstanding additions to this critical corpus, see World Bank, *Bureaucrats in Business* [1995] and Light [1994].

7. Along the way have come impressive studies in the political economy of policy dynamics: e.g., Hirschman [1968, 1-32], Mallon and Sourrouille [1975], Webb [1977], Kuczynski [1977], FitzGerald [1979], Sigmund [1980], Aspe and Sigmund [1984], Sikkink [1991], Schneider [1991], and Dornbusch and Edwards [1991].

8. There is now a lengthy literature on the conditions that forced policy change, and not all interpretations are the same. For early views, see Bela Balassa et al. [1985], Williamson [1990], Nelson [1990], and White [1990]. For a representative sampling of recent readings, see Pereira [1995] and Edwards [1995].

9. It would be simplistic to see this program as manufactured in Washington and exported to the Third World. In point of fact, most of it grew out of the experience of the developing and newly industrialized countries and was an indigenous product of the economics professionals therein as they tried to grapple with the circumstances of the day. See, for example, an account of structural change in one of the first cases in Luders and Hachette [1993].

10. The efficiency conditions are derived from two major recent studies of privatization: Galal, Jones, Tandon, and Vogelsang [1994] and Megginson, Nash, and van Randenborgh [1994, 403-43].

11. See Glade [1986] for a concise discussion of four types.

12. For the implications of a number of the studies see Glade [1995], and Baer and Birch [1994], as well as Galal and Shirley [1994].

13. Schumpeter [1954] recognized the research methodology required to explore these relationships, or the fiscal sociology of Goldscheid [1958]. The methodological requirements of research on such questions was largely anticipated by economists of the German historical school as well as by Veblen, Commons, and others of the American school of institutional economics.

14. The behavioral constraints examined in the new institutional economics elaborated by North and others are all constructed realities, not constraints given by nature, and hence are part of the process of social ordering in which public authority articulates the working rules of the transactional framework.

15. See Israel [1987] for a distillation of World Bank experience in this regard and Ostrom, Feeny, and Picht [1988] for a detailed examination of much actual field experience that demonstrates how important it is for the state's responsibility in rule making to be discharged in a manner sensitive to the impact of public policy on private behavior.

16. Chapter five in Frydman and Rapaczynski [1994] provides an especially thoughtful examination of this problem in a context somewhat less heated than that of Russia.

17. Aspe [1993] points out that the post-1982 period was actually salutary in that it brought a painful but necessary corrective turnaround in policy.

18. The Chilean economy, wherein the restructuring policies were pioneered, had collapsed almost a decade earlier for different reasons: namely, the poorly-thought-out program of rapid nationalization, which the Allende regime instituted for ideological reasons.

19. Compared with Hungary and Poland, Yugoslavia had introduced more significant reforms even earlier, while the Soviet Union had toyed with a variety of more modest reforms somewhat later. All apparently proved unavailing. Schroeder [1990, 35-43]; Bornstein [1985], Hewett [1988].

20. See Portes [1993] for an early assessment of intercountry differences.

21. Earle, Frydman, Rapaczynski, and Turkewitz [1994] provides an unusually detailed and informative view of structure both before and after the end of central planning, with good insight into intercountry differences. The description of pre-reform Czech organization is especially rich.

22. Bosworth and Ofer [1995] credit the existence of a private sector and the decentralization of decision-making in state-owned enterprises as factors speeding up the supply response to price liberalization in Poland and Hungary.

23. The problems this posed for the German economy have come to light in a number of excellent studies. See Smyser [1993] and Giersch, Paqué, and Schmieding [1993].

24. Politically and ideologically inspired control, censorship, and the interposition of official foreign trade organizations buffered Soviet firms and their managers from contact with both the structure and the meaning of market prices and shielded them from information on innovations in product specifications and design as well as production technologies and organization in the West. In an era of accelerating change these filters kept Soviet firms from benefiting from the fructifying influences of international trade that had favored Western growth since at least the Commercial Revolution. See Lopez [1971] and Cipolla [1980].

25. Guroff and Carstensen [1983] records the spurt of industrial and business growth that took place in late Czarist Russia.

26. Berliner [1976]. See also Amann and Cooper [1982]. The disinclination to decentralize investment decisions to the enterprise level routinely deprived the system of the familiarity of managers with the amount and direction of investment that would further productivity and helped stifle innovation.

27. Censorship and repression to ensure conformity were, of course, additional impediments to information flows, as was the pro-forma nature of governmental assemblies.

28. For three sensitive assessments of this situation, see Angresano [1992, 55-76], Angresano [1994, 79-100], and Clague and Rausser [1992].

29. Variations in policy outcomes, because of differing national circumstances, are well depicted in Frydman, Rapaczynski, Earle, et al. [1993].

30. The reference is to the set of behavioral or procedural rules that governs information-processing relationships among the organization's members and between them and the organization's environment, i.e., the standard operating routine that makes the organization work and perform. Berliner [1957], Kornai [1959], Richman [1965], and Granick [1979] all provide useful perspectives on the behavioral constraints that configured the management process in central planning. Granick [1975] reveals significant differences from Soviet experience in the satellite cases.

31. Among the studies that document the generally good performance of Western European state-owned enterprises are Mazzolini [1979], Vernon and Aharoni [1981], and Lamont [1979].

32. The growth of manufactured exports from Mexico, which could be observed in the late 1960s and early 1970s, was set back thereafter by the adverse movements in the exchange rate and domestic prices that ensued with the oil boom.

33. Trebat [1983] reaches a generally favorable assessment of much of the Brazilian parastatal sector, wherein, for example, the state agency to promote film-making also enjoyed a certain measure of international success.

34. The kind of research discussed in Chandler [1992] is ripe for the undertaking in most of the major Latin American economies, especially in, say, the Brazilian firms that succeeded early in penetrating export markets and in the adaptive strategies used for survival by Chilean manufacturing firms during the 1970s and '80s. Of special interest is the learning by doing evident in Mexican manufacturing during restructuring and accession to the GATT and NAFTA.

35. Though virtually all administration was left in a shambles by the Allende episode, CORFO's industrial holdings proved to be generally well run, and the brevity of the breakdown was such that they could fairly readily be restored to a sound condition.

36. As the recent World Bank research reported in *Measuring Environmental Progress* [1995] now recognizes, social capital--meaning the value of human organizations or institutions--constitutes along with natural capital, produced assets, and human resources, a major component of wealth. John Tomer [1987], in an important but under-recognized study, has explored the same conceptual territory to good effect.

37. It is relevant to note that the process characteristic of Latin American development has stood out in bold relief elsewhere. "While the policy reform process is certainly not complete, there is growing recognition that such reforms alone will not generate an efficient and broad-based supply response by private traders and processors. This is leading both African governments and international donors to move toward more direct measures to promote private sector agribusiness development. To intervene successfully in this area, a greater understanding of the private sector in Africa is needed--the constraints it faces, its modes and strategies of operation, and its varied responses to trade and market liberalization." This forthright acknowledgement of the importance of institutional research and institutionally focused policy comes from the World Bank's "Findings," *African Region, #50* (October 1995) but would seem equally applicable to the situation of the ex-CPEs.

38. The extensive efforts of the European Community (European Union) and the United States to upgrade academic training in business and the social sciences, to spread the study of English, German, and French in order to provide access to the rich inventory of instructional materials on technical subjects in those languages (as well as in translation), to mount intensive (re-)training conferences and seminars in the ex-CPEs, to multiply the scope

of international exchanges for leadership development in all the fields needed for building civil society, to increase by several orders of magnitude the opportunities for short-term and long-term study in the West, even the establishment of new Western-style universities and centers for advanced specialized training have contributed to the capacity of many countries to develop new project design and management capabilities (in both the public and private sectors). Assistance has also helped establish stock exchanges and the associated regulatory regimes, to reorganize commercial banking and the supervision of financial institutions, to promote small business development, to renovate press, broadcasting and publishing industries, and to introduce the possibility for a comprehensive overhaul of the legal system. Some assistance has been provided by programs such as the MBA enterprise corps and by retired business executives. By the same token, the reorganization of business operations through foreign direct investment and joint ventures, strategic business alliances, management contracts, and the transmission of organizational and technical information through the growing volume of cross-boundary commercial transactions, have contributed much to reordering the institutional structure of the ex-CPEs in ways that borrow heavily, if unconsciously, from the development experiences of Latin American countries, South Korea, and Taiwan, the most advanced parts of the Third-World.

REFERENCES

Aitken, Hugh G. J., ed. *The State and Economic Growth*. New York: Social Science Research Council, 1959.

Amann, Ronald and Julian Cooper, eds. *Industrial Innovation in the Soviet Union*. New Haven, CT: Yale University Press, 1982.

Angresano, James. "Political and Economic Obstacles Inhibiting Comprehensive Reform in Hungary." *East European Quarterly* 26 (March 1992): 55-76.

———. "Institutional Change in Bulgaria: a Socioeconomic Approach." *The Journal of Socio-Economics* 23 (1994): 79-100.

Aspe Armella, Pedro. *Economic Transformation the Mexican Way*. Cambridge, MA: MIT Press, 1993.

Aspe Armella, Pedro and Paul Sigmund, eds. *The Political Economy of Income Distribution in Mexico*. New York: Holmes & Meier, 1984.

Baer, Werner and Melissa Birch, eds. *Privatization in Latin America: New Roles for the Public and Private Sectors*. Westport, CT: Praeger, 1994.

Balassa, Bela A. et al. *Toward Renewed Economic Growth in Latin America*. Washington, DC: Institute for International Economics, 1986.

Banerjee, Abhijii V. and Michael Spagat. "Productivity Paralysis and the Complexity Problem: Why do Centrally Planned Economies Become Prematurely Gray?" *Journal of Comparative Economics* 15 (December 1991): 646-60.

Berliner, Joseph S. *Factory and Manager in the USSR*. Cambridge, MA: Harvard University Press, 1957.

———. *The Innovation Decision in Soviet Industry*. Cambridge, MA: MIT Press, 1976.

Bornstein, Morris. "Improving the Soviet Economic Mechanism," *Soviet Studies* 37 (January 1985): 1-30.

Bosworth, Barry P. and Gur Ofer. *Reforming Planned Economies in an Integrating World Economy*. Washington, DC: Brookings Institution, 1995.

Brada, Josef C., Edward A. Hewett, and Thomas A. Wolf, eds. *Economic Adjustment and Reform in Eastern Europe and Soviet Union: Essays in Honor of Franklyn D. Holzman*. Durham, NC: Duke University Press, 1988.

Chandler, A. D. "Organizational Capabilities and the Economic History of the Industrial Enterprise." *The Journal of Economic Perspectives* 6 (Summer 1992): 79-100.

Cipolla, Carlo M. *Before the Industrial Revolution: European Society and Economy, 1000-1700*. New York: Norton, 1980.

Clague, Christopher and Gordon C. Rausser, eds. *The Emergence of Market Economies in Eastern Europe*. Cambridge, MA: Blackwell Publishers, 1992.

Dornbusch, Rudiger and Sebastian Edwards. *The Macroeconomics of Populism in Latin America*. Chicago: University of Chicago Press, 1991.

Earle, John S., Roman Frydman, Andrzej Rapaczynski, and Joel Turkewitz. *Small Privatization: The Transformation of Retail Trade and Consumer Services in the Czech Republic, Hungary, and Poland*. London: Central European University Press, 1994.

Edwards, Sebastian. *Crisis and Reform in Latin America: From Despair to Hope*. New York: Oxford University Press for the World Bank, 1995.

FitzGerald, E. V. K. *The Political Economy of Peru, 1956-78: Economic Development and the Restructuring of Capital*. Cambridge: Cambridge University Press, 1979.

Frydman, Roman and Andrzej Rapaczynski. *Privatization in Eastern Europe: Is the State Withering Away?* London: Central European University Press, 1994.

Frydman, Roman, Andrzej Rapaczynski, John S. Earle, et al. *The Privatization Process in Central Europe*, Vol. 1. London: Central European University Press, 1993.

Galal, Ahmed, Leroy Jones, Pankaj Tandon, and Ingo Vogelsang. *Welfare Consequences of Selling Public Enterprises: An Empirical Analysis*. New York: Oxford University Press, 1994.

Galal, Ahmed and Mary Shirley, eds. *Does Privatization Deliver? Highlights From a World Bank Conference*. Washington, DC: World Bank, 1994.

Gerschenkron, Alexander. *Economic Backwardness in Historical Perspective*. New York: F. Praeger, 1965.

Giersch, Herbert, Karl-Heinz Paqué, and Holger Schmieding. *The Fading Miracle: Four Decades of Market Economy in Germany*. Cambridge: Cambridge University Press, 1993.

Glade, William. "The Role of Public Sector Firms in the Integration of Latin American Industrial Structure." In Mihály Simai and Katalin Garam, eds., *Economic Integration: Concepts, Theories, and Problems*. Budapest: Akadémiai Kiadó, 1977

Glade, William, ed. *Bigger Economies, Smaller Governments: The Role of Privatization in Latin America*. Boulder, CO: Westview Press, 1995.

———. *State Shrinking: A Comparative Inquiry Into Privatization*. Austin: University of Texas, Institute of Latin American Studies, 1986.

Goldscheid, Rudolf. "A Sociological Approach to the Problem of Public Finance." In Richard A. Musgrave and Alan T. Peacock, eds., *Classics in the Theory of Public Finance*. New York: St. Martin's Press, 1967.

Granick, David. *Enterprise Guidance in Eastern Europe: A Comparison of Four Socialist Economies*. Princeton, NJ: Princeton University Press, 1975.

Granick, David. *The Red Executive*. New York: Doubleday, 1961.

Guroff, Gregory and Fred V. Carstensen, eds. *Entrepreneurship in Imperial Russia and the Soviet Union*. Princeton, NJ: Princeton University Press, 1983.

Hausner, Jerzy, Bob Jessop, and Klaus Nielsen, eds. *Institutional Frameworks of Market Economies: Scandinavian and Eastern European Perspectives*. Brookfield, MA: Avebury, 1993.

Hewett, Edward A. *Reforming the Soviet Economy: Equality Versus Efficiency*. Washington, DC: Brookings Institution, 1988.

Hewett, Edward A. with Clifford G. Gaddy. *Open for Business: Russia's Return to the Global Economy*. Washington, DC: Brookings Institution, 1992.

Hirschman, Albert O. "The Political Economy of Import-Substituting Industrialization in Latin American Countries." *Quarterly Journal of Economics* 82 (February 1968): 1-32.

Israel, Arturo. *Institutional Development: Incentives to Performance*. Baltimore, MD: Johns Hopkins University Press, 1987.

Jessop, Bob, H. Kastendiek, K. Nielsen, and O. K. Pedersen. *The Politics of Flexibility: Restructuring State and Industry in Britain, Germany, and Scandinavia*. Hants, England: Edward Elgar, 1991.

Kuczynski, Pedro Pablo. *Peruvian Democracy under Economic Stress: An Account of the Belaunde Administration, 1963-1968*. Princeton, NJ: Princeton University Press, 1977.

Lamont, Douglas E. *Foreign State Enterprises: A Threat to American Business*. New York: Basic Books, 1979.

Light, Paul C. *Thickening Government*. Washington, DC: Brookings Institution, 1994.

Lockwood, William W. *The Economic Development of Japan: Growth and Structural Change*. Princeton, NJ: Princeton University Press, 1968.

Lopez, Robert Sabatino. *The Commercial Revolution of the Middle Ages, 950-1350*. Englewood Cliffs, NJ: Prentice-Hall, 1971.

Lord, Montague. "Manufacturing Exports." In Inter-American Development Bank, *Economic and Social Progress in Latin America, 1992 Report*. Baltimore, MD: Johns Hopkins University Press, 1992.

Luders, Rolf and Dominique Hachette. *Privatization in Chile: An Economic Appraisal*. San Francisco: ICS Press, 1993.

Maclean, Mairi. "Privatisation in France 1993-94: New Departures or a Case of Plus ça Change?" *West European Politics* 18 (April 1995): 273-91.

Maddison, Angus et al. *The Political Economy of Poverty, Equity, and Growth: Brazil and Mexico*. New York: Oxford University Press, 1992.

Mallon, Richard D. and Juan V. Sourrouille. *Economic Policymaking in a Conflict Society: The Argentine Case*. Cambridge, MA: Harvard University Press, 1975.

Mazzolini, Renato. *Government Controlled Enterprises*. New York: Wiley, 1979.

Megginson, William L., Robert C. Nash, and Matthias van Randenborgh. "The Financial and Operating Performance of Newly Privatized Firms: An International Empirical Analysis." *The Journal of Finance* 49 (June 1994): 403-43.

Nelson, Joan M., ed. *Economic Crisis and Policy Choice: The Politics of Adjustment in the Third World*. Princeton, NJ: Princeton University Press, 1990.

Olson, Mancur. *The Rise and Decline of Nations: Economic Growth, Stagflation, and Social Rigidities*. New Haven, CT: Yale University Press, 1982.

Ostrom, Vincent, David Feeny, and Hartmut Picht, eds. *Rethinking Institutional Analysis and Development: Issues, Alternatives, and Choices*. San Francisco, CA: ICS Press, 1988.

Pereira, Luiz Carlos Bresser. *Economic Crisis and State Reform in Brazil: Toward a New Interpretation of Latin America*. Boulder, CO: Lynne Rienner, 1995.

Portes, Richard, ed. *Economic Transformation in Central Europe: A Progress Report.* London: European Communities, Centre for Economic Policy Research, 1993.

Ranis, Gustav, ed. *Government and Economic Development.* New Haven, CT: Yale University Press, 1971.

Schneider, Ben Ross. *Politics Within the State: Elite Bureaucrats and Industrial Policy in Authoritarian Brazil.* Pittsburgh, PA: University of Pittsburgh Press, 1991.

Schroeder, Gertrude E. "Economic Reform of Socialism: the Soviet Record." In Jan S. Prybyla, ed., "Privatizing and Marketizing Socialism." *The Annals of the American Academy of Political and Social Science* 507 (January 1990): 35-43.

Schumpeter, Joseph A. *Capitalism, Socialism, and Democracy.* New York: Harper, 1950.

Schumpeter, Joseph A. "The Crisis of the Tax State." Reprinted in *International Economic Papers* 4 (1954).

Sigmund, Paul. *Multinationals in Latin America: The Politics of Nationalization.* Madison: University of Wisconsin Press, 1980.

Sikkink, Kathryn. *Ideas and Institutions: Developmentalism in Brazil and Argentina.* Ithaca, NY: Cornell University Press, 1991.

Smyser, W. R. *The German Economy: Colossus at the Crossroads.* New York: St. Martin's Press, 1993.

Swann, Dennis. *The Retreat of the State: Deregulation and Privatization in the UK and US.* Ann Arbor: University of Michigan Press, 1988.

Tomer, John F. *Organizational Capital: The Path to Higher Productivity and Well-Being.* New York: Praeger, 1987.

Trebat, Thomas J. *Brazil's State-Owned Enterprises: A Case Study of the State as Entrepreneur.* New York: Cambridge University Press, 1983.

Vernon, Raymond and Yair Aharoni, eds. *State-owned Enterprise in the Western Economies.* New York: St. Martin's Press, 1981.

Webb, Richard C. *Government Policy and the Distribution of Income in Peru, 1963-1973.* Cambridge, MA: Harvard University Press, 1977.

White, Louise G. *Implementing Policy Reforms in LDCs: A Strategy for Designing and Effecting Change.* Boulder, CO: Lynne Rienner Publishers, 1990.

Williamson, John, ed. *Latin American Adjustment: How Much Has Happened?.* Washington, DC: Institute of International Economics, 1990.

World Bank. *Bureaucrats in Business: The Economics and Politics of Government Ownership.* New York: Oxford University Press, 1995.

World Bank. *Measuring Environmental Progress.* Washington, DC: 1995.

World Bank, African Region. "Findings," #50 (October 1995).

CHAPTER 11

INSTITUTIONAL REFORM OF THE INTERNATIONAL MONETARY REGIME

Anthony Scaperlanda
Northern Illinois University

International monetary regimes seem to change more frequently than observers of institutional change in other economic realms might anticipate. As Barry Eichengreen has observed,

> The quarter century leading up to World War I was the heyday of the classical gold standard, when exchange rates were pegged to gold and to one another over an increasing portion of the industrial and developing world. The war provoked the breakdown of the gold standard and was followed by an interlude of floating rates. Countries returned to gold in the second half of the 1920s, only to see their laboriously constructed fixed-rate system give way to renewed floating in the 1930s. The Bretton Woods Agreement of 1944 inaugurated another quarter century of exchange-rate stability. The next episode of floating began in the early 1970s and now seems to be in the process of being supplanted, mainly in Europe, by a move back toward fixed rates [1995, 3].

The International Monetary Fund (IMF) continues to explore modifications that can be made to its operations, whether "target zones," a new Special Drawing Rights (SDR) allocation, new lending facilities, or some other change. In this chapter, I use institutional economic analysis to join the discussion on the direction of the IMF's evolution if it is to be effective in the twenty-first century.

INSTITUTIONAL ECONOMIC ANALYSIS

Wendell Gordon [1958, 275-419] and Anthony Scaperlanda [1978, 679-90] are institutionalist economists who have written on international monetary regimes.[1] This area of inquiry has attracted only modest attention from institutionalists because the frequent changes in regimes that Eichengreen describes are, in a sense, institutionalist prescriptions. When conditions changed, policy makers had the good sense to reform the exchange rate regime to accomplish the goals they had established. A brief digression to summarize relevant institutional analytical tools reveals the connection between specific endogenous changes and exchange rate regime modifications.

Wendell Gordon's summary of the theoretical foundations of institutional economics [1980, 9-36] identifies value theory and a theory of economic progress as central. The value theory, as Gordon explains it,

> is dynamic in the manner of the pragmatism and instrumentalism of C. S. Peirce and John Dewey. . . . what is valued by people changes with the passage of time as conditions and, in particular, technology (knowledge) change. . . . value judgments are made by individuals (and by institutions), and re-evaluations of the appropriateness of a given technology [or institution] for dealing with a given problem are made as technologies (and methods) are used and reused in dealing with problems [Gordon 1980, 9-10].

In the international monetary world, at least in the post-World War II era, policy prescriptions suggest that multiple values are expressed at any one time. An overriding value has been that a system works to minimize resistances and obstructions between countries to the movement of goods, people, and factors of production. Other values such as stability and predictability of a currency's worth, national governments being subjected to the regime's discipline, and a preference for smooth and gradual adjustments rather than sudden and more volatile adjustments were also operative. Still other values like linking economic development aid to the operations of the international monetary system have been debated but never warmly embraced, at least by the industrial countries that dominate decision-making.

Changes in the international monetary regime during the last half century can be seen as institutionalist in the sense they have been pragmatic. In July of 1944, in Bretton Woods, New Hampshire, the two principal choices for a post-war regime did not include a classical gold standard. Instead a faux gold standard was established. The fixed, but adjustable, exchange rate regime that emerged from Bretton Woods seemed appropriate to the times, at least after relatively realistic post-war parities were determined. Yet the rebuilding of Europe and Japan with modern industrial technology, together with slower modernization in the United States, began to shift comparative advantage and trade patterns so that the United States dollar-centered Bretton Woods system became increasingly cumbersome and inappropriate. Scholars offered a variety of solutions that included Milton Friedman's advocacy of freely fluctuating exchange rates [1953], and Wendell Gordon's [1958] and Robert Triffin's [1960] arguments for an international currency. And within the IMF institutional framework, policy alternatives were being developed using the ideas of these and other scholars to design modifications in the system. Two-tier gold pricing, in effect for a short period, as well as the conceptualization and creation of the SDR can be seen as attempts to modify the regime and adapt the IMF to the evolving geographic distribution of industrial power without modifying the package of values embraced at Bretton Woods. The modifications that began in August and culminated with the Smithsonian Agreement in December 1971 admit of a similar reading. Finally, in March 1973, the international trade and investment pressures emanating from cumulative technological developments were too strong to permit giving equal weight to all of the Bretton Woods values. Pragmatically, the community of nations, through the IMF, chose to value open, unobstructed interchange among nations over stable and predictable currency values, and the major currencies were officially allowed to float. Between then and April 1, 1978, when the Second Amendment to the IMF's Articles of Agreement was adopted, the IMF members changed the regime to one that allowed each member to use the exchange rate regime of its choice as long as the integrity of open international markets was maintained.

Implicit in my description of the evolution of dominant values manifested in the international monetary regime is the Thorstein Veblen-Clarence Ayres theory of economic progress. In this theoretical framework the accumulation of all rational (including technical) knowledge, which is assumed to be continually improving, is an endogenous dynamic force that is continually challenging the status quo institutional arrangements. Existing institutions, because they reflect an adaption to earlier technological pressures, must continue to adapt if the newer technology is to be efficiently and effectively organized. That is, existing institutions will, by definition, resist change and will adjust to the new technology, but with a time lag. The two other variables in this theoretical framework, resources and humans, are themselves shaped by global technological and institutional adjustments. According to Tom DeGregori, in chapter 7 of this book, resources are technologically and culturally defined. So are human beings. Take just two examples: (1) medical technology has modified life expectancy that, in turn, shapes the way other technology and institutions are incorporated into decision making; and (2) the participation of humans in cyberspace will modify human communication and learning processes and, in turn, other technology and institutions.

Eichengreen, seeking to endogenize the factors responsible for shifts in international monetary regimes, has recently advanced "six hypotheses with the capacity to explain the alternating phases of fixed and flexible exchange rates into which the last century can be partitioned" [1995, 4]. As he points out, his six factors (leadership by a dominant power, international cooperation, an intellectual consensus, the behavior of the macroeconomy, fiscal policy and monetary rules, and distributional politics) are not mutually exclusive. Indeed, he says that "an adequate account of the endogeneity of exchange-rate regimes will have to incorporate several explanations [1995, 4]. His six factors are compatible with the Veblen-Ayres theory of economic progress and implicitly with institutional value theory. For example, in this century extensive use of advanced technology is a prerequisite to a country's becoming dominant and exerting leadership. What is clear is that the analytical perspective forwarded by institutional economics can be very useful in organizing and analyzing the multiple forces endogenously determining changes in the international monetary regime. This is important because in Eichengreen's judgment "monocausal explanations are unlikely to provide an adequate account of the endogeneity of exchange-rate regimes. Blending the competing theories thus becomes an important task for subsequent research" [1995, 29].

THE IMF AND INSTITUTIONAL CHANGE, THE LATE 1970s[2]

When the fixed exchange rate regime, created at Bretton Woods, was abandoned in March 1973, the IMF Board of Governors and its Interim Committee began work to adapt policies to fit a world of floating exchange rates. In addition to short-run decisions and activities such as establishing a special oil facility, decisions of long-run importance were made. Principal among them were: establishing a new formula for valuing SDRs; increasing the Fund's quota by 33 percent; disposing of one-third of the Fund's existing gold stock; establishing a Trust Fund for poor countries; and amending the Fund's *Articles of Agreement*. The amendment, the second (the first having established SDRs in 1969), was a broad recasting of the Fund's *Articles* aimed at adapting the intellectual and organizational infrastructure of the Fund to the conditions of a floating exchange rate world. The sum of these changes can be read as establishing the basis for the IMF becoming a central bank for national central banks.

I base this interpretation on the premise that "the essential nature of central banking . . . is to regulate whatever banking business it does for the sole aim of furthering whatever seems best for the economy" [Galbraith 1963, 354]. With this principal purpose of influencing the level and rate of change of economic activity by managing credit and monetary conditions, the "distinguishing characteristic of a central bank is its unstable reserve ratio" [Galbraith 1963, 347]. Another important characteristic is that a central bank is the source and creator of banking reserves. Moreover, central banks may also possess certain attributes that ease the tasks of influencing credit and monetary conditions and regulating monetary activity. The attributes include: (1) creator of the medium of exchange, (2) banker to banks, (3) government banker, and (4) lender of last resort. Central banks also have (5) restricted commercial business and (6) public ownership and control [Galbraith 1963, 352].

The purpose of the IMF had always been (and continues to be) compatible with the purpose of a central bank. As section (ii) of Article I, unchanged by the Second Amendment, states, one of the purposes of the IMF is:

> To facilitate the expansion and balanced growth of international trade, and to contribute thereby to the promotion and maintenance of high levels of employment and real income and to the development of the productive resources of all members as primary objectives of economic policy [IMF, 2].

To this, section (iii) adds stability, order, and "fair play" perspectives; section (iv) recognizes the need for a multinational payments clearing system; and section (v) provides for short-term loans (a discount window) [IMF *Articles*, 2; IMF *Survey Supplement* Fall 1976, 1, 7-9].

Since the IMF's stated purpose has always been consistent with that of a central bank, it is necessary and sufficient that its practices evolve if it is to become recognized as a central bank. Such an evolution became possible, even necessary, as soon as the Bretton Woods fixed exchange rate regime collapsed (March 19, 1973).[3] Under the Bretton Woods regime, lending transactions were focused almost exclusively on exchange rate stability. With the disappearance of fixed exchange rates, the possibility arose that the Fund could adapt to the changing world by entering into loan arrangements that were more directly related to the growth and stability of the borrowing country's economy than was possible under the Bretton Woods regime. Put differently, the Fund had to become a channel of not-for-profit lending to members for reasons other than exchange rate maintenance. Doing so, it took on yet another of the characteristics of a central bank -- an unstable reserve ratio. All that remained in order for the IMF to possess all of the characteristics and most of the attributes of a central bank was to become a primary source of international reserves.

The IMF, that is, was tending toward becoming an international central bank in the second half of the 1970s. IMF lending practices after 1974 show the extent to which the Fund's lending practices changed during that period of time, as do data on the SDR's role in the post-Second Amendment regime.

IMF Lending Facilities After 1973

On June 13, 1974, the Fund established what was known as the Oil Facility to assist members in financing essential petroleum imports. To fund the Oil Facility, the IMF borrowed SDR 6.9 billion from 17 member nations. These financial resources were made available to 55 member nations, 37% of which were developing countries, over the next two years. As a condition for drawing from the Facility, the recipients agreed to avoid the use of restrictions on trade and payments and to demonstrate that they would develop medium-term policies to improve their external payments position. They also agreed to repay the amount drawn from the Facility in quarterly payments over a four year period beginning at the end of the third year after drawing from the Facility. There was an interest subsidy available in 1975 to assist the "most seriously affected" nations drawing from the Facility. And all of the interest paid on 1974 borrowings and all but .5% (7.25%) paid on 1975 borrowings was channelled to the 17 nations that had funded the Facility [IMF *Survey* April 5, 1976, 97, 102]. This process exerted central-bank-like control because norms and goals established and implemented collectively resulted in financial resources being funneled from cash surplus to cash deficient member nations on the condition that recipient nations adhere to the collective norms.

In September 1974, the Extended Facility was created for nations that needed to draw on the Fund's resources but would have difficulty repaying within the year permitted in normal IMF stand-by agreements. This little-used facility was designed for countries like the Philippines, which borrowed SDR 217 million in April 1976, that were experiencing either slow growth or were trying to restructure a sector of their economies. Although it was not much used, the concept on which the facility was created, lengthening the time horizon for repayment, had a central bank quality.

During the late 1970s, the Fund also expanded its lending to compensate a member nation for export income lost because of a sudden drop in the price of an export commodity. Although the lending facility (the Compensatory Financing Facility) had been in existence since 1963, it was rarely activated until the conditions applied to borrowers were liberalized in December 1975. Between February 1976 and January 1977, 48 members drew SDR 2.35 billion, approximately twice the total drawn in the previous 13 years [IMF March 7, 1977, 66-69]. The amount drawn from this facility in 1976 exceeded by nearly SDR 1 billion the amount drawn under the Fund's expanded credit tranches. The advantage for a borrowing nation was that the funds drawn from this facility did not affect a nation's normal tranche position. In a sense the Compensatory Financing Facility became a specialized discount window.

In May 1976, a fourth relevant facility, the Trust Fund, was established to provide additional balance of payments assistance to developing member countries. This facility was financed by a partial sale of the Fund's gold stock in which all proceeds in excess of SDR 35 per ounce were allocated to the Trust Fund. Eligible borrowers were originally defined as those countries with per capital income of SDR 300 or less, in need of balance of payments assistance, and in the process of making a reasonable effort to strengthen its external payments position.

In August 1977, the Fund established the Supplementary Financing Facility, which like the Oil Facility was funded by members' contributions that are in addition to their quota obligations. This facility entered into force in February 1979. Intended to be used in conjunction with the Fund's ordinary resources, the resources of this facility were available "only under a stand-by or extended arrangement reaching into the upper credit tranches and subject therefore to the usual policy conditions, phasing, and performance criteria." The facility was "designed to assist those members which, because of the seriousness of their payments problems, can be expected to need resources in larger amounts and for a longer period than could be available to them under the regular credit tranches" [IMF *Survey* February 7, 1977, 39-42; August 1, 1977, 251].

Between the demise of the Bretton Woods IMF regime and 1980, the IMF broadened significantly both its financial intermediation and lending activities. The Oil Facility and the Supplementary Financing Facility both involved new intermediation and each entered a lending area that was clearly an extension of the IMF's scope. The Trust Fund used the capital gains derived from the sale of an IMF asset to engage in a new lending activity. And the Compensatory Financing Facility and the Extended Facility used Fund resources to expand the credit that could be made available. These five ventures are considerable extensions of or departures from the lending practices through gold and credit tranches that existed within the framework of the Bretton Woods regime. Together, these ventures had an extra-quota value of SDR 18.3 billion, which amounted to approximately one half of cumulative tranche drawings from the Fund. The nature and variety of these five lending facilities coincide closely, perhaps entirely, with the purpose of a central bank.

The stand-by arrangement that the Fund approved for the United Kingdom on January 3, 1977 admits a similar interpretation. The SDR 3.36 billion agreement for the United Kingdom was the largest ever approved by the Fund and involved one of the countries that had made the most use of the Fund's resources. Because of the importance of the agreement, the conditions placed on the United Kingdom were specific and relatively stringent. The United Kingdom was required to cut public expenditure, reduce public sector borrowing, and restrain the growth of domestic credit. Essentially, the commitment was to a constant public budget in real terms over the intermediate term with some reduction in public sector borrowing (PSB) achieved by selling British Petroleum shares to cover needed expenditures [IMF *Survey* January 10, 1977, 1-5; January 24, 1977, 17]. On the monetary side, the reduction in PSB was meant to somewhat slow the growth of monetary aggregates and to reduce the public presence in competition for loanable funds. In general, the conditions that the Fund imposed on the United Kingdom aimed at altering the structure, at least marginally, of the British economy. Overall, the conditions projected the relative ascendancy of the private sector. The conditions set by the Fund were in the tradition of those that had always been possible under the credit tranche guidelines and procedures. They assumed a central-bank-control quality because of the specificity of the conditions and because of the purposes for which the loans were made.

In the second half of the 1970s the IMF also began to have greater influence on the decisions of the world's 40 or so largest commercial banks. Although this change effectively by-passes national central banks, it is worth noting because it is a sign that the Fund was assuming the trappings of a central bank, albeit not a central bank for national central banks. Throughout the 1970s, private commercial banks substantially increased their relative importance in international lending even as total borrowing in international capital markets was burgeoning. As Michael Dooley has observed, "the emergence of [commercial] banks as financial intermediaries in the 1970s can best be understood as a process in which the banks replaced the governments of industrial countries as lenders to developing countries" [1995, 263]. Private bankers were relatively more disposed to lend in developing countries where national "authorities are embarking on appropriate adjustment policies, particularly if such policies are supported by access to Fund resources" [IMF June 6, 1977, 178]. Essentially, the fact that the IMF found a country worthy of having access to Fund resources, either credit tranche or from one of the special facilities, was an imprimatur for that country. Private banks "with the approval, encouragement, and implicit support of the[ir home] governments" [Dooley 1995, 263], could assume they were even safer if IMF funding was also present in the recipient country.

The IMF as a Creator of Reserves in the 1970s

The ability of the International Monetary Fund to create bank reserves has existed at least since the First Amendment to the *Articles of Agreement* was adopted in 1969, when it acquired the ability to create Special Drawing Rights Although the quantity of SDRs allocated has always been minuscule, their magnitude grossly understates their importance on the international monetary scene.

The ascendance in importance of the SDR in the 1970s was, in part, due to the deliberate diminishment of the role of gold in the international monetary regime. The Fund's sale of one-third of its gold stock beginning in 1976 treated gold as a non-monetary commodity. In addition, since a portion of the sales were by auction, there was an explicit abandonment of an official gold price. These actions reinforced the Fund's 1974 decision to have a basket of currencies, rather than the U.S. dollar, determine the value of the SDR. These changes in the treatment of gold were codified in the Second Amendment. Explicitly, the revised *Articles* (1) prohibited the pegging of any currency to gold, (2) prohibited the Fund from acting to manage the price of gold, and (3) relieved the Fund from any obligation to buy or sell gold [Witteveen 1976, 8].

Since June 1974 when the Fund began valuing the SDR in terms of a basket of currencies, it has published daily the SDR value of a number of currencies.[4] This "service" rather firmly established the SDR as an important unit of account for international transactions as indicated by the fact that some countries peg their national currency to the SDR. In addition, it has been used as a unit of account by the International Air Transport Association, in some private contracts, and by other international organizations [IMF *Survey Supplement* Fall 1976, 7]. A number of the transactions for which the SDR was used as a unit of account involved deferred payment. This was explicitly true for all borrowings from and repayments to the Fund. And the SDR functioned as a store of value for any national central bank or "Prescribed Holder"[5] that held them. The SDR's stature as international money was enhanced by the adoption of the Second Amendment that had an "objective of making the SDR the principal reserve asset of the international monetary system [Witteveen 1976, 5].

Between January 1, 1970 and January 2, 1981, a total of SDR 21.4 billion was allocated to 141 member nations. This relatively small amount, equaling 2.6 percent of the total non-gold reserves as of April 20, 1995 [IMF *Survey Supplement* September 1995, 20], had an effect far in excess of its magnitude. The importance of SDRs could have been much larger if the Substitution Account proposed in the late 1970s had been ratified. This account would have exchanged national currencies used as international reserves for SDRs. A Substitution Account would have changed the composition of international reserves in use rather than increasing them, as does an SDR allocation. For the Substitution Account to have been effective, national governments, especially that of the United States, would have had to exert enough domestic discipline to limit imbalances in international payments. Needless to say such discipline was not embraced by Presidents or Congresses of the United States during the 1980s, and this alternative route to greater SDR creation was never tested.

AN INTERNATIONAL MONETARY REGIME FOR THE 21st CENTURY[6]

A recent and prescient article in *IMF Survey*, "Revisiting Proposals for Monetary Reform," is evidence that the "system" in existence at the end of 1995 is less than perfect and is likely to change [November 6, 1995, 350-53]. The article features three alternatives. John Williamson is reported to favor the IMF being at the "center of a system of international policy coordination or surveillance . . . [that] would be based on exchange rate target zones" [350]. Robert Solomon's position is that the present system should be strengthened so that there is "a more central role for the IMF." He is critical of the target zone approach because a nation's compliance with achieving the target "would periodically require [national] monetary policy to be diverted from its principal function of maintaining economic growth and domestic price stability" [351]. Charles Dallara argues that "the IMF needed to expand its role in two directions: by extending it surveillance of the major industrial countries; and by establishing a closer rapport with participants in the private market that supply potentially destabilizing flows of capital to emerging market economies" [352]. Stanley Fischer, First Deputy Managing Director of the IMF, concluding the meeting at which these views were expressed, noted "that the incremental reforms that the IMF has been pursuing in recent months--expanding its financial resources, developing an emergency financing mechanism, redefining the role of the SDR--are all on the plate, and will make a difference over the next few years" [353].

From a Veblen-Ayres, institutionalist perspective, the Williamson, the Solomon, and the Dallara-Fischer ideas should be evaluated at least within the context of technological developments of recent decades and those that are expected to continue. Most relevant here are the striking advances in communications technologies. Not only does CNN take nearly everyone on the planet to each new "hot spot," but we are becoming ever more capable of reaching anywhere individually with cellular voice technology and communications through cyberspace. Transportation technology has also improved in recent years, though less dramatically than communications technology. I expect, however, that in the early part of the next century, advances will be made to shorten dramatically the time required for international transportation. The possibility of virtually instant communication together with fast, efficient, and safe transportation have combined, in a relatively peaceful world, to unleash the firm-based industrial and organizational technology that has spawned an explosion of multinational enterprise (MNE) activity in the last three decades.

From SDR 67.7 billion in 1960 worldwide foreign direct investment (FDI) increased 18 times to SDR 1,283.9 in 1991 [Rutter 1993 Appendix table 2]. The value of MNE assets is approximately twice that amount if the FDI-total assets ratio has remained constant since the Bretton Woods fixed-exchange-rate regime ended (FDI equalled about 52 percent of total assets at that time) [Scaperlanda April 1974, 52; June 1974, 55]. The growth of international portfolio investment, permitted by the changes in communication technology, changes in the instituted structures of national capital markets, by mutual fund growth, and by other changes in investment practices, has probably paralleled the growth of FDI. Regardless of the precise magnitudes, these developments suggest that private international financial stocks now dwarf substantially the resources available to the IMF. Currently those resources are SDR 145 billion from members' quota subscriptions and SDR 18.5 billion available to borrow from 12 counties [IMF *Survey Supplement* September 1995, 23]. IMF financial resources are, of course, complemented by reserves held by national central banks. Recognizing the growth of private international financial holdings, it seems certain that exchange rates cannot be kept in a target zone if the target is unwarranted.

Technological changes suggest, then, that the IMF should not be reformed around a target zone design. As Richard Cooper has argued, "from the perspective of the well-being of ordinary people . . . [there are] microeconomic disadvantages of the current arrangements of market-determined floating exchange rates" [1995, 85]. In his view, the additional costs travellers incur converting currencies are important. More important is the same type of costs incurred by MNEs. But most important are "the indirect, long-term costs [that are a result] of exchange-rate uncertainty on investment decisions" [1995, 85]. To avoid exchange-rate-induced, long-term costs, Cooper envisions an MNE pursuing one of three strategies: (1) the level of MNE investment could be reduced; (2) the investment could be geographically distributed to spread the risk of exchange rate fluctuations (investment artificially distorted by exchange rate uncertainties would be less productive than investment located for technological reasons); or (3) by encouraging governments to separate markets, MNEs may try to preserve rents obtained from a previous entrepreneurial activity because unconstrained markets make their loss possible through unpredictable exchange rates [1995, 86-7].

Cooper concludes that the "ultimate solution is to establish a single currency, at least among the major manufacturing regions" [1995, 87]. One of the issues raised by his proposal is how to organize and implement a single monetary policy. Cooper's approach is compatible with Solomon's call, mentioned earlier, for a more central role for the IMF. Also supportive of efforts to establish a single currency is the Dallara-Fischer call for greater financial resources for and strengthened surveillance by an IMF that has an emergency financing mechanism and a redefined SDR available. In general, the calls for a single currency and enhanced authority in the IMF are consistent with the IMF's evolution in the late 1970s and have implications for an IMF-based monetary policy. That is, these proposals could be synthesized into a call for the evolution of the IMF into a central bank for national central banks in order to handle expanding international financial demands and maintain the stability and harmony required for prosperity and growth in the twenty-first century.

Although not committed to becoming an international central bank, the International Monetary Fund is in the process of reconsidering the role and function of the SDR in the world financial system, and will sponsor a seminar on the subject in March 1996 [IMF *Survey* October 23, 1995, 316]. Even though the stock of SDRs continues small, their use is expanding. The IMF reports that "SDR transfers [from the General Resources Account, among participants, and among prescribed holders] nearly doubled to SDR 20.3 billion in 1994/95 from . . . the previous financial year" [IMF *Survey Supplement* September 1995, 20-2].

As we look to the future of the IMF, it is useful to note that the broadening of the Fund's financial intermediation activities that were active in the late 1970s has continued. Since then a policy of enlarged access to Fund resources, a Structural Adjustment Facility for use by low-income developing countries, an Enhanced Structural Adjustment facility for those low-income developing countries undertaking a serious three-year economic restructuring program, a Compensatory and Contingency Financing Facility in 1988, and a Systemic Transformation Facility in 1993 have been implemented. The IMF has strengthened its surveillance of the policies of members that affect exchange rates [IMF *Survey* May 22, 1995, 153-6]. And the SDR has continued to grow in importance, especially recently.

Of central importance as the contemporary international monetary regime adapts for the twenty-first century will be expanded use of the SDR. It seems likely that another allocation will be made in coming years. This approach could easily be complemented by a revived Substitution Account. If nations were permitted to convert national currencies now held as reserves into SDRs, there would be a gradual uncoupling of international clearing balances from national currencies. This uncoupling stands to reduce the domestic policy limitations currently imposed on countries sponsoring reserve currencies. At the same time, the private use of the SDR as a unit of deferred payment should introduce additional stability into international capital markets. The substitution-account approach should accompany any new allocations of SDRs in order to increase the relative prominence of SDRs more quickly.

If a substitution account were implemented, the IMF could evolve into a bank of issue of a single currency of the sort proposed by Cooper. Together with ever more vigilant surveillance and the specialized lending windows provided by the various lending facilities, the IMF can handily evolve in the central-bank direction. In the longer run, the evolution may accelerate if borrowing by the Fund to supplement Quota subscriptions generates securities that are available for the equivalent of open market operations. If a reduction in the international volume of dollars seemed desirable, for example, SDR securities could be sold for dollars. The ability to issue such securities would give the IMF an additional tool to promote exchange rate stability and to insure adequate international balances for transactions purposes.

While placing the responsibility for controlling the supply of money for international transactions with the IMF will seem an apparent loss of sovereignty to some, it is in fact a relatively small extension of authority and responsibility. For those who fear that such a transfer of monetary authority may be inflationary, established IMF voting procedures should be reassuring. Further, IMF directors have shown their prudence, even conservatism, through their stress on firm surveillance and on anti-inflation policy stances. There is little danger, that is, of undisciplined behavior. It seems likely, therefore, that the evolution of the IMF into a central bank for national central banks is probably an event whose time has come. Such an institutional adjustment would more adequately reflect the technological developments in communication, in industry, and in transportation that have accumulated as of the end of the twentieth century.

CONCLUSION

Exchange rate regimes can be viewed as institutional arrangements that facilitate the movement of goods, people, and factors of production across national borders. They have changed over time, to some degree in response to changing technologies. If the latest technologies are to be organized and used efficiently, institutions must adapt. Arguably, the IMF has been adapting. The fixed rate regime with which it began its existence was superseded by a flexible-rate regime to a large extent because of the changing distribution of industrial capacity around the globe. Since 1973, when the floating-rate regime began, the IMF has continued to adapt, facilitating international contact relatively free of artificial barriers. A reasonable next stage, given the evolution of technology, is for the IMF to become, fully and explicitly, a central bank for national central banks.

ENDNOTES

1. A political scientist, James A. Caporaso, has used a similar institutionalist approach in reference to international organizations, including the IMF [1992]: 620-30.
2. This section of the chapter is an adaptation of Scaperlanda [1978].
3. A useful chronology of the highlights of the IMF's evolution through April 1995 is available in [IMF *Survey* September 1995, 25-28].
4. Initially there were 16 currencies in the basket used to value the SDR. On January 1, 1981 the basket was reduced to five currencies (German deutsche mark, French franc, Japanese yen, British pound sterling, and United States dollar).
5. As of April 30, 1995, 15 international organizations like The African Development Bank, The Bank for International Settlements, and the World Bank had the designation "Prescribed Holder."
6. This section is an updating and extension of Scaperlanda [1979].

REFERENCES

Caporaso, James A. "International Relations Theory and Multilateralism: The Search for Foundations." *International Organization* 46 (Summer 1992), 599-632.

Cooper, Richard N. "Comments on One Money for How Many?" In Peter B. Kenen, ed., *Understanding Interdependence: The Macroeconomics of the Open Economy*. Princeton, NJ: Princeton University Press, 1995, pp. 84-8.

Dooley, Michael P. "A Retrospective on the Debt Crisis." In Peter B. Kenen, ed., *Understanding Interdependence: The Macroeconomics of the Open Economy*. Princeton, NJ: Princeton University Press, 1995, pp. 262-87.

Eichengreen, Barry. "The Endogeneity of Exchange-Rate Regimes." In Peter B. Kenen, ed., *Understanding Interdependence: The Macroeconomics of the Open Economy*. Princeton, NJ: Princeton University Press, 1995, pp. 3-33.

Friedman, Milton. *Essays in Positive Economics*. Chicago: University of Chicago Press, 1953, pp. 157-203.

Galbraith, John A. *The Economics of Banking Operations: A Canadian Study*. Montreal: McGill University Press, 1963.

Gordon, Wendell C. *Institutional Economics: The Changing System*. Austin: University of Texas Press, 1980.

———. *International Trade: Goods, People, and Ideas*. New York: Alfred A. Knopf, 1958.

International Monetary Fund. *Articles of Agreement*. Washington, DC: International Monetary Fund Board of Governors, 1968.

———. *Survey*. Washington, DC: International Monetary Fund, various issues.

Rutter, John. "Recent Trends in International Direct Investments: The Boom Years Fade." Washington, DC: U.S. Department of Commerce, International Trade Administration, Trade Development, August 1993.

Scaperlanda, Anthony. "The IMF: An Emerging Central Bank?" *Kyklos* 31 (1978): 679-90.

———. "The International Monetary Fund in the Contemporary World: Its Evolution and the Related Implications." *International Financial Conditions*. In United States Senate, Hearings before the Subcommittee on International Finance of the Committee on Banking, Housing, and Urban Affairs, December 12 and 14, 1979: 202-20.

———. *The Financial Structure of the Foreign Affiliates of U.S. Direct Investors*. Washington, DC: U.S. Government Printing Office, April 1974.

———. *The Financial Structure of the Foreign Affiliates of U.S. Direct Investors in 1972*. Washington, DC: U.S. Department of Commerce, Office of Foreign Direct Investments, June 1974.

Triffin, Robert. *Gold and the Dollar Crisis: The Future of Convertibility*. New Haven: Yale University Press, 1960.

Witteveen, H. Johannes. "The Emerging International Monetary System." *Finance and Development* 13 (September 1976): 7-9.

CHAPTER 12

A WORLD OF NATIONS AND[1] THE UNITED NATIONS

Wendell Gordon
University of Texas

The United States is part of one world, this world in particular, whether we like it or not. This essay has to do with the implications of the existence of this one world. Is the world likely to be better off if the people can freely interact worldwide and make decisions applicable to the world as a whole? Or is it, in some sense, more likely to be better off if particular nations can and do make decisions that are designed to benefit their nation even though they may adversely affect the world, and the world has no leverage for saying to them: Nay?

The United States has been ambivalent on this matter. Representatives of this country were crucially active in the creation of the League of Nations after World War I and the United Nations after World War II. Woodrow Wilson was responsible for the very coming into existence of the League of Nations, even though his own country then disowned his League. The United States delegation to the San Francisco Conference in 1945 was responsible for the addition to the United Nations Charter of a Preamble that had not been present in the Dumbarton Oaks Draft. It read in part:

> We the Peoples of the United Nations determined . . . to promote social progress and better standards of life in larger freedom, and for these ends to practice tolerance and live together in peace with one another as good neighbors . . . have resolved to combine our efforts to accomplish these aims. . . ."

In the first years after World War II the United States could command a working majority in the U.N. General Assembly. It was, however, frequently frustrated in the Security Council by the so-called "great power veto," which the Soviet Union frequently exercised. But then, the United States had been a leader along with the Soviet Union in inserting the great power veto in the Charter. The United States as well as the Soviet Union wished to be able, at its pleasure, to quash such U.N. action as it considered undesirable, regardless as to whether the measure in question had majority support.

The crucial development in turning the United States negative on the United Nations was its loss of an automatic majority in the General Assembly. This development occurred in the 1960s and 1970s when the number of new small independent nations began to proliferate as the result of most of the colonies of the great powers obtaining their independence. And speeches denunciatory of the United States began to proliferate in the General Assembly. The Third World had become a voice, if not a force, to be reckoned with. The United States began to fudge on payment of its U.N. assessments, and the absence of the United States-Soviet Union cooperation prevented the U.N. from developing an independent military capability of its own to use to prevent aggression.

An early, identifiable turning point in the behavior of the United States toward the United Nations occurred in 1964-65. The General Assembly majority proved unwilling to enforce the penalty of deprivation of voting rights against the Russians and the French, who at that time were seriously delinquent in meeting their U.N. assessments. In 1964, this refusal of the General Assembly to penalize the delinquents resulted in a stalemate that rendered the General Assembly incapable of voting on anything during that year. The United States gave up in its effort to penalize the Soviet Union and France and on August 16, 1965, the United States ambassador to the U.N., Arthur Goldberg, announced: "If any Member can insist on making an exception to the principle of collective financial responsibility . . . the United States reserves the same option."[2]

The United States from then on became a leading delinquent and used its delinquency actively as leverage to force the United Nations to accede to policies in accord with United States views. Especially relevant over many years has been the United States' repeated insistence on the principle that there should be no "increases in international organization budgets beyond zero real growth.[3] The zero-real-growth concept, even though not fully implemented, represented a not helpful attitude if the U.N. was really to become an effective instrument for implementing the creation of a civilized society in the world, one free of war and tyranny, and a protector of the environment.

The years from 1945 to the present have seen a progressive rejection by the United States, and other countries also, of the commitment the world made in 1945 to a meaningful United Nations. The United States has continued ostensibly to endorse the freeing of trade, as witness the approval of the North American Free Trade Organization and the World Trade Organization, successor to the General Agreement on Tariffs and Trade. At the same time the Executive Branch, the Legislative Branch and the general population have become increasingly derogatory of and uncooperative with the United Nations, in word and action and failure to act.

In the 1990s, the end of the Cold War and the apparent collapse of Soviet power have had as counterparts, not a world in which peaceful nations are cooperating under the aegis of a benign United Nations, but rather, one in which the U.N. is widely flaunted and starved and left with inadequate resources to confront a world of troubles.

What the United Nations has gained has been the power to practice peacekeeping and what peacekeeping turns out to mean is the begging for troops at the last minute at the time of crisis from nations reluctant to provide them unless they are well paid. Those troops, utterly untrained for the work they are to do, go from India, Pakistan, and various other generally underdeveloped countries, to Somalia, Rwanda, or Bosnia to perform impossible tasks. The exception occurs when a great power decides it personally will implement and command a *peacemaking* operations—in the Persian Gulf, or Somalia, or in Haiti. United States hunger for the oil of Arabia or interest in keeping Haitians with AIDS off its shores may lead to an apparently successful mission but one which has provided the U.N. itself with no experience in the execution of such missions or organization for the effective conducting of such missions.

PRESENT WORKING OF SYSTEM

The manner in which many of these difficulties might have been dealt with is elaborated in Chapters IX and X, Articles 55 through 72, of the U.N. Charter. Article 55 says that "the United Nations shall promote . . . higher standards of living, full employment, and conditions of economic and social progress and development" and "solutions of international economic, social, health, and related problems. . . ."

Articles 56, 57, 58, and 63 provide for coordinating the activities of the various agencies dealing with economic and social problems. Included in the effort to provide for coordination are the so-called specialized agencies which have been established by special treaties and have a legal existence independent of the U.N. Also included of course are the agencies which are more immediately part of the U.N. organizational structure and whose employees and budgets are handled by the United Nations.

This coordination of the agencies is supposed to occur primarily through the Economic and Social Council (ECOSOC), which is one of the so-called principal organs of the United Nations (Art. 7). The special agencies are:

International Monetary Fund (IMF);
World Bank (International Bank for Reconstruction and Development [IBRD], International Finance Corporation [IFC], and International Development Association [IDA]);
World Trade Organization (WTO); formerly General Agreement on Tariffs and Trade (GATT);
Food and Agriculture Organization (FAO);
International Atomic Energy Agency (IAEA);
International Civil Aviation Organization (ICAO);
International Fund for Agricultural Development (IFAD);
International Labor Organization (ILO);
International Maritime Organization (IMO);
International Telecommunication Union (ITU);
United Nations Educational, Scientific, and Cultural Organization (UNESCO);
United Nations Industrial Development Organization (UNIDO);
Universal Postal Union (UPU);
World Health Organization (WHO);
World Intellectual Property Organization (WIPO);
World Meteorological Organization (WMO).

Then, in addition to these specialized agencies, there are those units which are an integral part of the United Nations systems. Some of these agencies are:

The various regional economic and social commissions such as the Economic Commission for Latin America and the Caribbean (ECLAC);
Commission on Transnational Corporations;
Office of the United Nations High Commissioners for Refugees (UNHCR);
United Nations Center for Human Settlements, i.e., housing (UNCHS);
United Nations Children's Fund (UNICEF), which does a lot more than sell Christmas cards;

United Nations Development Program (UNDP);
United Nations Environmental Program (UNEP);
Committee on the Peaceful Uses of Outer Space;
Global Environmental Facility (joint with World Bank);
Disarmament Commission;
International Civil Service Committee;
High Commissioner for Human Rights;
World Food Programs and World Food Council;
United Nations Conference on Trade and Development (UNCTAD);
United Nations Population Fund (UNPD); and,
United Nations University (UNU).

It may help to place the power (and some will say, usefulness) of these organizations in perspective to mention a few matters in which some have played a major and influencing role. The IMF has been a chief actor in determining how much real aid Russia has received since the collapse of communism. The World Bank has been a powerful advocate of big projects: big dams, big river development projects, heavy industry in the developing world. It has not "thought small." The General Agreement on Tariffs and Trade, the predecessor organization for the World Trade Organization, tried to lower trade barriers by agonizingly long, product by product, country by country negotiations.

The Food and Agriculture Organization has produced a Nobel Prize winner in the person of Norman E. Borlaug. Other agencies, as agencies, have also won Nobel prizes: United Nations Peacekeeping Forces, the International Labor Organization, the United Nations Children's Fund, the Office of the U.N. Commissioner for Refugees. Officials who have won Nobel prizes for work with the United Nations include Dag Hammarskjøld of Sweden and Ralph J. Bunche, an American black.

By contrast, the United Nations Educational, Scientific, and Cultural Organization (UNESCO) had for many years been subject to ongoing denunciation by the United States, primarily it seems for being too representative of U.S.S.R. and Third-World radical views. During the Reagan administration, the United States withdrew from UNESCO and ended its financial support for most UNESCO activities.

The specialized agencies are involved in a formal association with the United Nations, a situation which at first glance would seem to mean coordination at the world level in the handling of a major range of important international economic and social problems. The U.N. Charter reads as though it was authorized to play this co-ordinating role. The appearance is deceptive. Mostly the specialized agencies, each established by its own treaty, and financed directly by governments rather than by the United

Nations, go their own freewheeling way. The nations, and for this the great powers and especially the United States are primarily responsible, have not given the U.N. the leverage to ensure that the specialized agencies follow policies the U.N. has endorsed.

Consequently, for example, the chief activity of ECOCSOC is the collection, discussion, and filing of reports. Many people are acquiring knowledge about operations and desirable policies, at the same time that they must feel rather futile. ECOSOC cannot itself establish enforceable policies for dealing with the problems which are brought to light as a result of its procedures. It may prepare draft conventions for the General Assembly's attention. The General Assembly may then submit them to the nations for possible adoption as treaties. The United States Senate is the graveyard of many such efforts. Only after nations adopt a treaty is there enforceability, and such enforcement as there is will be up to the national governments rather than the United Nations and may well be virtually nonexistent.

For the United Nations to amount to something constructive and effective, it must be capable of enacting and enforcing legislation in areas where the world has decided it should have jurisdiction. An important, equally prevailing condition is the frequency with which there are two or more U.N. organs plus independent non-governmental organizations (NGOs) working in an uncoordinated manner on the same problems: refugees, natural disasters, health, persecution, tyranny, the environment. One cannot necessarily expect an individual or an NGO, which is prepared to try to do some good work in a crisis situation, to pause to coordinate its efforts with all the other good work being done by others. The situation is different when, in one organization such as the U.N. which is continually involved over the long run in dealing with crises, it should be possible and useful to coordinate.

We like to assess blame. It is easy to blame the United Nations for its failure to have well thought-out and co-coordinated plans for dealing with crises. And the U.N. generally gets its orders to deal with particular crises on a hurry-up, ad hoc basis from the Security Council. It is notorious that the governments which assign these chores to the U.N. fail to provide it with the resources necessary to do the work. For example, when it comes to budgeting, the United States regularly pressures for a no-increase-in-real-expenditures principle. Then, on top of this, when it comes time to pay up on the assessments which have been voted and thus become a treaty-sanctioned legal obligation of the United States, the United States Congress is likely to drag its feet in voting for the necessary payments or to demand some special behavior by the U.N. before it will vote for such payments. The United Nations Educational, Scientific, and Cultural Organization (UNESCO) has been a favorite target of the United States

Congress in such situations. Of course other countries can and do practice the same behavior, but given the relatively large size of the United States assessment, a failure to pay by the United States hurts the U.N. more than does such behavior on the part of other countries.

HIERARCHY OF LEVELS OF GOVERNMENT

The organization that best represents the interests of the world, in these times the United Nations, should be the ultimate authority in world decision making. But the world owes it to itself to make sure that this is a democratically based organization.

This does not imply, and should not be allowed to imply, a large bureaucracy and a powerful, everywhere present, military and police force. It does not mean that the United Nations legislates on all subjects. It does not mean that U.N. courts handle most cases or even very many cases. It does not mean a U.N. police force capable of patrolling all the streets of the world, or even very many of them. It does not mean a level of U.N. taxes that makes U.N. taxes the dominant tax on the world scene, or even a major player on the tax scene. To repeat, it does not mean a huge U.N. bureaucracy, or even a particularly large bureaucracy.

For example, in this new world order, worldwide free trade should result in elimination of considerable employment at the level of national governments, to wit, the elimination of those working in the customhouses of the world to regulate and limit imports and monitor exports. Such elimination can happen without an offsetting increase in U.N. bureaucracy. Worldwide free trade should not require a lot of administration. Surely that proposition need not be argued at length. It is obvious, is it not?

Beyond such specifics, the general rule that should apply says: Governmental control should be administrated at the lowest level of government which can usefully administer that activity. Schools and education should be administered in quite small districts with a most minimal amount of high level supervision. The same goes for street repairs and garbage collection. Come to think of it, these are important, even though largely scorned, needs. Many problems can better be dealt with by a hands-on approach at the level of quite small governmental units. There is much to the proposition that variety is a welcome phenomenon. There does not need to exist any hidden power (like the force of competition or U.N. police) to force the low levels of government to practice uniform policies in dealing with all problems. Tolerance of diversity should be welcome along with general freedom of interchange. Both are desirable. They should not be considered conflicting approaches.

CRITERIA IN SELECTION OF POLICY

Given the state of the world, which problems should be dealt with at the world level and which at the lower levels?

It is probably not helpful to try to specify a formula (or a rule or a "value floor") that is supposed to have long-run applicability as a criterion for passing judgment on policy proposals. One may be led into trying to apply all too simplistic criteria (such as the desirability of the continuity of human life and of noninvidiousness) as though those concepts provided an operational basis for making specific judgments in specific problem situations. Examples might be the desirability of a health care system that bends over backward to retain insurance companies as major players in the reformed health care system or the possibility of the use of force by world society to stop Brazil from devastating the tropical rain forest or the United States to stop devastating the virgin forest in the Pacific Northwest.

We need to understand that each significant problem needs to be looked at de novo (anew, afresh) under conditions which perforce are slightly different from those that prevailed last week or last year. We should not try to use the crutch of an already formulated principle (even if we recognize that the principle is subject to change) that has gained some aura of authority as a result of having been around in a determinate form for, say, fifteen years.

The basic understanding should be that we are creatures of nature caught up in a process, whether we like it or not, in which the crux of the matter is ongoing continual change. The necessity of adaptability is a concept we need to understand. And there is no fundamental nature to this "life process," which we are capable of putting into a formula.

AREAS APPROPRIATE FOR WORLD COOPERATION

Areas where it would seem desirable for the world organization at the present time to have the power to make laws (at least in significant aspects of those areas) include:

- passing judgment on the totally unacceptable behavior of national rulers;
- coordinating aid to the victims of terrible catastrophes; fostering improvement in the welfare of people (especially emphasizing the poorest countries);
- controlling the spread of disease; preserving and protecting the worldwide environment;

- a dominating role in regulating the exploitation of the oceans, the Arctic and the Antarctic (the ozone hole, ocean mining, and contamination of the oceans);
- the behavior of ships at sea and plane and rockets; the use of the atmosphere to communicate;
- collecting and disseminating weather information;
- insuring the free flow of international mail and communication;
- regulating atomic energy;
- regulation of the production of exhaustible resources;
- playing a significant role in controlling (or eliminating of control over) international migration and the refugee problem;
- collecting revenues to support itself independently of the cooperation (or lack of it) of national government;
- and, as circumstances dictate, many other matters such as international trade.

The United Nations and other international agencies are already involved, frequently ineffectively, in many of these activities. Experience and the passage of time will influence the identification of problem areas which should be added to or deleted from such a list, or where the degree of worldwide control needs to be increased or decreased relative to local control. There will still be plenty of things to do for the multitudinous other levels of government.

To detail the situation of one industry, a good example is the international mail transmission system where, typically, governments collect postage from shippers but are not in a position to provide delivery in the recipient country. Providing a solution in the form of payment of a reasonable percentage of the postage originally collected by the shipping country to the receiving country would create an unmanageable administrative problem. The original ingenious solution to the problem was that each shipping country would retain the entirety of the money it collects. And the rather cavalier judgment was made that when that was done everywhere, all the countries would end up with an, arguably, fair share of the proceeds, a solution scarcely imaginable in the workings of the competitive free market. Also, of course, as a solution, it is a little too good to be true: nations have found ways to complicate this too felicitous, simple solution. Even so, surely most people would agree that this is a market-type problem that requires an international and cooperative, not a competitive, solution. Furthermore, the process of setting the rules for handling international mail would work better if there existed a legislative body capable of enacting enforceable law to establish those rules. The process involving the negotiation of international treaties to accomplish this is unnecessarily cumbersome and time consuming.

In a case in which it is decided that it is desirable for the world to operate as a whole, the world operation must have the police power to enforce its rules. Otherwise, the facade of world regulation in appropriate areas becomes a joke. The existence of enforcement compliance, imposed by a worldwide organization, has the potential for alarming people. It sounds like the coming of a heavy hand from on high. But, on the issue of which level of government will be more tyrannical, if it has the chance to be tyrannical, and which will be more obnoxious, are we so sure which level of government is the more intimidating? Did the people of the United States circa 1800 find the new federal government more objectionably intimidating than the state governments had been before 1789? Or was there a great sigh of relief because squabbling and fighting among the states became less common than had been the case before 1789? The federal government did set up a system of federal marshals to enforce federal laws. (The general attitude with regard to federal marshals does not seem to have been that Matt Dillon was an unwelcome and unwanted intruder on the local scene.) Federal prisons were eventually established, but meanwhile it was not uncommon for the federal marshals to house their suspects in state or local incarceration facilities. These problems can be worked out if there is the will to make the world a more civilized place.

As the years pass, the pendulum may well swing back and forth between a tendency to vest more power in the center and more power in the lower levels of government. Where power should lie involves issues that do not have permanent, definitive solutions. There is not any ideal solution at which we can arrive and relax. External vigilance by well meaning individuals remains important. The need for whistle blowers has not passed.

A more standard example of economic activities in the international area that may appropriately be matters of United Nations concern is international trade. Let us eschew extended treatment of the standard comparative cost argument for free trade. The current vogue for managed trade has hardly shaken that standard argument. The world is more likely to be a friendly place in which to live if the nations are not eternally playing Machiavelli for nickels and dimes in the foreign trade arena. It is worth dwelling a little bit more on an argument that is more institutional. This has to do with explaining why nations generally and individually go to great lengths to foster exports and discourage imports. Such effort is largely self-defeating because it fails to explain how the difference between money value of exports and money value of imports is financed. And we are, it seems, indisposed to giving away the goods involved in order to generate the export trade balance. Yet, where can the financing of the difference come from?

The institutionalism argument tries to explain why an irrational behavioral pattern, the pressure for a favorable trade balance, exists. The crux of the matter is found in the relative strength of producer-oriented and consumer-oriented pressure groups. Almost all of the effective lobbying pressure groups in Washington and in state capitals are producer-oriented and, believe it or not, employers and workers see eye-to-eye in this matter. Employers, interested in increasing profits, lobby to keep out competing imports. Labor unions, with an interest in expanding employment and in raising wages also desire to restrain imports. And it is feasible, it is what is going on, that employers and workers are organized and lobbying in self-serving trade associations and labor unions. Legislative bodies listen to them and ride to the rescue and the legislators claim the votes of the trade association and labor union members who want the tariffs, quantitative restrictions, embargoes, and what not on imports and are not adverse to picking up export subsidies when and where possible. So, the result of their activity is policies oriented to discouraging imports and encouraging exports. To oversimplify a little, it is the whole (almost) population that is doing this, since we all play a self-serving role as profit makers and wage earners.

Also, to continue with the same oversimplification, all of us are consumers. We all produce (don't hold me to that too literally) and we all consume (although some more than others). But it is not easy effectively to organize all of the consumers of, let us say, sugar, to finance a trip to Washington to lobby some congressional committee for a measure designed to force the import of more sugar so consumers can buy more sugar at lower prices. Then visualize how many consumer organizations it would take to lobby for lower prices for all the products. And each person has to be involved in all of them to match the lobbying efficacy of the producer-oriented groups. The League of Women Voters or representatives of Consumers Union may make an appearance and a nice, politely applauded statement the first day of the hearings, pleading for importation of more lower priced sugar. Then, all the congressional committee hears for the next two weeks or two months is the pleas of the workers for their jobs in the Louisiana cane fields, and the Colorado sugar beet fields, and Jesse Helms's backyard. The result is great effort to discourage imports and foster exports, an effort which is quite unrelated to the question whether it is, in fact, possible to discourage imports and encourage exports at the same time without explaining how the difference is to be financed.

The author claims, that is to say, *makes*, the value judgment that the logical difficulty is resolved by opting for genuine free trade and a monetary system that either involves exchange rates that fluctuate freely (except perhaps for a limited amount of central bank market intervention to slow down the rate of change of, but not reverse the direction of, exchange rate change) or involves a uniform worldwide currency administered by a restructured International Monetary Fund. But the justification for those recommendations is a long story.

Of course there are going to be disturbing incidents involving international financial and trade crises as long as each nation is pursuing independent trade and financial policies. National sovereignty as a justification for autonomy in policies in these matters is an infallible preliminary to shooting oneself in the foot by a willful sovereign nation.

AN AREA INAPPROPRIATE FOR WORLD REGULATION: THE NATURE OF THE WORLD MARKET ITSELF

What kind of a market system is desirable for a world that is striving to improve the welfare of people? A purely competitive market system, or a not so purely competitive market system, a regulated economy, an unregulated economy, socialism, communism, a mixed economy, government ownership or government operation of some or parts of some industries, one practicing free trade, one practicing trade restrictions? The range of possibilities is infinite.

How should it be determined what the system should be? Is it desirable for there to be a uniform system for the world? May some variety in systems be healthy, at least as long as the systems are compatible? Was something that might be called a free market system incompatible with Marxian socialism? Is either one of those systems a neat understandable system anyway? Or have either or both been hodgepodges of varieties of methods of doing things?

Unbridled profit-seeking entrepreneurs are not the ideal linchpin for an economic system. For one thing the entrepreneurs need a few rules of the road to protect themselves from each other. We hear about cooperation and brotherly and sisterly love on our various Sabbaths, then the rest of the week, quite sanctimoniously, endorse a competitive economic system. We denounce government regulations in general and find ourselves indignantly supportive of a lot of government regulations in particular, like, by golly, bumpers should be a uniform height off the road. Or, let us keep out those unwashed immigrants that want to come in and help us enjoy the land of the free and the home of the brave.

Here follows an alleged answer or two: Things will work out better if the world does not try to legislate or impose some particular type of marketing system on everybody. American statesmen (secretaries of state, presidents, senators, what have you) should stop shouting at other nations, especially those currently escaping from the heavy hand of Marxism, that they should commit themselves to the market system (as though they did not have a marketing system while they were still ostensibly Marxist). Frequently, our statesmen are more specific. The commitment, they say, should be to a *free* market system, or a competitive system, or pure competition (à la the elementary economics course). It is not desirable to get bogged down arguing this issue. The economy is going to involve a mixture of "free market" pricing, planning, state ownership and operation, regulation, and what have you. The proportions of these options over time and place will vary and change. We can hope that those ongoing changes will be made thoughtfully in a setting of half-way democratic political processes.

NATURE OF THE DEMOCRATIC PROCESS

If the worldwide organization is going to do a credible job in regulating the areas of political, economic, and social activity which are its appropriate domain, it requires a legislative body with the power to enact laws applicable to the world and enforceable against individuals as well as governments, enforceable by law enforcement officers and courts beholden to the worldwide organization. Such a legislative body needs to be elected by some halfway meaningful democratic procedures that bypass national rulers. One of the reasons the United Nations has not been able to operate effectively is that the General Assembly and the Security Council members have been the appointees of national rulers and the national rulers have directly controlled the action or failure to act of the U.N. The failure up to now of the U.N. is a failure in the willingness of assertive national rulers to cooperate and reach reasonable compromises.

Also, the head of the worldwide organization must be selected by this democratically elected body rather then being the least common denominator in a process dominated by the national rulers. Independence of the control of national rulers must be built into the process by which all those who are trying to run the worldwide organization are selected. Such a major overriding of the national sovereignty concept and its implications is necessary if the government of the world is to become an institution serving the world in a halfway constructively useful manner. It would probably be desirable in an essay of this type to say more about the legislative process, but it is hardly feasible here to dwell on the details, especially of the working of the selection process, except to say that there will be a lot of backing and filling on the way to acceptable procedures.

THE REAL CULPRIT: NATIONAL SOVEREIGNTY

The implication of national sovereignty is that national governments cannot be called to account for their behavior, however vicious, terrible, and arbitrary it may be. Dictators may murder large numbers of their own people. Nations may contribute to contaminating the world environment, while the rest of the world is obligated to stand idly by. The egos of members of the United States Senate are inflated by the idea that they can act in ways that affect the world without their being accountable to the world. The Charter of the United Nations in Article 2, par. 7, that "Nothing contained in the present Charter shall authorize the United Nations to intervene in matters which are essentially within the domestic jurisdiction of any state. . . ."

After the Tiananmen Square Massacre in Beijing in 1989, China used the national sovereignty argument to justify the position that the affair was none of the business of the rest of the world, the United Nations, or the United States. The political leaders of small countries relish brandishing their national sovereignty status any time it has the faintest usefulness. Also, the United States, Britain, France, and you name it among the larger countries are not about to permit the United Nations to intervene in their handling of minority problems, however vicious.

Another thing might be said to speak to the idea of downgrading the power of national governments to sabotage measures in the general interest of the world. It seems that national leaders delight in frustrating efforts to implement policies that would be useful to the world merely because they do not want to lose a jot of the power that they have enjoyed wielding arrogantly and irresponsibly. After the Persian Gulf War the United States failed to foster the establishment of a reasonable world order in a world desperately needing order. It preferred merely to retain the power to undermine efforts by others to deal with problems. It preferred to remain the one country with the leverage to interfere in the business of everybody else, without placing Americans serving in the American all-volunteer army at risk, and without being subject to the necessity for participating in the solution of difficult problems when it chose to abrogate its leadership role, as in the cases of Yugoslavia and Rwanda.

United States citizens should realize that they are the basic sinners in the failure to generate a pleasantly livable world. The President and the Congress are accurately reflecting public opinion as they frustrate the action of a workable United Nations. What do the American people want? The ego gratification of knowing they are citizens of the dominating country at the same time that they feel no obligation to participate in the solution of problems if they choose to abstain. Meanwhile countries generally, including the United States, delight in making certain that the U.N. does not have the power to enforce peace or decisively resolve social and economic problems.

Let us stumble and lurch in the direction of a friendlier, more charitable world where reasonable taxes are paid quietly and where peacemaking has replaced peacekeeping, but where peacemaking is less and less needed. In this world the United Nations will be permitted decisively to resolve such social and economic problems as call for "world level" solutions.

Much of this involves, and is heavily dependent on, the attitudes of people. We are the people and we are responsible for our attitudes.

All this is easy to say.

The world hereafter will be as civilized as people make it.

ENDNOTES

1. Wendell C. Gordon, *The United Nations at the Crossroads of Reform*. Armonk, N.Y.: M.E. Sharpe, Inc., 1994.

2. Thomas M. French, *Nations Against Nation*. New York: Oxford University Press, 1986, pp. 85-86.

3. United States Department of State, *United States Participation in the UN . . . 1990*. Washington: Government Printing Office, 1991, p. 69.

EPILOGUE: THE INFLUENCES OF WENDELL C. GORDON

John Adams
Northeastern University

> *And it came to pass on the third day of the morning, that there were thunders and lightnings, and a thick cloud upon the mount, and the voice of the trumpet exceedingly loud; so that all the people that was in the camp trembled* [Exodus 19:16].

This concluding chapter offers an epiphanic account of the transmission of ideas and values between one teacher, Wendell C. Gordon, and his students in the Department of Economics at the University of Texas during its institutionalist Eden. That those ideas and values are alive, and being deepened and exercised, by overlapping generations of apostles, each of whom perceives the faith somewhat differently, is attested by the chapters in this book, our New Testament, if you will. (In the references, IT refers to Wendell C. Gordon, *International Trade: Goods, People, Ideas* [1958] and EIV to *Economics from an Institutional Viewpoint* [1973]. The italicized text in this chapter represents quotes from Gordon's work.)

GENESIS

Much hinges on what economists learn in graduate school. Continued reading, contact with other economists in one's workplace, the development of ideas in the profession, and the annual rounds of conferencing do fertilize the mind, but for most, if not all, of those economists who are not mere technicians, the DNA of beliefs--of transmitted principles--is established during graduate incubation. What is taught and learned is a set of precepts derived from prior professorial learning, experience, and judgement, which then constitutes intellectual DNA, since replication through subsequent generations is what is involved in the process. Following Exodus 19:16, as quoted, Moses receives the Ten Commandments from God while the children of Israel wait anxiously at the foot of the mountain. The Ten Commandments are, of course, very powerful bits of cultural DNA; this is true even if there are other conflicting bits of DNA--of the natural as well as the cultural sort--that confound the encoded message and lead God's sheep astray.

Did Wendell C. Gordon play the Moses part in the drama of the Texas classrooms? Or did he have The Even Higher Role during those formative days, first on Mount Garrison, later on Mount BEB?[1] Some light, if not a blinding light, may be shed on this mystery of mysteries by examining text and legacy in a search of the decimic tablets inscribed long ago. If Gordon's Ten Commandments can be reconstructed and deciphered, then we may have advanced at least a portion of the distance towards answering these questions. Come then, let us rest not until our quest is done.

LATER

Some time passed before my crusade for a remnant of the Holy Text was successful, after many tribulations. Providently, I found my original copy of *International Economics: Goods, People, and Ideas*, signed *John Q. Adams, U. of Texas, 1962.* Even more remarkably, and undoubtedly with some divine aid, I have located my 1963 class notes from Economics 384L, Studies in International Economic Theory. Most wondrously of all, I find that there are Ten Commandments, or, Ten Principles of International Economics, if you will, that register plainly, as if written by a finger of fire, across the dust and crumble of these sacred slates. I will now convey these to you replete with appropriate exegeses. Yea, Listen Up, O Host!

THE FIRST COMMANDMENT--CONSTRUCTIVE FREE TRADE

The international trading policy which modifies the pure free-trade position to the extent necessary to achieve maximum world well-being might be called the "constructive free trade" position [IT, 87]. The orthodox theory of comparative advantage has powerful appeal, even if many of its assumptions are questionable. It is unlikely that national economies are fully competitive, that factors move frictionlessly internally, or that trade does not affect the distribution of income. In addition, the theory outrageously assumes that technology does not change and that all nations have access to the same shelf of technologies.

Wendell Gordon's constructive free trade argument adduces that these failings, and others, must be taken into account in setting trade policies. At the same time, the popular public interest is best served by movements toward freer trade, and the burden of proof must be on those who seek tariffs or subsidies. Because private and public interests may differ, there is scope for social oversight in such fields as research and innovation, monopolization, and correcting a maldistribution of burdens resulting from labor-force adjustments arising from trade. The ultimate rationale for free trade is not that it is trade but that it is free. Bostonians should be as unobstructed in buying French wine as they are in buying California wine. The comparative advantage argument is therefore useful not because it is absolutely correct but because it is sometimes serviceable in debates.

In retrospect, it is a little surprising that the phrase "constructive free trade" has not caught on. In a different world, say the world of 1993, with a new (hypothetical) Texan President seeking to make a gesture to demonstrate that the United States is switching to a more active approach to trade policy, the nation might have witnessed a different--but equally shocking--appointment to the chairpersonship of the Council of Economic Advisers. A strategic trade policy implies the adoption of a combative stance, but a constructive free trade policy implies working usefully towards collective ends. LBJ would have understood.

THE SECOND COMMANDMENT--THE BALANCE OF TRADE

Changes in the institutional organization of western European society led to an international trade policy called mercantilism which involved a change over to a "fear of goods" psychology which still prevails, coloring our attitude on such subjects as the balance of trade [IT, 45]. The balance of trade (BOT), exports (X) minus imports (M), expressed formally as

$$BOT = X - M, \quad (1)$$

was the first quantitative expression in economics designed to measure the effectiveness of a set of economic policies. Unfortunately, it was not the last. Following (1), the mercantilists advocated that protection of imports and stimuli to exports be employed to suppress imports (M) and to raise exports (X), thereby levitating the balance of trade. The effect was to run a favorable balance of trade (BOT > 0) and to ensure an influx of precious metals in the form of coins, ingots, and plate.

This outcome amounts, as Gordon says, to a "fear of goods." It can be recognized equally as a direct welfare loss since more goods are being given than got, so there is nothing particularly favorable about a favorable balance of trade. I have been teaching international economics to graduate and undergraduate students for 30 years. I remain amazed that even the best have trouble disconnecting themselves from the mercantilist belief. Economic journalists, and many economists, make the same mistake. A prevalent recent example is the discussion of the problem of the United States' trade deficit with Japan. How can it be a problem to get more goods than we give (BOT < 0)?

THE THIRD COMMANDMENT--THE TRANSFER OF PURCHASING POWER

It would be a great help in analyzing the problem of balance of payments adjustment if the various factors would interrelate in some regular and predictable pattern. Unfortunately, they do not [IT, 328]. One of the bedeviling aspects of trying to learn and teach international economics is that the logic and certainties associated with the real, or trade, side of the discussions disappear when one moves to the financial side. A valuable aspect of the training at Texas was the very thorough review and critique of the various ways of handling international exchange markets and international adjustments: specie-flow, income interdependence, and fluctuating rates. Gordon's sympathetic treatment of Ohlin's transfer-of-purchasing-power argument cut through the sophistry and jargon associated with international finance. If the Italians buy something from the Spanish, then the Spanish have purchasing power, which more likely than not they will use to buy something from the Italians. End of discussion. How often this simple circuit is overlooked; always, I have found it helpful as a small rock to stand on in an ocean of raging confusion.

In passing through chapter 16 in IT, I see on page 287 a note in Gordon's hand. I must have asked a face-to-face question about his view of the United States as a financial center and pointed to the text. He wrote in the margin: "U.S.--creditor at long-term, debtor at short-term," presumably so that I, qua village idiot, would not forget. I have not. Many others have. The nation as bank is an important notion, especially when that nation is the United States and the dollar is the currency.

THE FOURTH COMMANDMENT--COSMOPOLITANISM

Our problem is to civilize ourselves. Our problem is to make world society pleasantly livable, in a setting where, in spite of ourselves, we are generally opulent. And this may take a bit of doing [EIV, 40]. One of the lost concepts in today's world is cosmopolitanism. One of the flaws of conventional international economics is that it cleaves to the national viewpoint in making welfare assessments. Policies and their effects are judged on the same basis. In all of Gordon's work in the international field he not only appraises the effects of the movements of goods, people, and ideas on nations as wholes, but moves down to the level of groups and individuals, and up to the global plane. He argues that it is up to the people of the world to make better lives for themselves through a worldwide democratic process.

I will not describe the various institutional arrangements that Gordon advocated to create and implement such a global order. Rather, I state, indefensibly, that if we collectively pursued cosmopolitan aims we could reduce and avoid a great deal of international strife, too much of it involving persons of various intense religious or ethnic persuasions. The operating and literal principle is "live and let live." My Biblical opening notwithstanding, people are more important than gods.

Likewise, by adding only one more "c" word, civility, to our code of conduct we could escape the toils of one of the fruitless exercises of my lifetime, and yours: the irruption of those foolishnesses associated with the movement called political correctness, at least by its critics. Cosmopolitanism addresses the obligation of coping decently with other collectivities of persons; civility deals with the day-to-day routines of navigating through our relationships with immediate and singular others. Civility, as Gordon describes it, is employing one's "freedom to do the decent thing" [IT Introduction: 4]. If there is genuine, widespread civility, then there is no need to legislate correctness.

THE FIFTH COMMANDMENT--GOVERNMENT AND BUSINESS

In governing ourselves, in making democracy work, we do not have the problem of choosing once and for all between freewheeling enterprise and paternalistic government, but the continuing problem of weighing each decision our society makes in the light of the total impact, in the light of the desirable balance between let-it-alone-to-take-care-of-itself and group or government planning [IT, 7]. Wendell Gordon has thought a great deal about the relationship between government and the private market system and its agents. It is his powerful wisdom that there is no single, correct, once-and-for-all resolution to this dilemma which lies at the heart of all modern societies' struggles to frame economic and social policies. This amounts to the espousal of open-ended, value-free, principle-free instrumentalism [Gordon and Adams 1989, chs. 7-8]. Human actions and decisions continuously reassess and remodel institutions, including national governance, in light of failures and successes experienced. Because values are never absolute and permanent, there is not a single rule or set of rules, a Value Principle, a Golden Rule, or even a Ten Commandments that always guides public policy. Social movements and political forces push the boundaries between state and market back and forth as circumstances warrant. Karl Polanyi [1944] termed this "the double movement." Laws, customs, and due process all evolve.

THE SIXTH COMMANDMENT--WATCH THE BAT

Now we will add trade and draw the welfare implications for a given set of production possibilities and patterns of consumption--the indifference curves [384L notes, Tuesday, 3 December 1963]. At Texas, along with H. H. Liebhafsky in price theory, Gordon believed that the advanced course in international economics should cover not only institutional ideas and critiques but what is usually called a solid grounding in the prevailing neoclassical theory. Looking back, one is astounded by how much was covered in one semester. After parading through mercantilism, classical thought, and Bertril Ohlin, we confronted the derivation of Marshallian offer curves from the two-country two-commodity model, explicated with production possibilities curves and indifference curves, with a strong dose of being thoroughly warned about the pitfalls of the techniques. When it came time to make the derivation on the chalkboard it was necessary to manipulate the two countries' production frontiers located in the northwest and southeast quadrants of a pair of X-Y coordinates. In order to accomplish this, Gordon conjured a flying bat into the classroom. This bat was actually a cardboard template that he waved about and moved on the board in order to trace precisely the derivation of the offer curves. Of course, lacking something equivalent, it was all but impossible to replicate in our notebooks what was being done at the board.

THE SEVENTH COMMANDMENT--TRADE AND DEVELOPMENT ARE DIFFERENT

No country need have a falling level of living as a result of the development of other countries, although there may be a tapering off in the rate of growth. If the level of living in the United States fifty years from now is not higher than it is today, in a setting where the rest of the world is much better off, then we have failed to show that initiative for which we are so widely self-acclaimed [IT, 543]. One of the nice things about Gordon's *International Trade* is the unclouded distinction he makes between trade and growth or development. I have become convinced recently that trade has been greatly oversold as a curative. You want jobs? Then we need trade. You want growth? Then we need trade. You want to be more competitive? Then we need trade. The standard free trade argument has little to do with employment, growth, or competitiveness. There is nothing in the neoclassical model about jobs, since full employment is assumed and the transition from one job to another, as from an import-lost job to an export-created job, is seamless. There is nothing in the neoclassical model about growth. The transition from autarky to free trade involves a once-and-for-all gain in allocational efficiency; plus, technology never changes.

Gordon devoted the six chapters of part VII of his text [IT, chs. 30-35] to growth. He discussed the Veblen-Ayres theory of technological change and the role of institutions. He recognized that international movements of people, ideas, skills, and technologies were the fundamental determinants of comparative levels of living and growth rates. Capital played a role only to the extent that it facilitated technological diffusion. Offering a lesson that many forgot in the debt-ridden 1980s, if they ever knew it, Gordon argued with force that the acquisition of tools, machines, and process knowledge should be funded by poorer countries on a pay-as-you-go basis, not by international credits or reliance on foreign investment.

By the way, Gordon's 50-year forecast of broad global growth has so far proven correct. Although from 1958 we have travelled only to 1996, not to 2007, the United States is better off, and much of the world is better off. Despite these gains, angst continues to infect our supposedly bravado-ridden businesspersons as they grapple with global forces, international competition, and the Japanese enigma.

THE EIGHTH COMMANDMENT--RELATIVE STRENGTH OF PRESSURE GROUPS

The number of producers is sufficiently limited so that it is feasible for them to organize effectively; a substantial degree of organization is not only possible, but seems to occur in the natural development of the production side of most industries [IT, 169]. One of the defects in standard international trade-policy theory is that it cannot explain why there are trade barriers. The logic of the comparative advantage and free trade case is plain and the sheer pursuit of profit will drive economic affairs towards a welfare optimum. Why would tariffs exist in such a world? The answer is, of course, that the industrial and commercial interests, including unionized workers, will gain if they can act together and secure protection. In the phrase quoted, Gordon points out that pressure groups have a great deal to gain from tariffs or quotas; at the same time, consumer groups have a great deal to lose, but little clout because their memberships, though large, are scattered and underfunded. Precisely the same arguments are made today by social choice theorists and international political economists who are working on the theory and empirics of protectionism.

THE NINTH COMMANDMENT--POLICY COORDINATION

The policy which satisfactorily solves one problem may worsen another. . . . We need to utilize a pattern of policies co-ordinated in such a way that they do not tend to offset or negate each other [IT, 623]. So far as I know, Gordon is the only person who has laid out, in the context of international economics and development, a full set of coordinated policies designed to lead the world towards a higher standard of living with enhanced security and enlarged freedom of action. He has offered a complex discussion of aims and instruments, following Jan Tinbergen's and James Meade's contributions. This stratagem cannot be adequately parsed here, but some of its highlights may be furnished. Gordon recommended a universal international monetary unit, or alternatively, freely fluctuating rates, and constructive free trade. For global development, he suggested facilitating technology exchange, more education, freer movements of persons, and the adoption of social welfare programs. Avoidance of wars and the planetary dispersion of the Bill of Rights should go hand-in-hand with material improvement. Although Gordon made these strikingly contemporary proposals in 1958, sadly, the world has made little progress on most of these fronts.

THE TENTH COMMANDMENT--FLOATING THE RUPEE

Price comparability is a situation in which the price of a particular commodity will be the same--except for differences corresponding to legitimate costs of transportation--everywhere in the world. Price comparability is important for effective planning by both business and government [IT, 261]. There is a burgeoning literature on liberalization and policy reform emanating from such august organizations as the International Monetary Fund. A topic of gravity has been the sequencing of reforms: fiscal balance, privatization, free internal capital and stock markets, delicensing, tariff reduction, exchange convertibility. Either I have failed to grasp key points, or I am correct in concluding that there is not much that is international in it. What is going to happen in each country is to be driven by internal forces: the winners and losers from policy change, the strength of institutional resistances, the degree of isolation from the world's channels of communication and information, and the relative strength of pressure groups.

As one example, consider India. Since 1991, the Indian government has adopted a number of economic reforms. The most forward of these has been the freeing of the rupee and the amassing of over $20 billion in reserves to underwrite the stability of the rupee at about 31 to the dollar. For reasons I cannot fully fathom, I have reached a conclusion that is as strong as any I ever have held in my time of India-watching. IMF panjandrums apart, I am convinced that the freeing of the rupee is the most critical step the Indian government has taken in a very long time. It does not matter what "theory tells us" and whether the rupee has been more-or-less freed "too soon" or "too late." The tenth commandment's message is accurate. India's government and its agencies and India's businesspersons will be much better off, after a period of adjustment, by knowing what the rupee equivalents of world prices are; and, India's businesses and families will be better off from being able to use their rupees as they see fit in the international arena: to buy the best machine tools, to pay to send children to the United States for graduate education, or to jet to Monte Carlo and lose $1 million at the tables.

CONCLUSION

We who have contributed to *The Institutional Economics of the International Economy* are by no means all of those who have been influenced by and are indebted to Wendell C. Gordon. We are grateful to have had the opportunity to know him as teacher, as guide, and now as almost-contemporary. We marvel at his lifelong and continuing industry, and admire his robust integrity and peerless vision. The zeal with which he has advocated decency, civility, equality, and peace springs from a reformist spirit and a sanguine nature. His commitment to the pursuit of a better world has been unflinching. If there is one transcendent lesson he has conveyed, it is that freedom above all else is that which makes us human and opens the prospect of our collective betterment. It is this transmitted and now-shared commitment that has made our work on the economics of the international economy worth doing.

Thanks, WCG.

ENDNOTE

1. The Texas economics department was located in Garrison Hall until the early 1960s when it moved into a joined pair of buildings: BEB was shorthand for the Business and Economics Building, which housed classrooms. BEOB, adding an "O" for "Office," was the higher-rise location of faculty and graduate student offices. The economics department was administratively part of the arts and sciences college.

REFERENCES

Gordon, Wendell C. *International Trade: Goods, People, Ideas.* New York, Alfred A. Knopf, 1958.

———. *Economics from an Institutional Viewpoint.* Austin, University Stores, Inc., 1973.

Gordon, Wendell C. and John Adams. *Economics as Social Science: An Evolutionary Approach.* Riverdale, Maryland, The Riverdale Company, 1989.

Polanyi, Karl. *The Great Transformation.* New York, Rinehart, 1944.

INDEX

MIX
Papier aus verantwortungsvollen Quellen
Paper from responsible sources
FSC® C105338

If you have any concerns about our products, you can contact us on
ProductSafety@springernature.com

In case Publisher is established outside the EU, the EU authorized representative is:
Springer Nature Customer Service Center GmbH
Europaplatz 3, 69115 Heidelberg, Germany

Printed by Libri Plureos GmbH
in Hamburg, Germany